Ekklesia In Glorious Revival

DR. NOVA DEAN PACK

Table Of Contents

Table Of Contents

Dedication

I dedicate this book to my constantly encouraging wife, Linda, who has allowed me the time to rewrite, revise, and clarify the truth in this book. She reminds me that Believers need to know the truth in the Bible in order to experience the freedom and liberty in their souls. I know that God sent me Linda as an abundant blessing in these final years of my life.

I also dedicate this book to my three wonderful, spiritual children, Brandon, Joshua, and Destiny, who grew up while our family ministry had a building for the Believers to fellowship that I did not call "Church." Church was "*Ekklesia*" and meant God's Kingdom government assembly and God's Kingdom military assembly of Believers. They were there to experience dynamic home fellowships with other families. Each of my children remember my teachings for years; and now as adults, they have a solid foundation of not living in a religion but living in the relationship with the King and His kingdom

The Religious Attraction of the Jonathan Syndrome That Frustrates Ekklesia Revival

The Religious Attraction of the
Jonathan Syndrome That Frustrates *Ekklesia* Revival

THE STORY OF KING SAUL'S SON, JONATHAN,
IS ONE OF THE SADDEST AND MOST
DISAPPOINTING STORIES IN THE BIBLE

Jonathan saw the coming of a new order and King, named David, yet he missed the next movement of the Holy Spirit because he failed to come out of the old religious order.

Jonathan loved the new future King David, who had been anointed by the Prophet Samuel to be the next King of the Israelites, but Jonathan also loved his father, Saul, the current King of the Israelites, who had previously been anointed by the Prophet Samuel, but now was managing symbolically the old religious order. With Jonathan's story comes the harsh warning to the saints of today. There are sobering questions that you need to answer for your spiritual betterment and enlightenment.

Are you one of those Believers who sees the move of the Holy Spirit? Are you one of those who knows what it is to feel the anointing of the new move of the Spirit? Are you one of those Believers who is in great danger of missing this next new movement of the Holy Spirit because you refuse to come out of the comfort of your old Church structure and religious order?

Are you one of those Believers, like Jonathan, who only will casually dabble in the anointing of this next new movement of the Holy Spirit? Are you one of those Believers who is content to hang around the edges of God's Kingdom in these last days, but never enter in with zeal and full commitment? Are you one of those Believers who wants the baptism of the Holy Spirit but not the baptism of God's holy, cleansing fire?

Are you one of those Believers, like Jonathan, who is satisfied only to keep in touch at a distance with those truly anointed of God who are going through a wilderness experience bearing the reproach of the leaders of the previous movement of the Holy Spirit? Are you one of those Believers who wants the anointing of the next new move of the Holy Spirit, but are not willing to bear the persecution and reproach by dwelling in Adullam's Cave for a season? Are you one of those Believers who fear change?

Instead, are you one of the Revival Believers who will let go of the pull of the temptations in the world to follow Christ Jesus and to minister under the anointing of the Holy Spirit? Are you one of those Believers who is battle ready for spiritual warfare against the Kingdom of darkness? Are you one of those Believers who will preach both the gospel of the Kingdom of God (Matthew 24:14), along with repentance and remission of sins (Acts 24:47)? Are you one of those Believers who will minister to other Believers to activate them as leaders in God's Kingdom government and God's Kingdom army instead of followers of your religious ministry? Are you one of those Believers who are willing to change the old wineskin for new wineskin for the new wine of the Spirit, which requires Kingdom community relationships to experience the resurrected life flow that comes from Jesus' humanity nature and brought to you by Christ's divine nature and the entire Godhead?

JONATHAN LOOKED LIKE HE WOULD BE THE RIGHT HAND MAN IN DAVID'S KINGDOM AND WOULD PARTICIPATE IN THE BLESSINGS OF THE PROMISED EVERLASTING THRONE

At first, Jonathan was truly one of the finest and most admired young men in Scripture. He was never charged with one intentional sin in scripture. Jonathan was a man of vision, courage, faith, unselfishness, loyalty, discernment, deeply spiritual, and was originally the natural heir apparent to Saul's throne as his eldest son.

However, Saul failed to be one hundred percent obedient in a particular mission of God and lost his anointing and Kingship, and Jonathan thereby lost his position as the next in line to be King.

At first, Jonathan laid his desire to be King aside for the love and friendship of David, as he saw that God had anointed David to be the next King. Jonathan loved David as his "soul buddy."

JONATHAN, LIKE HIS FATHER, WAS ORIGINALLY GOD'S ANOINTED WARRIOR AGAINST THE ENEMIES OF GOD'S PEOPLE

In 1 Samuel 13:2-3, one can see Jonathan as a great captain, leading the army of Israel to victory against the Philistines. "Saul chose for himself three thousand men of Israel. Two thousand were with Saul in Michmash and in the Mountains of Bethel, and a thousand were with Jonathan in Gibeah of Benjamin. The rest of the people he sent away, every man to his tent. And Jonathan attacked the garrison of the Philistines that was in Geba, and the Philistines heard of it. Then Saul blew the trumpet throughout all the land, saying, 'Let the Hebrews hear!'"

On another occasion, one can see Jonathan defeating the Philistines in battle as a mighty, courageous warrior as the account continues. 1 Samuel 14:1, 12-15, 20 says, "Now it happened one day that Jonathan the son of Saul said to the young man who bore his armor, 'Come, let us go over to the Philistines' garrison that is on the other side." But he did not tell his father...then the men (Philistines) of the garrison called to Jonathan and his armorbearer, and said, 'Come up to us, and we will show you something.' Jonathan said to his armorbearer, 'Come up after me, for the Lord has delivered them into the hand of Israel.' And Jonathan climbed up on his hands and knees with his armorbearer after him; and they fell before Jonathan. And as he came after him, his armorbearer killed them. That first slaughter which Jonathan and his armorbearer made was about twenty men within about half an acre of land. And there was trembling in the camp, in the field, and among all the people. The garrison and the raiders also trembled; and the earth quaked, so that it was a very great trembling...then Saul and all the people who were with him assembled, and they went to the battle; and indeed every man's sword was against his neighbor, and there was very great confusion."

Therefore, in the beginning, Jonathan moved under the gift of his father's anointing and favor of God, and the Lord's miraculous hand even caused an earthquake at the right time to insure Jonathan's victory in battle. Then Jonathan's father, Saul, started listening to the demands of the people instead of the commands of God through His prophet, Samuel.

"GIVE US ORGANIZATION AND A KING LIKE ALL THE OTHER NATIONS"

God had originally desired to speak to His people directly, but the people said they did not want to be in the presence of God because they were afraid. They told Moses they wanted him as their special prophet to speak to God and return and speak to the people what God says. Exodus 20:18-22 says, "Now all the people witnessed the thundering, the lightning flashes, the sound of the trumpet, and the mountain smoking; and when the people saw it, they trembled and stood afar off. Then they said to Moses, 'You Speak with us, and we will hear; but let not God speak with us, lest we die.' And Moses said to the people, 'Do not fear; for God has come to test you, and that His fear may be before you, so that you may not sin.' So the people stood afar off, but Moses drew near the thick darkness where God was. Then the Lord said to Moses, "Thus you shall say to the children of Israel: 'You have seen that I have talked with you from Heaven.'"'"

God's desire was to speak to the people directly, Himself, but the people insisted on having an organized group of special leaders to take care of the responsibility to hear correctly from, and to rule according to the dictates of God in a theocratic nation. These special leaders were called Prophets and Judges. Samuel was one of these special Prophets of God. Judges seemed to work to some degree for about 450 years with such leaders as Samson, Gideon, and Deborah. Judges 21:25 says, "In those days there was no king in Israel: every man did that which was right in his own eyes." Solomon said in Ecclesiastes 7:29, "Lo, this only have I found, that God hath made man upright; but they have sought out many inventions (schemes)."

The people of Israel later were dissatisfied with being ruled as a theocracy through God's Judges and Prophets. The people wanted to further "organize" and establish a secular government and have someone other than God to rule over them to fight their enemies and to help the people from disobeying God. 1 Samuel 8:5-7, 9 says, "Then all the elders of Israel gathered themselves together, and came to Samuel unto Ramah, And said unto him, 'Behold, thou art old, and thy sons walk not in thy ways: now make us a king to judge us like all the nations. But the thing displeased Samuel, when they said, 'Give us a king to judge us.' And Samuel prayed unto the LORD. And the LORD said unto Samuel, 'Hearken unto the voice of the people in all that they say unto thee: for they have not rejected thee, but they have rejected Me, that I should not reign over them. According to all the works which they have done since the day that I brought them up out of Egypt even unto this day, wherewith they have forsaken Me, and served other gods, so do they also unto thee.... Now therefore hearken unto their voice: howbeit yet protest solemnly unto them, and shew them the manner of the king that shall reign over them.'" God's warning was what would happen with a bad King instead of a benevolent King who obey God, such as King David and later his perfect Greater Grandson, King Jesus.

The above verses were God's words concerning the whole idea of organizing the people under a secular government instead of a theocratic benevolent rule through God's Judges and Prophets. God told His Prophet, Samuel, to protest and "solemnly forewarn" the people what a worldly King with his secular government would do. With a King to obey, the people thought they could be less responsible for their disobedience to God and avoid His judgment and wrath.

In history, the Believers in the old religious order demanded a spiritual leader like a secular President of a country or a President of a corporation in the world. Today, in much of the denominations, we have the professional Pastor, Teacher, or Priest (or other title for leaders), who the Believers hope that in the office he or she has will cause him or her to have the power from the Holy Spirit to cast out devils, heal the sick, and teach a fresh Word when all Believers themselves are required to also do these things and to study the word of God by themselves and in Kingdom community fellowship with other Believers (Ephesians 4:12-16; 2 Timothy 2:15). The religious tradition of the old religious order leaders is to make followers of their ministries, not leaders in God's Kingdom. Instead, the Ephesians 4:11 Ministers are office gifts from the Lord, chosen to perform their special engiftments and functions as apostles, prophets, evangelists, pastors and teachers "for the perfecting of the saints, for the work of the ministry (of establishing the Kingdom of God and to be Kingdom Ambassadors and Soldiers as the *Ekklesia*), for the edifying of the Body of Christ: till we all come in the unity of the faith, and of the knowledge of the Son of God, unto a perfect man, unto the measure of the stature of the fullness of Christ."

Some religious Believer Leaders today remember the "good old charismatic or Jesus Movement days" when they were "led by the Spirit" through hearing from the Holy Spirit, hearing a prophetic word, or obtaining a *rhema* word from studying the Bible; and they knew their born again spirits were being taught directly by the anointing of the Holy Spirit (1 John 2:27). After the fire of every revival dies down, then many religious leaders involved consider it was proper to put a name on the revival and start new denominations as the religious organizations with established rituals to follow to keep the congregation thinking they are okay in their souls. When they place a name on a Revival, they steal the recognition for themselves of the Holy Spirit's sovereign, special work; and in so doing they start the end of that Holy Spirit Revival movement.

The children of Israel essentially told Samuel, "We want a King like the other nations." Samuel's warning was like the mechanics warning: "If it works, don't fix it." However, the people wanted a change into a natural government with a natural King they could see and hear like other nations because they did not want to change their hearts and be obedient directly to God. The people wanted a King that God would speak with and judge through God's prophets instead of God speaking to the people and judging the people directly.

In effect, God was saying to the Israelites and the Believer Leaders today, "Go ahead and try to organize the move of My Spirit if you have a mind to do it. Try and legislate the gifts of the Spirit. Try to put a harness on the power of God through your ecclesiastical religious structure if you think you can. But in a short time I will make you so sick of the organization you have built, that you will cry out for deliverance." 1 Samuel 8:19-20 says, "Nevertheless the people refused to obey the voice of Samuel; and they said, 'No, but we will have a King (only a single Ephesians 4:11 minister instead of the fivefold ministers of Apostle, Prophet, Evangelist, Pastor and Teacher who are dedicated to the responsibilities in Ephesians 4:12-13) over us, that we also may be like all the nations (corporations and denominational Churches), and that our King (only a single Ephesians 4:11 minister) may judge us and go out before us and fight our battles.'"

The prophet Samuel obeyed God and anointed Saul to be King over Israel and anointed him with oil in a "vial" that was made by man (1 Samuel 10:1) and not a horn from a sacrificed animal as was used to anoint David (1 Samuel 16:13). King Saul was very nice in the beginning and did great exploits under the anointing of God. He defeated the Philistines (which represent the devil and his demons) in many battles. However, Saul was disobedient in his mission against the Amalekites (which represent the flesh) in that he became a "man pleaser" instead of the "God pleaser" by allowing King Agag and the best of the sheep, the oxen, the fatlings, the lambs, and all that was good to live instead of "utterly destroying" them as commanded by God through the prophet, Samuel. Because of his disobedience, Saul lost his appointed Kingly anointing, which is the presence of the Holy Spirit. Saul was never allowed further contact with God's prophet who had the presence of the Holy Spirit until his visit at Samuel's funeral (and with Samuel's visitation with Saul through the medium). 1 Samuel 15:35 says, "And Samuel went no more to see Saul until the day of his death. . . ."

This historical Bible story is a picture of almost every major movement of the Spirit in the *Ekklesia's* history since Pentecost. For a time, even after a revival is named and organized, God seems to bless it; and the leaders seem to have a measure of victory over the strategies of the devil and his demons for a season. Yet, the spiritual leaders in every Revival Movement seem to fall victim to the temptations of the natural world and their own lust of the flesh, lust of the eyes, or the pride of life (1John 2:15-16). They always seem to have their "Agags" and their "good sheep," who are committed tithers in the natural. These are the ones they want to please to insure they remain as their committed workers and financial supporters in the new religious order they call church. "Tithing sheep" generally insist on having their "money's worth" by demanding organizational religious structure and their personal positional authority. Therefore, some religious leaders are led by the demands of the people instead of being led by the Holy Spirit. Very few religious leaders would ever admit this and I believe most pastors are indeed led by the Holy Spirit.

Yet, in the midst of all this religious structure organizing activity, God still maintains His special anointed Ephesians 4:11 ministers, especially His Apostles and Prophets who try to repair the breach of the foundation of the Ekklesia. They continuously speak forth the Word of God to try to cleanse and mature the souls of the new Believers that came in during the Ekklesia Revival. Often, the greatest debilitating move for Apostles and Prophets of God is to place themselves in the bondage of an ecclesiastical old religious structure, often just to secure a steady income for his family.

"SEND ME YOUR ANOINTED SON, DAVID, WHO IS WITH THE SHEEP."

God's functioning prophet, Samuel, was instructed by the Lord in 1 Samuel 16:1 to go to the house of Jesse who lived in Bethlehem and anoint one of his sons as the new King of Israel. The son finally anointed as King was so small, so insignificant, and so weak looking in the natural and outward appearance that at first Jesse did not even bother calling him from the wilderness where he had been "watching over the sheep that belonged to the family." Besides, he was not very popular amongst his brothers because all he wanted to do was write and sing psalms in the Spirit to the Lord. This young teenage shepherd boy was David.

David's older brothers were committed to King Saul's army, the "old religious structure." They were busy battling the Philistines for King Saul. In today's old religious order structure, they are busy passing out fliers, knocking on doors, building up the children's ministry, and increasing

Church attendance while the "Davids" are just "resting in the lord," waiting on the leading of the Holy Spirit. While he shepherded his father's sheep, David had been learning how to be led by the Spirit while training for warfare by sharpening his skills by killing the lion and bear. Whatever David did in his preparation to be a Shepherd, Warrior, Priest, and King, he did by the power of the Spirit. His older brothers did not understand David who did everything differently.

When the functioning Prophet, Samuel, came to Jesse's house in Bethlehem, he examined all the older sons of Jesse and liked what he saw in the natural. However, God was looking at the hearts of David's brothers, and there was ambition, competition, selfishness in them all; and they were full of their own plans for promotion in Saul's old religious order. God saw that David was a man after His own heart (Acts 13:22). 1 Samuel 16:12-13 says, "So he sent and brought him in. Now he (David) was ruddy, with bright eyes, and good looking. And the Lord Said, 'Arise, anoint him; for this is the one!' Then Samuel took the horn of oil and anointed him amid his brothers; and the Spirit of the Lord came upon David from that day forward…." The horn containing the anointing oil represented a vessel from a sacrificial Ram, where blood was spilt, whereas Saul's anointing oil was poured from a fabricated vial. There seems to be a prophetic difference.

David was Jesse's eighth Son. Eight is a special number. It is the number of resurrection life out of death, a new beginning. David was the chosen anointed one for the new beginning of the movement of God's Spirit to bring revival to the land.

After his anointing by the prophet, what did David do? He went back to the wilderness pasture and continued watching his Father's sheep because he knew that the timing for his promotion was in the hands of God. Today, there are many anointed shepherds of God working in the wilderness alone watching a small herd of God's sheep who will rise to the forefront in this next great revival of the Spirit of God.

In the meantime, because of Saul's disobedience, God allowed the old Church structure to be visited by a religious demonic spirit. 1 Samuel 16:14 says, "But the Spirit of the Lord departed from Saul, and a distressing spirit from the Lord troubled him." Then all those in the old religious order in Saul's Palace agreed that the old religious order structure needed someone with God's anointing living in the same household, as their King (Pastor) had lost his anointing. 1 Samuel 16:18-19 says, "Then one of the servants answered and said, 'Look, I have seen a son of Jesse the Bethlehemite, who is skillful in playing, a mighty man of valor, a man of war, prudent in speech, and a handsome person; and the Lord is with him.' Therefore, Saul sent messengers to Jesse, and said, 'send me your son David, who is with the sheep.'"

Some Believers think you can return to the old religious order structure if you bring God's anointed leader into the structure. Sometimes, you can put new wine in the old religious order structure, but you have to rub a lot of the anointing oil on the old wineskin bag to make it pliable. There is a possibility that it will become pliable and will not break when the new wine is poured into the old religious order structure. However, this is a rare exception, and much time and anointing oil is often wasted.

At first, Saul liked the anointing on David to be around him, as he missed its presence. Saul did not know immediately that David was anointed and was chosen of God to be the next King instead of his son, Jonathan. 1 Samuel 16:21 says, "So David came to Saul and stood before him. And he loved him greatly, and he became his armorbearer… And so it was, whenever the spirit from God was upon Saul, that David would take a harp and play it with his hand. Then Saul would become refreshed and well, and the distressing spirit would depart from him." Scripture reveals that living in Saul's old religious order structure was not the destiny of David.

If you come to the old religious order with a fresh anointing from the Holy Spirit, it may excite and soothe the troubled minds of Believers in the old religious order structure with its religious spirit for a season or time, and you may even cause a measure of renewal changes to come in. However, if you stay in Saul's palace by taking a position of authority in the old Church structure, you may lose all God has given you, or called you to inherit, for your life here on earth and in the everlasting Kingdom of God when Jesus' humanity nature sits on His throne in the New Jerusalem.

FIVE SMOOTH MINISTRY STONES
IN THE SHEPHERD'S BAG

In 1 Samuel 17 is the famous battle between David and Goliath. This Story tells of the present condition of God's people in the old religious order structure, visited by the devil, but then has a warrior Believer from God who enters the scene with the Kingly anointing who is not religious but lives seeking the whole heart of God. While the members of the old wineskin church are fearful of sickness, poverty and demonic possession, the Believer with the anointing has no fear against the oppressing devil. The Believer with the fresh anointing has the Kingly anointing, and whatever he or she says or does, it is by the leading of the King of kings and God the Holy Spirit. The Believer with the kingly anointing from God knows because "…greater is He that is in (or on) you, than he that is in the world" (1 John 4:4).

In 1 Samuel 17:1 the Philistines were "… gathered at *Sochoh*, which belongs to Judah; they are encamped between *Sochoh* and *Azekah*, in *Ephes Dammim*." The Philistines represent the devil and his demons, and they are on God's property, Judah.

Today, in America, a spiritual battle is going on; and Satan is camped in God's land of Judah, as America is where the greatest percentage of people are joined in the Tribe of Judah, having accepted Christ as Savior and Lord. The devil is tormenting God's people with sicknesses, temptations, afflictions, poverties, stresses, and all kinds of sufferings, and tribulations. The word *"sochoh"* means "hedge." If it were not for God's hedge of protection, the old Church members could suffer harm. The word *"ephes dammim"* means "boundary of blood." Therefore, the then army under Saul (or under the old Church religious structure) was protected from Goliath. Today, the members in the old Church religious organizations are being protected by the "boundary of blood" established by Jesus. This land belonged to Judah, and Judah means "praise," and I believe that we can see the people in America worshiping the King of the Tribe of Judah and declaring America is the land of Judah. This land belonged to the praise for the Lord's Glory, and the man of praise, David, had come to the battle scene.

No one in Saul's army would go up against the devil, Goliath, for they did not have David's anointing or faith to fight Goliath, but David knew that since God had anointing him to be king of Israel, this devil, Goliath, would not defeat or kill him. Saul lost his anointing. The old Church religious structure has no anointed power inherent within it to fight Satan. God's Temple is each Believer and simultaneously collectively every Believer in the local Church (1 Corinthians 6:19; 1 Corinthians 3:16; 2 Corinthians 6:16; Ephesians 2:21) and universally in world Church. God anoints people, not buildings, or religious structures.

Weak Ministers with little anointing try to think up solutions to solve the issues and problems facing the old religious Ministry instead of praying long hours, having an intimate, daily relationship with the Lord, activating the rank-and-file members to take on some of the burdens and work, to hear clearly and be led by the Holy Spirit. Instead, they fill their calendars with meetings after meetings with their "captains" as to how to strengthen the old religious Ministry, but they end up continuously being attacked by the devil. These hirelings of the old religious order structure would suggest, "Perhaps we could have an 'old fashion Camp Meeting' or perhaps we could 'have more advertisement' or perhaps we could have a 'T.V. Evangelist' come to do a meeting." However, none of these activities or personalities can bring the anointing of the Holy Spirit to bring renewal or restructure. These religious leaders are not seeking first the Kingdom of God and His righteousness; they are seeking and uplifting their cherished religious rituals that they hope attract new Believers, or more so, transplanted old Believers who are hoping for a change.

In 1 Samuel 17:8 Goliath actually spoke a correct fact about the Israelite army; he referred to them as "the servants of Saul" instead of "the servants of the Most High God." This is actually an indictment against the Believers in the Church today. Some Christian leaders have sold out their spiritual birthrights for a small bowl of ecclesiastical pottage just like Esau had done and have replaced God's anointing with Church titles, social activities, and religious rituals that only appear to be are holy and sanctified. They may be saved, but they have missed the pleasure in serving the Lord in the Kingdom of God. They will not miss the tribulation that comes to every man and woman which is common in the world, but out of mercy the Lord will see them through (1 Corinthians 10:13).

However, God rewards obedient Believers with certain "crowns" in the life to come, including the "Crown of Life" (James 1:12), "Crown of Glory" (1 Peter 5:4), "Crown of Exultation" (2 Timothy 4:8), "Incorruptible Crown" (1 Corinthians 9:25), and "Crown of Rejoicing" (1 Thessalonians 2:19) because they were truly Ambassadors and Soldiers in the Kingdom of God, which they sought every day as Kingdom Citizens and rejected joining religious structures with their sanctimonious religious rituals.

David enters this devil's challenge scene in 1 Samuel 17:12. David had left the palace and had gone back to feed, lead, and protect his father's sheep, as God's training to be King is to be first a Shepherd of sheep. Goliath had challenged the army of Israel for forty days, and David's father tells him to run and feed his brothers in Saul's spiritually weak army. What David's older brothers needed was much more than natural food for their bodies. They needed the anointing that David possessed.

The number 40 is the number that represents a time of trial and testing. God had put the old religious order structure represented by Saul's army to a trial; and Saul's soldiers lacked courage. Saul's army was tested, and they failed to meet the challenge of the devil, represented by Goliath.

However, David had the kingly anointing because He recognized and used God's omnipotent power and authority and found life in seeking the very heart of God in God's Kingdom. David learned how to be a King in God's Kingdom by the King, Himself. David was not one who would settle for a little mountain behind a hedge of protection. He was not satisfied with just being saved and waiting for the so-called Rapture of Believers to come. David saw Goliath's challenge as the devil challenging God Almighty, Himself, and God's chosen people. David was in love with God; and David worshiped God with new songs while playing the string instrument. He temporarily got rid of the religious demon attacking Saul. David was of the Tribe of Judah that meant praise, and God enters the praises of His people. Psalms 22:3 says, "But Thou art holy, O Thou that inhabitest the praises of Israel."

Saul was embarrassed, frustrated, and without faith or hope. Saul and Jonathan had seen victories on the battlefield against the Philistines before, then here appeared Goliath and stopped the small revival from going on. The people were looking to Saul, as King, for deliverance; just like Believers mistake the office of Pastor as the source for their deliverance. Saul knew that he did not have the anointing anymore, and his organized army (or religious order structure) was lacking the power (or anointing of the Holy Spirit) in the natural to defeat Goliath (or the devil). Saul was hiding in his tent instead of leading his army against the Philistines. Saul's army thought Saul was making his battle plans. Yet, Saul allowed the enemy to dictate the terms of the battle, by agreeing that only one soldier on each side would battle against each other and the outcome would determine who won the war. However, not one Soldier volunteered, and surely the Soldiers did not require Saul, himself to do battle against this ugly giant, did they?

If you think about it, Goliath's challenge was very risky and put a lot of pressure on the individual person doing the fighting for the whole nation. However, this is often what Believer Leaders in the old religious order structure do today. Believers expect their leader (weak, tired, worn out, once anointed Pastor) to produce a solution, to do the battle, himself, for them as their representative, or to form a committee of intellectuals who can analyze a problem in the natural and come up with an educated natural solution. Intellectual natural remedies are not enough against the devil. Only the anointing of the Holy Spirit can break the devil's yoke (Isaiah 10:27). Most old religious order structure Believers expect to reap the benefits of a fight with the devil without fighting themselves. The old Church structure leaders have taught the Believers that Christianity is a spectator sport, where you come to a "Church" building to watch other Believers perform on stage.

Believers wrongfully are taught that Jesus already destroyed the works of the devil (1 John 3:8), so there are no more battles to be fought, ignoring scriptures, such as 2 Corinthians 10:3-6; Ephesians 6:10-18, 2 Timothy 2:3-4, and James 4:7. This anemic teaching goes like this, "Didn't Jesus do it all when we were saved? Man is not saved by works, so why should we work? Isn't the devil a defeated foe, so why should we need to do battle against him and his kingdom of darkness?" No wonder many Pastors hide out in their offices with administrative agendas that do not require an anointing. No wonder Believers see little or no miracles, prophesies, operation of spiritual gifts, anointing of the Holy Spirit, spiritual victories, and activation into ministry of leaders of this or the next generation.

David's first opposition was "jealousy" from his own brother, Eliab. 1 Samuel 17:28 says, "Now Eliab his oldest brother heard when he spoke to the men; and Eliab's anger was aroused against

David, and He said, 'Why did you come down here? And with whom have you left those few sheep in the wilderness? I know your pride and the insolence of your heart, for you have come down to see the battle.' And David said, 'What have I done now? Is there not a cause?'"

David's oldest brother did not say, "I am with you. If your faith gets weak, I will intercede for you. I will be by your side, and I will encourage you. Do not let people call you a fanatic. I remember in the former years when I was called a 'tongue talking fanatic' and of the devil, so do not be discouraged and do not listen to the critics. You can do it, for you have the anointing from God. You have been anointed King; so, God will protect you because you becoming King is in the future. Your victory against this Giant devil will be a victory for all of us. May God's power be with you!"

There is a lesson here. What happened to David can happen to you, so do not expect the support and encouragement from your brethren in the Lord when you have had a new present realization of a new move of the Holy Spirit unto revival that will eventually fall upon the whole world. It is not a new revelation to God, but it is a new illumination to you from God. God has planned this end time revival from the beginning, prophesied about it; and He will send forth the Holy Spirit to execute it in due season. Notwithstanding, sometimes you might have to follow what David did. You might have to turn away from your brethren who headed up the last movement altogether (verse 30) or risk discouragement, doubt, and losing the glory of the hour. You must seek daily the Kingdom of God and stay away from the religious rituals of the organized religious Church and do not be enamored by an offered position in the Old Church Religious Structure. It will become your religious prison.

The next thing David had to battle against was the tradition of how Saul had fought the enemy in the past. Saul represented the organized religion of the past movement of the Spirit. Saul said to David in 1 Samuel 17:33, "... You are not able to go against this Philistine to fight with him; for you are a youth, and he a man of war from his youth." David knew that God had prepared him for battle while he was out watching the sheep in his wilderness time alone with God. "Moreover, David said, 'The Lord, who delivered me from the paw of the lion and from the paw of the bear, He will deliver me from the hand of this Philistine'" (1 Samuel 17:37).

Saul was no longer depending on the supernatural or spiritual anointing of the Holy Spirit to fight his battles. He had organized a large army that looked good in the natural, but in the spiritual realm, he was bankrupt. By comparison, a Pastor may have a large membership, a good music director, competent youth ministers, and every activity is organized to run smoothly. Saul told David to wear his bronze helmet, his coat of mail, and his sharp sword, which were the best pieces of manmade armor in Israel. In other words, Saul essentially said, "David, you have no experience running a religious order structure. Let me show you how to put on a revival. I will give you my natural wisdom from my experience, and I have had some success." Saul did not say or realized that his success was during the time he had the anointing from the presence of the Holy Spirit. The battle is the Lord's! David said to Goliath in 1 Samuel 17:47, "And all this assembly shall know that the LORD saveth not with sword and spear: for the battle is the LORD's, and He will give you into our hands."

Saul was from the tribe of Benjamin (1 Chronicles 12:2). The tribe of Benjamin did not use modern armor as Saul was using, as Saul's armor was the modern armor that Goliath and the

Philistines were also using. You cannot beat the devil by using carnal weapons. However, a close cousin to David's Tribe of Judah was the tribe of Benjamin; and David learned from one of them how to be very proficient with the slingshot. David already had killed the bear and lion to protect his sheep. Judges 20:16 says, "Among all this people there were seven hundred chosen men lefthanded (of the tribe of Benjamin); everyone could sling stones at a hair breadth, and not miss." Why did not Saul and the Benjamites in Saul's army use a sling shot to kill Goliath? They may not have been trained in using the slingshot. Yet, the primary problem was because they feared the Giant and feared losing their lives. Besides, this was a spiritual battle between God and the Giant representing the devil. 2 Corinthians 10:4 says, "For though we walk in the flesh, we do not war after the flesh: (For the weapons of our warfare are not carnal, but mighty through God to the pulling down of strong holds.)" David knew he would win the battle because God was on his side and the battle was the Lord's, but the victory would be David's and the army of Israel.

David removed the natural armor of Saul, or the old religious order Saul tried to put upon him. As it relates to the old religious order, David concluded, "King Saul, this armor didn't work for you, and it won't work for me. If religious organizations could have brought the body of Christ to perfection, it would have been perfected centuries ago. If forming denominations could have cut Goliath's head off and put Satan where he belonged, under our feet, then leaders of the organized old religious order had far too many opportunities to do so but failed. You see, Saul, now that your anointing is gone, no amount of armor and religious structure will make up for the loss. You cannot make up for the lack of anointing with committees, departments, missionary boards, youth activities, etc."

When David started down the mountain to meet Goliath, he had only his SHEPHERD'S STAFF in his hand and an empty SHEPHERD'S BAG on his side. He was clothed with faith and the knowledge that God had anointed him to be King over Israel. God is not a man that He would lie. Being King was sometime in the future, so David trusted God and had faith that he would come on the other side of this battle victorious. David was led by the Holy Spirit, and the Holy Spirit had anointed him to battle Goliath. Therefore, he rushed down the mountain toward the valley to fight full of faith, anointing, and confidence that he would be victorious.

When David reached the brook that ran at the foot of the mountain, he stopped to pick up some ammunition-five smooth stones. These stones represent the Fivefold Ministry Functions of the Apostle, Prophet, Evangelist, Pastor and Teacher (Ephesians 4:11). Today, the good Shepherd, Jesus, still uses five smooth ministry stones to be thrown at the satanic forces, which have come up against Believers. These five stones had been tumbling in the stream of living water, and all their sharp edges were knocked off, as result of being thrown against the other stones for many years. When they were tossed from David's sling toward the Giant, the stone selected would not fly off course and miss the target with any wind (of doctrine) that might be blowing at the time (Ephesians 4:14). These five stones had been in the working process of the living water for many years and had been polished and washed by the water of the word of God (Ephesians 5:26). This slingshot was a weapon that Goliath did not know how to defend against, so he had no defensive moves against the rock being hurled at his forehead at the speed of a bullet. God can reveal to you new weapons of warfare that the devil does not know about and has no defense against to bring you victory over the enemy of the Kingdom of God. God's Kingdom Soldiers always win because God is the greatest strategy planner in war. God can cause a sandstorm as He did to stop the Egyptian Army during the six-day war against Israel in June 1967 when Israel won and captured and occupied the Golan Heights, the West Bank (including East Jerusalem), the Gaza Strip, and the Sinai Peninsula. God can cause a flood to drown the enemy as He did Pharaoh's army when following the Israelites crossing the Red Sea.

For Believers to be used by God in this new movement of the Holy Spirit, they must preach both the gospel of the Kingdom of God (Matthew 24:47) and repentance and remission of sins (Luke 24:47). Then after receiving a born again spirit, Believers will have to submit to the Godhead's process of transformation of their minds, emotions, hearts that houses the will, of knocking off all of the rough edges; so, they can be anointed Kingdom Soldiers to go up against the Goliaths that is attacking them, their families, their communities, their businesses, their church members, and against the issues that are against the laws of God's kingdom and word.

Isaiah 57:6 says, "Among the smooth stones of the stream is your portion; they, they, are your lot!" It did not matter which smooth stone (or fivefold minister) David would use against Goliath; for the remaining stones could be used later against Goliath's four other giant brothers. Each stone when throne would be directed by the anointed guiding hand of God. The five stones were not jealous of each other as the rough edges of jealousy had already been worn off. There were many other sharp stones lodged in the side of the mountain with the sharp edges of their stubborn independence protruding outward, which David knew he could not use. There are some ministers in the Body of Christ who take immense pleasure in using their sharp edges to cut other ministers at every opportunity. However, the smooth stones would not cut each other, but were well rounded spiritually in their personalities to rub up against each other and learned to love other Ministers in the same bag or spiritual fellowship in the Kingdom of God without competition or jealousy.

Now, Goliath, the devil, was expecting to go up against the old religious order structure. Goliath had graduated from seminary school and learned all about religion. He had studied all the right methods to fight in the religion politics and win, as he was possessed of a demonic religious spirit. The devil spends a lot of time in the old religious order structure learning how to deceive the leaders and stop a revival. Goliath thought that his enemy would come out to battle fully armed with shield, helmet, sword, spear and coat of mail. Goliath thought that you cannot even start an old religious order structure nowadays without extensive advertisement, a core of tithing families, committees, assistant pastors, a choir and music director, a youth director, and a lot of other machinery and ecclesiastical structure. So, Goliath thought David would wear and use the traditional armor and weapons to which Goliath was accustomed and experienced.

What Goliath saw and heard was this small in physical stature Shepherd Teenager who had no traditional armor or weapons, other than a slingshot and a shepherd's staff, claiming he was God's anointed, with the bold praises of God in His mouth. Goliath said, "Am I a dog that you come to me with sticks?" (Verse 43) or to make it relevant to the old religious order today, the devil would say, "What kind of old time religion meeting is this? I expected at least 1500 people to show up for your healing crusade! I am the mighty devil (Goliath) who has been oppressing people with sickness since I caused Adam and Eve to sin in the Garden of Eden. This small group is an insult to my fame and reputation. My intention was to show you Believers in Jesus how weak the old religious order structure is against me by not allowing one person to be healed at this so-called miracle crusade! I have many Believers who already believe that miracles are not for today, and this meeting will confirm their belief. Isn't this meeting televised? How come you called only these five prayer Intercessors to come to this meeting? They do not look like they are sick to me. I thought this was going to be a healing crusade! What do you mean they are here to pray against me on behalf of all the Believers in the Ekklesia who are sick of me? Do you mean that these little closet Intercessors are here to try to defeat me and try to reveal my deceptive ways? This is a waste of my time. What do you mean they are here to cut off my head? I have kept sickness and disease in the old religious oder structure for almost two thousand years. What do you mean that these five little stones have been chosen by God to stop me? Who are these guys? In what wilderness have they been hiding? I doubt if they even have seminary training. What is the name of their old religious order organization? I think you are bluffing! I do not believe they have any spiritual weapons of warfare, so let us fight!" Then the devil is self-deceived and has to run away because of the anointing on these five prayer warriors is too much for him to defeat. Isaiah 10:27 speaks of victory, "…and the yoke shall be destroyed because of the anointing."

1 Samuel 17:45 says, "Then David said to the Philistine, 'You come to me with a sword, with a spear, and with a javelin. But I come to you in the name of the Lord of host, the God of the armies of Israel, whom you have defied." In other words, David's weapons of warfare were "... not carnal but mighty in God for pulling down strongholds, casting down arguments and every high thing that exalts itself against the knowledge of God, bringing every thought into captivity to the obedience of Christ" (2 Corinthians 10:4-5). David continued in verses 46-47, "This day the Lord will deliver you into my hand, and I will strike you and take your head from you. And this day I will give the carcasses of the camp of the Philistines to the birds of the air and the wild beasts of the earth, that all the earth may know that there is a God in Israel. Then all this assembly shall know that the Lord does not save with sword and spear; for the battle is the Lord's and He will give you into our hands." In other words, David told the devil that he was looking for an unanointed religious leader with traditional natural religious weapons with which to do battle, but he, David, came with the anointing of God. He would prove that God does not use as a weapon an organization or hierarchical religious structure.

David did not even boast that in his bag of ammunition was God's ordained anointed fivefold ministry stones ready to be used by God to kill Goliath's brothers. All of the fivefold ministry stones would be eventually used, but the glory goes to the Lord. David spoke with His Kingly anointing, with confidence that God had ordained victory to His anointed in this battle. The people likewise were amazed at Jesus' confidence and kingly anointing: "And they were astonished at His teaching, for He taught them as one having authority, and not as the scribes (those in the old religious order structure)" (Mark 1:22).

1 Samuel 17:49-51 says, "Then David put his hand in his bag and took out a stone; and he slung it and struck the Philistine in his forehead, so that the stone sank into his forehead, and he fell on his face to the earth. So David prevailed over the Philistine with a sling and a stone, and struck the Philistine and killed him. But there was no sword (old Church religious structure) in the hand of David. Therefore, David ran and stood over the Philistine, took his sword and drew it out of its sheath and killed him, and cut off his head with it. And when the Philistines saw that their champion was dead, they fled." James 4:7 says, "Therefore submit to God. Resist the devil and he will flee from you." The old religious order structure cannot stand on the same level as the anointed ministers of God that are led by the Holy Spirit as Kingdom Soldiers of Christ against

the kingdom of darkness.

The true fivefold Minister must speak with authority and anointing as he or she hears God's *rhema* word from the Spirit of God; because when he or she speaks, God's word will be confirmed with signs following (Mark 16:20). When you are truly anointed of God, being led by the Holy Spirit, everyone will know it, as Christ's divine nature in you, through the power of the Holy Spirit, simply goes forth preaching the gospel of the Kingdom (Matthew 24:14) and repentance and remission of sins (Luke 24:47), casting out devils, healing the sick, raising the dead, slaying your Goliaths, such as the influence of the god of mammon in people's lives.

Look at the effect one anointed Believer of God can have on a true *Ekklesia* fellowship. It is the anointing that breaks the yoke of the enemy (Isaiah 10:27). Did not God say, "...Do not touch My anointed ones, and do My prophets no harm" (Psalm 105:6). Christ means the "Anointed One" or "Messiah, the Anointed." Therefore, a Believer not only is a follower and disciple of the Anointed One, Christ Jesus, but the Believer has been born again as a new creature in Christ, Who is anointed by God with the Holy Spirit like Christ's humanity nature (Acts 10:38; 1 John 2:20). A Believer is a new creature in Christ (2 Corinthians 5:17), meaning a Believer has taken on a different and new form of everlasting life in his born again spirit as a new man, "which is renewed in knowledge after the image of him that created him" (Colossians 3:10). A Believer's born again spirit is in and from the resurrected Second Man, Christ Jesus (1 Corinthians 15:47) and no longer is in the fallen first man, Adam (1 Corinthians 15:45). The everlasting life in Christ Jesus' resurrected humanity nature is in the Believer's new born again spirit which is born perfect (Hebrews 12:23) from Christ's incorruptible seed from His resurrected humanity nature (1 Peter 1:23). Jesus' resurrected humanity nature is the everlasting Father of the Believer's born again spirit (Isaiah 9:6; Hebrews 2:13). The Believer's born again spirit does not sin because he is born by the power and design of God (1 John 3:9). The Believer's born again spirit, as the new man, is joined with Christ's humanity nature spirit as one spirit (1 Corinthians 6:17). The Believer's born again spirit, as the new man, is righteous and holy (Ephesians 4:24). Colossians 10:13 says, "And have put on the new man, which is renewed in knowledge after the image of Him that created Him."

The Believer should petition in prayer that he or she be endowed with the manifestation of the Holy Spirit's anointing and gifts wherever and whenever he or she ministers as Christ's Ambassador here on earth (2 Corinthians 5:20). A Believer has the entire Godhead, the source of the anointing, living inside of the Believer as the Temple of the Godhead (John 14:17, 23; 1 Corinthians 6:19-individually; 1 Corinthians 3:16- collectively in local *Ekklesia*; and Ephesians 2:21-collectively in the universal *Ekklesia*).

Goliath paid the price of trying to touch God's anointed. The Lord will do battle for whom He has anointed. One anointed Believer trusting God and walking out in faith caused the army of Israel to suddenly have faith and courage that results in victory. "Now the men of Israel and Judah arose and shouted and pursued the Philistines as far as the entrance of the valley and to the gates of Ekron. And the wounded of the Philistines fell along the road to Shaaraim, even as far as Gath and Ekron" (1 Samuel 17:52).

JONATHAN COULD NOT LEAVE THE LUXURY,
COMFORT, AND NATURAL BLESSINGS DERIVED

FROM LIVING AS A LEADER IN KING SAUL'S PALACE.

Jonathan recognized God's anointing and became David's "soul buddy." 1 Samuel 18:1 says, "Now when he had finished speaking to Saul, the soul of Jonathan was knit to the soul of David, and Jonathan loved him as his own soul. Saul took him that day and would not let him go home to his father's house anymore. Then Jonathan and David made a covenant because he loved him as his own soul. And Jonathan took off the robe that was on him and gave it to David, with his armor, even to his sword and his bow and his belt."

Jonathan saw and understood the divine kingly anointing upon David. Jonathan came to know that David was the one who was to sit on the throne as the next King, and not himself. Jonathan accepted David's calling to be King with gladness. Even though David and Jonathan were the best of friends, Jonathan had no experience living off the grid. Jonathan did not want to rough it in the wilderness with David. Jonathan liked the comfort of the palace and his own home. 1 Samuel 23:16-17 says, "And Jonathan, Saul's son arose, and went to David into the wood, and strengthened his hand in God. And he said unto him, 'Fear not: for the hand of Saul my father shall not find thee; and thou shalt be king over Israel, and I shall be next unto thee; and that also Saul my father knoweth.' And the two made a covenant before the LORD: and David abode in the wood, and Jonathan went to his house." Thus, David lived in the woods and at times hid in Adullam's cave, while Jonathan lived in luxury in his own house being supported by King Saul. Unfortunately, Jonathan never would leave the old religious order structure which had lots of riches and power in the natural, but in so doing Jonathan tried to pour new wine, representing the anointing, into old wine skins, representing the old religious order structure, but the old religious order structure could not hold the new wine that David had.

Jonathan loved David and saw that David was God's chosen anointed King, but obviously Jonathan could not manage the rejection and reproach David was receiving from Saul, Jonathan's father. Jonathan loved his father and David, but he chose poorly who to be with and failed to fulfill the will of God. Today, among old religious order leaders, there are many "Jonathans." They want the anointing and the fullness of God as their inheritance. They are willing to pray, fast, give, go on ministry teams, and sacrifice. However, they will not let go of the old religious order structure and go and suffer in the wilderness and be a reproach for a season by the present old religious order leadership.

Many Believers in the old religious order structure, like Jonathan of old, do not lack courage or lack a great love for the Lord. These Believers are some of the finest resolute workers in the old religious order that is there. They just do not understand why these anointed "Davids" have to waste their time with a small band of followers in the wilderness when there is plenty of room in the old religious order structure for them to minister. The old religious order structure just needs "a good shot in the arm," they believe. Loyalty to a man or woman of God is what keeps a lot of Jonathans out of the new Movement of the Holy Spirit. Fortunately, sometimes the anointing of God comes upon and energizes a leader of an old religious order structure, and this leader risks everything, gives up the security of his religious order, and starts moving his congregation into this new Movement of the Holy Spirit. It is wonderful, and the Lord loves to see these mature leaders find a new lease on their spiritual lives. If they do, the Holy Spirit will mightily use them. Yet, they must be teachable, pliable, humble, and obedient to the Holy Spirit! Old things of religious tradition that the Holy Spirit tells them to discard has to be rejected and removed.

Too often, these leaders of the old religious order do not seek after the anointing of the Holy Spirit, but the religious traditions. Like so many Believers today who are caught in the "old wineskins" religious orders who were part of the organization of earlier movements of the Spirit, the thing Jonathan lacked was a hearing ear when God said, "Come out of her, My people, lest you share in her sins, and lest you receive of her plagues" (Revelation 18:4). The "Jonathans" think, "If these 'Davids' who are so anointed would just bring their anointing into the main-stream of the old religious order, they could draw big crowds, win substantial numbers of souls to the Lord and could sit at the tables of the 'King Sauls' who are the present leaders in power and wealth." Yet, what the Lord really wants is God's Kingdom Government, with His anointed leaders submitted under His power and authority with purified hearts, who want more than mere religion or denominational religious tradition. Jesus Christ wants to be on the throne in His King-dom, and He wants to mature His citizens of His Kingdom to be more like Him in their souls, like Believers' born again spirits. Jesus wants to be intimate with each Believer as a citizen of heaven and a citizen of the Kingdom of God here on earth. God wants to live in Believers as His Temple guiding the perfect, holy, and righteous born again spirit in Kingdom ministries and in making the soul spiritually minded, spiritually emotional, and spiritually heartfelt to be trans-formed to do the will of God (John 14: 16-17, 23; 1 Corinthians 6:19; 1 Corinthians 3:16; Ephe-sians 2:20-21; Romans 12:2; Romans 8:6).

Jonathan just could not see the necessity to separate himself away from the palace, servants, comfort of large houses, recognition as the King's son, fine clothes, wealth, and all that symbol-ized natural blessings from God, but can be an entrapment, especially during the Revival of the Holy Spirit. God wants Believers to steward His natural possession, but He does not want those natural possessions to become the primary focus of the Believers. Jonathan probably thought, "Why must David sit in Adullam's Cave? Is not poverty the sign of a curse? Besides, look at all the 'misfits' joining David. I love David with his wonderful anointing, but he has all of these 'second string players' joining his band of merry men."

1 Samuel 22:1-2 says, "David therefore departed from there and escaped to the cave of Adul-lam. So when his brothers and all his father's house heard it, they went down there to him. And everyone who was in distress, everyone who was in debt, and everyone who was discontented gathered to him. So, he became captain over them. And there were about four hundred men with him." Jonathan was not in distress, was not in debt, and really was not discontented in the natu-ral. He had everything he wanted in the natural living in Saul's Palace; except he did not have the anointing of the Holy Spirit, and he was not doing the work of the Lord as was his friend, Da-vid. Yet, it was Jonathan's choice not to join the Davidic Revival. The revival bunch of second-string Kingdom Soldiers did not look like they had enough resources to win any battle. They had no old religious order building, no money, and all of them looked like they needed about ten years of counseling before they could get up to ground level.

David had a motley band of 400 distressed, indebted discontents (1 Samuel 22:1-2) that grew to 600 anointed mighty men of war and members of his wilderness congregation. Most Pastors or Teachers today have less than 350 members in their congregations, and David's 400-600 mem-bers may seem like an adequate army of Believers. However, compared to the thousands that Saul, who had lost his anointing, could assemble, the size of David's army was very small. Yet, David's mighty men had the anointing of God and accomplished mighty exploits for the Lord and their generation. Many anointed "Davids," today, are frustrated when they see an old wine-skin religious order leadership which has little anointing, are doing essentially nothing except sitting around the King's table getting fat and burping up with size oriented obesity that spend forty million dollars on a religious building edifice when over 60% of the world population, mostly in Asian countries, cannot read or have a T.V. or a radio to hear both the gospel of the Kingdom and repentance and remission of sins. There are many nations that could be evangelized with only ten million dollars.

In America, under the established old religious order structure, according to Barnum Research it costs close to $10,000 in investment (radio, T.V., traveling evangelists and local religious building expenses) for each person to be saved. This is too expensive. If the rank-and-file Believers were activated to do the work of ministry in the workplace, school place, marketplace, and government place, then the cost would be minuscule. The big old religious order organization and building as the anemic *Ekklesia* have captivated the souls of many innocent sheep throughout history, and it is time for the truth to prevail and that the desire for intimate relationship with God liberate the souls from religious bondage.

Again, even though Jonathan knew that David was the anointed chosen King, he chose to stay in the comfort of his father's Palace. In the meantime, David and his mighty men were sitting in the wilderness around a campfire, singing praises and new songs before the Lord, having fellowship as the presence of the Holy Spirit was with them, and He anointed them as God's *Ekklesia* of Kingdom Soldiers. The Holy Spirit had left the Palace because He had left King Saul. Jonathan was busy socializing, attending Saul's banquets, participating in Saul's committee meetings, trying to sell Saul's promotions, watching Saul's political maneuvering, supporting Saul's policies, and avoiding Saul's demonic religious spirit.

Saul's old religious order structure was a fatal religious attraction for Jonathan. What Jonathan did not understand was that God was training through David His historical example of a chosen and anointed army and leadership to be future heroes of the faith and serve the King of Kings, the greater great great grandson of David (as the lineage from Mary), Who would sit on an everlasting throne. This time in the wilderness was the time of preparation for David and his mighty men of valor. From the spoils of war, David and his mighty men, along with inspired other leaders after David became King joyfully donated gold, silver, precious stones and other wealth to build Solomon's Temple, where God and His *Shekinah* glory became present (1 Chronicles 29:1-9; 2 Chronicles 7:1-3).

Has the old religious order structure you belong to become your fatal religious attraction? Furthermore, has the old religious order structure become your focus to serve instead of the Lord, Himself. Be very careful with that which makes you comfortable. Are you seeking first the comfort of your position in the old religious order structure instead of seeking first the Kingdom of God and His righteous?

In the old religious order structure, Jonathan first acted as a person with principles. Jonathan rejected his father's wishes that he, Jonathan, go and kill David. To his credit, Jonathan refused to come up against this new move of the Holy Spirit (1 Samuel chapters 19&20). 1 Samuel 20:30-33 says, "Then Saul's anger was aroused against Jonathan, and he said to him, 'You son of a perverse, rebellious woman! Do I not know that you have chosen the son of Jesse to your own shame and to the shame of your mother's nakedness? For as long as the son of Jesse lives on the earth, you shall not be established, nor your Kingdom. Now therefore, send and bring him to me, for he shall surely die.' And Jonathan answered Saul his father, and said to him, 'Why should he be killed? What has he done?' Then Saul cast a spear at him to kill him, by which Jonathan knew that it was determined by his father to kill David. So Jonathan arose from the table in fierce anger, and ate no food the second day of the month, for he was grieved for David, because his father had treated him shamefully."

David's exile from Saul's Palace (or main body of the old religious order structure) lasted ten years, but finally at age 30 David was crowned King over Judah in Hebron (2 Samuel 2:4). However, Jonathan missed his beloved friend, David's, coronation as King because Jonathan was already dead, having chosen to remain with the old religious order structure where he died with his father, Saul. Jonathan chose to experience the natural life comforts given by the old Movement of the Holy Spirit with Saul, which was now religiously organized to death; and Jonathan died with Saul in battle. Had Jonathan chosen to experience the discomfort of the wilderness along with David and his mighty men, Jonathan would have been chosen to serve as David's right hand of power and authority next to the Davidic Throne and Kingdom that was established by God as everlasting (2 Samuel 7:16).

Jonathan missed the conquering of the Jebusites to regain Jerusalem (2 Samuel 5:6-9). He missed seeing David reign as King over Judah from Hebron for seven and half years and as King over all Israel and Judah from David's Throne in Jerusalem for thirty three years (2 Samuel 5:5). He missed dancing with David before the Ark of the Covenant when it was brought to Jerusalem and placed in David's Tabernacle on Zion Hill (2 Samuel 6:14-15), where new songs of worship and praise were offered to the Lord daily (1 Chronicles 16:37) and was a type of a New Testament Ekklesia of Kingdom Government Assembly and Kingdom Soldiers anointed and sent by David's greater grandson, Jesus Christ to the whole fallen world.

In fact, Jonathan missed out during the entire time of the height of the New Movement of the Holy Spirit under David's reign, just like so many people will do today who try to hold on to the familiar, comfortable, settled practices of the organized old religious order structure which has little or no anointing because it merely is the present derivative of one of the last great movements of the Holy Spirit. Believers will miss out if they fail to listen to God and be led by the Holy Spirit as sons and daughters of Christ Jesus' resurrected humanity spirit. Believers mistake the display of the pomp and circumstance and religious rituals in the natural in the ecclesiastical organization for the works of the power of the Holy Spirit. The natural old religious order does have a false feeling of accomplishment, a feeling of order, a feeling of security, but these feelings are generated through the works of the natural inspirations of man, not by the leading of the Holy Spirit.

During the time of Moses' leading the children of Israel in the wilderness for forty years, when God notified through Moses that His Ark of the Covenant was moving, then the Israelites had to immediately pack up and be led by God or stay and die in the practices of some dying organized old religious order which has no present anointing or mandated direction by the Holy Spirit. The provision is wherever the Kingdom of God is, and the entire Godhead lives in the Kingdom of God and in each Believer with each Believer's born again spirit. Thus, foundationally for the anointing and the movement of the Holy Spirit, Matthew 6:33 says, "But seek ye first the kingdom of God, and his righteousness; and all these things shall be added unto you."

The new wine of the Spirit cannot be stored in the old wineskin religious order structure. Jesus said in Matthew 9:17, "Nor do they put new wine into old wineskins, or else the wineskins break, the wine is spilled, and the wineskins are ruined. But they put new wine into new wineskins, and both are preserved."

Everyone needs to have a spiritual checkup with Dr. Jesus. True Kingdom *Ekklesia* life and relationships are supposed to run under the close diagnostic eyes of God the Father, God the Word, and God the Holy Spirit. You may find some flesh that needs to enter the crucifixion of Christ to release more zoe life. Are there ideas, values, and old religious order traditions of which you must let go? Have you grown comfortable in your old religious order congregation setting? Are you set in your old religious order practices? Will you allow God to anoint you afresh and bring His Spiritual renewal into your soul? Will you become spiritually minded, emotionally stable, and willfully submitted to God in your soul? Will you change the library of beliefs in your heart? Are you willing to be baptized in the Lord's spiritual fire? Are you willing to experience reproach, persecution, rejection, defamation, and suffering from members of the old religious order structure for the sake of Christ and His Kingdom of God? Are you willing to be led into the wilderness by the Holy Spirit to resist the temptations of the devil to experience the Holy Spirit's anointing and power?

If you feel the spiritual fire in the hot furnace of circumstances has been turned up in your daily living, perhaps you are experiencing that the old briers and brambles of the old religious order structure have entrapped you and have been holding you back from being the Holy Spirit's anointed that has become aflame. It is God's holy cleansing fire within you that will burn and make clear God's pathway to reveal God's assignment for you in His next great Revival. When you become aflame, you are baptized with fire by the Lord; and you will walk in the fiery furnace without even the stench of smoke on your garments because the Lord's divine nature will be with you; and God's holy fire will consume you. So, natural fiery circumstances cannot burn out God's spiritual holy fire. Firemen fight forest fires by starting controlled fires to burn off the brush and dead wood ahead of the out of control raging fire, so there is nothing to consume in the path the menacing fire is traveling.

Become the Lord's anointed servant in His Kingdom whose only desire is to glorify the Lord and the entire Godhead and receive the fullness of your inheritance to again serve the Godhead and allow them through you to minister the gospel of the Kingdom and repentance and remission of sins. As you obey, you will go from carnality to godliness, glory to glory in the presence and under the anointing of the Holy Spirit. Do not be satisfied with an offer of a religious position for a salary in an old religious order structure, unless you clearly hear from God that this is your assignment. Be willing to suffer for a time in the wilderness as God prepares your destiny as part of His chosen generation, royal priesthood, holy nation, and peculiar people in the Spirit's Revival true *Ekklesia* of Kingdom Ambassadors and Kingdom Soldiers, and be free from religion. In the meantime, touch not God's once Anointed and do His Prophets no harm.

Revelation 1:6 says that as a Believer, you are a Priest and King of the Lord Jesus and God. Although you became a King and Priest upon initial salvation and a citizen of heaven, your office experience might take some time until your daily habit is to seek first the Kingdom of God and

His righteousness, which means being in right standing with God. Be like David and wait on the Lord, and your Coronation Day as an under-ruler in Christ's Kingdom will come when you least expect it.

Be thankful to God. Be like David, a man or woman after God's own heart. Be a worshipping King. Always take care of the sheep and lead them to the Kingdom of God, not into habitual religious rituals and lukewarm fellowship. Colossians 1:12-13 says, "Giving thanks unto the Father, which hath made us meet to be partakers of the inheritance of the saints in light: Who hath delivered us from the power of darkness, and hath translated us into the kingdom of His dear Son."

Ekklesia Has Been Mistranslated as "Church", and Ministers Have Failed to Preach The Gospel of the Kingdom

CHAPTER TWO

Ekklesia Has Been Mistranslated as "Church", and Ministers Have Failed to Preach the Gospel of The Kingdom

THE REAL *EKKLESIA*

When Believers discuss the end time Revival *Ekklesia*, then they need to know the truth as to what the Greek word, *Ekklesia*, really means. Being led by the Holy Spirit during Revival, Believers are commanded to witness and promote the truth of God's word, not religious tradition. Examine the Greek, Aramaic, Latin, and Hebrew meanings of English words to determine their true meaning. The English word "Church" is a mistranslation of the Greek word *Ekklesia*. The real *Ekklesia* is not a building, a lecture hall, or a music center, but involves Believers living in loving communal fellowship with each other by allowing Christ to live in them and through them while the Believers evangelize the lost in the world and lead them into the Kingdom of God. The *Ekklesia* also is the Lord's viable Kingdom of God spiritual government assembly and the Lord's obedient Kingdom of God spiritual army. When Believers study Scripture, the pretext, post text, and historical setting will determine the contextual meaning of a word or passage of Scripture written in English. *Ekklesia* also defines the Kingdom of God services that new Believers from the Revival are asked to perform as they mature in Christ after initial salvation, instead of just sitting in pews every service and paying tithes and offerings for stage performances of praise and worship and delivering sermons for the rest of their lives. Leaders have to disciple unbelievers by preaching both the gospel of the Kingdom of God (Matthew 24:14) in conjunction with preaching repentance and remission of sins (Luke 24:47). Colossians 1:13-14 says, "Who hath delivered us from the power of darkness, and hath translated us into the kingdom of His dear Son: (14) In Whom we have redemption through His blood, even the forgiveness of sins." Your healing and prosperity must take on the personality of Christ Jesus for the Kingdom power to manifest to bring the blessing in this time and in this natural world. You will have prosperity and health in the same proportion as your soul prospers (3 John 2), and your soul prospers by entering the Kingdom of God and by allowing Jesus to become everything to you, which you can only experience through loving submission to Christ in the Kingdom of God.

Jesus is the Believers' personal Physician, Advocate, Faith, Provider, Righteous One, Sanctification, and Wisdom, but God must dwell and rule from His throne inside of Believers for them to experience these blessings in a practical way. Jesus' divine nature is with Believers always (Matthew 28:20). Christ is the only Way into the Kingdom. The *Ekklesia* has to operate within the Kingdom of God, not outside the Kingdom of God. God expects Believers to bring the Kingdom of God to manifest God's power, love, and sound mind which is inside Believers wherever they travel, wherever they work, wherever they go in the marketplace, wherever they are educated, and wherever they go to have fellowship in the *Ekklesia* community.

After initial salvation the entire Godhead, along with the Ephesians 4:11 Ministers participate in the transformation, maturation, and sanctification of Believers' souls to become righteous and holy to be godly servants who operate their ministry functions with knowing the truth in God's word and expressing *agape* love in fellowship with other Believers. This book, and especially this chapter, will speak about the word "Church," wrongfully translated from the Greek word *Ekklesia*, who are commanded by the Lord to preach the gospel of the Kingdom (Matthew 24:14) and preach repentance and remission of sins (Luke 24:47), while they experience the ongoing transformation of their souls with these understandings.

Preaching the gospel of the Kingdom and preaching the repentance and the remission of sins are like the two wings of an airplane. The airplane will not fly with just one wing; it takes both, and on each wing are the engines that empower the plane down the runway and up, up, up into the spiritual heavens.

MANKIND'S CREATION
DOMINION MANDATE

The original mandate of God to Adam and Eve and their posterity was stated in Genesis 1:28: "And God blessed them, and God said unto them, 'Be fruitful, and multiply, and replenish the earth, and subdue it: and have dominion over the fish of the sea, and over the fowl of the air, and over every living thing that moveth upon the earth.'" This is still the foundational dominion mandate that the Believers are commanded to fulfill. The Hebrew word for "dominion" in Genesis 1:26, 28 is *"mamlaka,"* (Strongs H4467), from the primitive root words *"malak"* (Strongs H4427), *"melek"* (Strongs H4428), or *"mashal"* (Strongs H4910), which are the same or similar Hebrew words that elsewhere in the Bible are translated into English as "kingdom" (Exodus 19:6), "reign" (Exodus 15:18), "King" (Genesis 14:8), "rule" (Judges 8:22), and "realm" (2 Chronicles 20:30). Yet, all these Hebrew words are related to the Kingdom of Heaven becoming the Kingdom of God here on earth, as God's colony.

The point is that Adam and Eve's mission from Father God was to establish the Kingdom of God here on earth as it is in Heaven, and to have Believers become both citizens of Heaven and also citizens of God's Kingdom here on earth, Adam and Eve's dominion mandate was to be God's under rulers and as God's servant kings, lords, and priests. With the advent of Christ Jesus, Believers today are not just "members" of Jesus' Kingdom, as Christianity is not a religion. Believers are citizens of Heaven (Philippians 3:20), with citizenship responsibilities and rights that are blessings from God that He manifests here on earth to Believers from His heavenly Kingdom (Ephesians 1:3). Believers for over 1,800 years have failed for the most part in working as Jesus' *Ekklesia*, where Believers are commanded to serve as Kingdom spiritual Ambassadors and Kingdom spiritual Soldiers. Like Adam, Believers are mandated as God's chosen generation, royal priesthood, holy nation, and peculiar people (1 Peter 2:9) to be transformed in their souls with God's goodness, righteousness, and love; and with that motivation, to take dominion over the earth, the world system, every animal creature, fish, birds, plants, and all things here on earth but not other humans. To this end, with God's goodness, love, fruit of the Spirit, holiness, and righteousness, Believers' dominion mandate is to take over the world's financial centers, businesses, industries, movie productions, radio programs, newspapers, news media, Internet, schools, secular governments, and every other aspect of the nation in which each Believer lives, while submitting to the Holy Spirit as He leads their minds, emotions, heart, and Will in their souls in spiritual reality, as their souls are transformed, cleansed, matured, consecrated, and sanctified to make them better Kingdom servants in Christ for this great Kingdom service.

The dominion mandate of Jesus Christ as the Son of Man, along with the saints of the Most

High, was clearly written in a vision and prophecy by Daniel. Daniel 7: 13-14, 27 says, "I saw in the night visions, and behold, one like the Son of Man came with the clouds of Heaven, and came to the Ancient of days, and they brought him near before him. And there was given Him dominion, and glory, and a kingdom, that all people, nations, and languages, should serve him: his dominion is an everlasting dominion, which shall not pass away, and His kingdom that which shall not be destroyed… And the kingdom and dominion, and the greatness of the kingdom under the whole Heaven, shall be given to the people of the saints of the Most High, whose Kingdom is an everlasting Kingdom, and all dominions shall serve and obey Him." Jesus was referred to as the Last Adam and as the Second Man (2 Corinthians 15:45, 47). Jesus, and His disciples, preached the "gospel of the Kingdom" (Matthew 24:14) and preached the repentance and remission of sins (Luke 24:47).

For the authority of the *Ekklesia* to rise and subdue and take dominion over every aspect of a nation and culture, the apostolic and prophetic functions have to repair the breach in the foundation of the *Ekklesia*. Jesus said in Mark 2:22: "And no man putteth new wine into old bottles (wineskins): else the new wine doth burst the bottles (wineskins), and the wine is spilled, and the bottles (wineskins) will be marred: but new wine must be put into new bottles (wineskins)." This scripture will be repeated often in this book because of the importance of Jesus' statement about the harmfulness of pure religion instead of intimate relationship with God and Christ. Jesus came not to bring a new religion but rather to inaugurate the Kingdom of God here on earth and to die on a Roman cross for the remission of sins and as the witness to the world that He is King with the name above every other name (Philippians 2:7-11).

If there is going to be a repairing of the foundational beliefs of the Body of Christ to function as the Kingdom *Ekklesia*, it should come from the modern-day foundational functions of the Apostles and Prophets (Ephesians 2:20). Is there a crack in the foundation of the *Ekklesia* that leaders and denominations have ignored the last 1,800 years or so? If the foundation of the *Ekklesia* is weak or cracked, then what Believers traditionally call the "Church" is built on a weak foundation. The Body of Christ has been given the Creator's PRIME MANDATE to spread God's goodness, holiness, and love, while subduing and taking dominion of the earth and world system through preaching the gospel of the Kingdom and preaching repentance and remission of sins to evangelize new Believers. The Body of Christ has been mandated to make disciples of all nations, not just converts, which means that after initial salvation to mature Believers into God's Kingdom mandate to be servants motivated by holiness, righteousness, goodness, and *agape* love as the New Man in Christ Jesus. The world system is currently under the rule of the prince of this world, so why are those in the world outdoing the members of the Body of Christ in taking dominion and having control of the world's political and economic systems? Is it because leaders are preaching an anemic self-focused message of an atonement theology, which is good, but are they leaving out the preaching of the gospel of the Kingdom?

Nearing the time of His false trial, whipped with a Cat-o-Nine-Tails, and crucifixion, some Greeks (John 12:20) and Jews came to speak with Jesus. Jesus equally called the Greeks and Jews with a servanthood mandate as His followers, not religion. John 12: 26-35 says, "If any MAN (Jew and Gentile) SERVE Me, let him FOLLOW Me; and where I am, there shall also My servant be: if any man serve Me, him will My Father honour. Now is My soul troubled; and what shall I say? 'Father, save me from this hour: but for this cause came I unto this hour. Father, glorify thy name (Jesus).' Then came there a voice from Heaven, saying, 'I have both glorified it (Jesus' name), and will glorify it (Jesus' name) again.' The people therefore, that stood by, and heard it, said that it thundered: others said, 'An angel spake to Him.' Jesus answered and said, 'This voice came not because of Me, but for your sakes. Now is the judgment of this world: now shall the prince of this world be cast out (the mandate to take back possession of the earth, world system, and the fallen people living on earth). And I, if I be lifted up from the earth (on the Cross), will draw all men unto Me.' This he said, signifying what death he should die. The people answered him, 'We have heard out of the law that Christ abideth for ever: and how sayest thou, "The Son of man must be lifted up? Who is this Son of man?" Then Jesus said unto them, 'Yet a little while is the light with you. Walk while ye have the light, lest darkness come upon you: for he that walketh in darkness knoweth not whither he goeth.'"

WHAT GOSPEL DID CHRIST PRIMARILY PREACH? WHAT GOSPEL DOES THE CURRENT CHURCH PREACH?

Jesus spoke about the forgiveness of sins, and when Nicodemus came to Jesus in the night and stated that he knew that Jesus was a teacher that came from God, Jesus answered with a salvation message because Nicodemus was a Pharisee but was not saved because he had not yet been born again. Jesus said in John 3:3,5-6, "…Verily, verily, I say unto thee, 'Except a man be born again, he cannot see the kingdom of God.' … Verily, verily, I say unto thee, 'Except a man be born of water and of the spirit, he cannot enter the kingdom of God. That which is born of the flesh is flesh; and that which is born of the spirit is spirit.'" Jesus mentions both being born again and seeing and entering the Kingdom of God in the same discourse, so, seeing and entering the Kingdom of God is the purpose of being born again and being born of water and of the spirit.

Are the leaders in the Body of Christ preaching only repentance and remission of sins (Luke 24:47) without preaching the gospel of the kingdom at the same time (Matthew 24:47)? From God's perspective, the true dynamic, world changing, activating message is the gospel of the Kingdom? The gospel of the Kingdom is the "good news," as the "good news" is much more than just receiving the benefits of forgiveness of sins to obtain everlasting life and going to Heaven after Believers die. Yes, repentance and remission of sins to become God's citizens of heaven and children by adoption in the household of Father God are all important, as God wants to save them from infernal death by giving them a born again spirit and creating in them the new man in Christ (Colossians 1:13-14; 1 Corinthians 15:47; 2 Corinthians 5:17; Ephesians 2:15). Yet, from God's perspective, God wants Believers to seek first the Kingdom of God and God's righteousness, so Believers will be righteous servants, obedient children, who practice *agape* love and God's goodness as the new man in Christ Jesus. After being born again, Believers' souls must put on the new man (born again spirit), which is absolutely holy and righteous (Ephesians 4:24) and is renewed in knowledge after the image of Him that created his born again spirit (Colossians 3:10).

The "good news" is that Believers not only are saved, but that Christ Jesus grants authority now to Believers as spiritual members of Christ's Kingdom spiritual Ambassadors and Kingdom spiritual Soldiers. The prince of this world has deceived most leaders in the Body of Christ that the "good news" is instead just and only the traditional gospel of salvation and getting people saved so they go to Heaven, just the preaching of only repentance and the remission of sins by Jesus' death on the Cross, then afterwards all the Believers must do is sit in a pew and listen to praise and worship and a sermon on Sundays without the message of the Kingdom of God where they have been assigned as Kingdom Ambassadors, Soldiers, Kings, Lords, and Priests to do a kingdom work here on earth as led by the Holy Spirit. Jesus spoke very little about going to heaven, but He preached that heaven has come to earth in the form of the Kingdom of Heaven. Everlasting life and going to Heaven are wonderful benefits, but why leave out of the preaching the mandated gospel of the Kingdom? Discipleship training is to make born again Believers servants in the Kingdom of God here on earth while they are living, going to heaven for a season but returning to earth when Jesus returns to rule and reign on earth throughout eternity when believers receive their new bodies to live in the new heaven and new earth (1 Corinthians 15:23; Revelation chapter 21).

Indeed, Believers are saved and do go to Heaven for a season but return to the earth for all eternity; so, Heaven is not the final destination of Believers. This was taught by Jesus and the first century Apostles and taught, preached and emphasized in the "gospel of salvation" or "gospel of Heaven." Christ's functional gospel of the Kingdom message is that Jesus has inaugurated the Kingdom of God giving Believers the authority to rule and reign with Christ Jesus here and now on earth and throughout eternity when He and resurrected Believers return to earth in the Kingdom Age, when Jesus is coronated and sits upon His throne in the New Jerusalem. Revelation 5:10 says, "And hast made us unto our God kings and priests: and we shall reign on the earth." The *Ekklesia* should be training Believers to be Kingdom Kings, Kingdom Lords, and Kingdom Priests under the authority of Jesus Christ as the Head of the Church and the King of His Kingdom (Matthew 28:18; Ephesians 1:22-23; Colossians 1:13; 1Timothy 6:15; 1Peter 2:9; Revelation 1:6).

The gospel of the Kingdom of God is the opposite of self-aggrandizement if that is what Believers believe they are receiving by accepting Jesus as Lord and Savior. Galatians 2:20 says, "I am crucified with Christ: nevertheless, I live; yet not I, but Christ liveth in me: and the life which I now live in the flesh I live by the faith of the Son of God, who loved me, and gave Himself for me." The gospel of Christ that Paul preached is the gospel of the Kingdom and the repentance and the remission of sins (Romans 15:19, 29).

Again, I repeat the gospel mandate. Believers must preach repentance and the remission of sins (Luke 24:47), while not neglecting the preaching of the gospel of the Kingdom of God (Matthew 24:14). Believers should take themselves off the focus only on self-improvement and instead put their focus on Christ Jesus as His *Ekklesia* seeking first the Kingdom of God and His righteousness here on earth (Matthew 6:33). As Believers submit to the transforming work of the Godhead in their souls, their old, fractured personalities in their souls become more Christ like, as after initial salvation God's focus is developing the New Man in Christ in Believers' minds, emotions, and hearts to submit their wills to obedience unto God (John 14: 16-17, 23; Romans 12:2; John 15:2; Ephesians 5:26; Romans 8:13). When Believers become Christ like, then they exhibit fruit of the Spirit and become loving servants in the Kingdom of God as Christ's Ambassadors, Soldiers, and citizens of the Kingdom of Heaven and Kingdom of God here on earth.

The Kingdom of God is a spiritual government that came back to earth at the advent of Christ Jesus' humanity nature, the Son of God, Son of Man, and the Lamb of God, Who received a resurrected and ascended humanity nature as the Ascended One, while His divine nature, God the Word, is infinite and omnipresent and is both in Heaven and here on earth and lives inside and amongst Believers as the Present One, Who is in Believers' midst and lives inside them as

Believers are the Godhead's Temple (Matthew 18: 20; 28:20; John 14:16,17, 23; 1 Corinthians 3:16-17; 1 Corinthians 6:19; 2 Corinthians 6:16; Ephesians 2:21). With both Jesus Christ's resurrected humanity nature as the Ascended One in Heaven and His divine nature as the Present One both in Heaven and here on earth, He is the King of kings and Lord of lords (1 Timothy 6:15), the Apostle of our Profession and High Priest (Hebrews 3:1), the good Shepherd (John 10:14), and the ultimate Prophet of God prophesied to come by Moses (Acts 3:22). Jesus is the Head of His Body, His *Ekklesia*, is the King of His Kingdom and Lord over the whole earth (Ephesians 1:22-23).

Believers are mandated to preach repentance and the remission of sins onto the mission to transform Believers' souls to be better Kingdom loving and righteous servant leaders (Luke 24:47). If accepting the gospel of salvation with everlasting life and the gospel of Heaven made your entire being righteous, why would the Lord command His disciples to seek God's Kingdom and also God's righteousness after initial salvation? Jesus' gospel message was always about His spiritual Kingdom here on earth, along with getting people saved to receive the gift of everlasting life, to have the beneficial assurance of going to Heaven, and returning to earth to rule and reign with Christ as His under rulers. Both messages should be preached. Receiving everlasting life and going to Heaven and returning back here to a new heaven and new earth to receive a new resurrected body (Revelation 21) are the beneficial results of being born again, but they are not the only message commanded by Christ to be preached. Christ gave His disciples work assignments to do in establishing His and Father God's Kingdom here on earth as it is in Heaven. Accepting the invitation when the gospel of the Kingdom is preached grants to Believers the privilege of joining Jesus' merciful, ruling Kingdom spiritual government and Jesus' conquering Kingdom spiritual army, which always wins. Believers are employed as Christ's Kingdom Ambassadors representing the Kingdom of God. This is a political appointment, not mere religion.

In the famous discourse in Romans 10, which he continued from the same subject in Romans 9, Paul was speaking about salvation as a benefit to the Gentiles and Jews alike, and that natural Israelites are not saved without accepting Jesus as Lord and Savior. Paul taught that being obedient to the law will not save Israelites or anyone else (Ephesians 2:8-9). Good people may not go to Heaven or rule and reign with Christ in His Kingdom here on earth, but only those who accept Jesus as Lord and Savior, both Jews and Gentiles (John 14:6). Paul said in Romans 9:8 "That is, they which are the children of the flesh, these are not the children of God: but the children of the promise are counted for the seed." Paul in Romans 9:26 quotes Hosea 1:10 to inform the Israelites the truth that God saves people not because of their lineage in the flesh from Hebrew ancestors, but because of God's choosing. "And it shall come to pass in the place where it was said to them, 'You are not My people,' There they shall be called sons of the living God." Paul's purpose in Romans 10 and elsewhere was that salvation was by grace through faith not the obedience of the Hebrew laws (Romans 9:30-32; Ephesians 2:8-9). Paul's discourse in Romans 10 regarding being saved was not to replace Jesus' "gospel of the Kingdom" with a new only "gospel of repentance and remission of sins" but that both messages should be preached together. Paul's communication was to inform his Hebrew brothers and the Roman and Greek Gentiles that just because the Israelites were children of Abraham in the flesh does not give Israelites automatically the benefit of everlasting life or entry into the Kingdom of God.

The often-quoted verse by religious leaders in preaching the "gospel of salvation" that includes everlasting life is John 3:16, which says, "For God so loved the world, that He gave his only begotten Son, that whosoever believeth in Him should not perish, but have everlasting life." Everlasting life is eternal, but you can go to hell and burn in the Lake of Fire eternally, but that is not everlasting life; it is everlasting dying or everlasting state of death. Jesus' purpose was to bring the Kingdom of Heaven to earth. The atonement theology by itself does not give Believers a job assignment in the Kingdom of God after being born again, but the gospel of the Kingdom of God does. Ephesians 2:10 says, "For we are His workmanship, created in Christ Jesus unto good works, which God hath before ordained that we should walk in them." The good works are those that are assigned to Believers, after they receive born again spirits and submit to having their souls transformed. The good works always include the preaching of the good news of God as the King of His Kingdom through Jesus Christ as Lord over the entire heaven and earth as Christ Jesus' domain (Matthew 28:18).

When Adam and Eve were created, they both were created with immortal spirits and immortal souls, but they were created with mortal bodies. Since the Garden of Eden was a Temple of God because that was where heaven and earth met together, the Tree of the Knowledge of Good and Evil and the Tree of Life were supernatural, not natural trees. The Tree of Life was removed by God from the Garden of Eden and taken to heaven, so the bodies of Adam and Eve could not partake and cause immortality to come in their mortal bodies. Thus, as fallen humans, we already have immortality in our spirits and souls, so everlasting life in John 3:16 does not refer to never existing. The issue is whether people's spirits and souls continue to exist in everlasting infernal punishment in the Lake of Fire or everlasting vibrant living in the Kingdom and family of God? It is the acknowledgement that fallen humans either perish in the Lake of Fire with Satan and the kingdom of darkness (Revelation 20:15) or they believe in God's only begotten Son, Christ Jesus, and enjoy everlasting Kingdom Life and the life in Christ as His body. Confessing Christ Jesus as Lord in Believers' lives and believing in their hearts that God raised Jesus' humanity nature from the dead is a transfer from the power of darkness into the Kingdom of God's dear Son. Colossians 1:13-14 says, "Who hath delivered us from the power of darkness, and hath translated us into the Kingdom of His dear Son: In whom we have redemption through His blood, even the forgiveness of sins."

Therefore, in context, in Romans 10, Paul was not preaching through his letter only repentance and remission of sins. Paul was preaching life with God is an everlasting life and not everlasting infernal dying; and being forgiven of sins to avoid the Lake of Fire is an everlasting life "benefit." Jesus and Paul both preached Jesus' gospel of the Kingdom of God, and Paul wrote that Believers are translated from the kingdom of darkness into the Kingdom of God's dear Son (Colossians 1:13); he taught for two years the Kingdom of God in a synagogue and seminary school (Acts 19:8-10). Paul continuously preached the gospel of the Kingdom of God (Acts 28:23,31). Without preaching the gospel of the Kingdom of God and only a message of personal salvation, which has been communicated for over 1,800 years in Church history as religious tradition, Believers are wrongfully taught that furthering religious tradition is the goal and not the Commission of Christ because they believe initial salvation defines the full blessings. They are taught the religious traditional teaching that becoming a new creature in Christ is all there is in Christ's gospel message. Pastors and teachers do quote Matthew 6:33 for Believers to seek first the Kingdom of God for provision or as the primary message from God's point of view but not for work assignments as Kingdom spiritual Ambassadors and Kingdom spiritual Soldiers.

Believers usually are not schooled in ministry as to their rights and responsibilities as citizens of the Kingdom of Heaven. Pastors and teachers generally do not teach the importance of being translated from the power of darkness into the Kingdom of God's dear Son is for the purpose of serving as Kingdom spiritual Ambassadors and as Kingdom spiritual Soldiers, but this is God's *Ekklesia* mandate. Pastors and teachers normally do not want their memberships to be "called out" because they want them to "stay put" and continue supporting the local religious practice with their tithes and offerings. As is in practice today, the so-called "Church" is not the true *Ekklesia* but has developed into a world-wide religion. Jesus did not come to the earth to start a new religion but came to earth to inaugurate the Kingdom of God here on earth as it is in Heaven and to cause people to accept Him as Savior and Lord through repentance and remission of sins, and to become servants of His Kingdom in the Kingdom colony called "earth."

Addressing the issue of belief of heart and confession with mouth for personal salvation with the remission of sins should be preached but with the preaching also of the blessings and responsibilities of seeing and entering the Kingdom of God. Then one would have to ask, "What is the real purpose to reconcile people back to God? What does God benefit from Believers personal salvation?" Father God wants His creation mandate ministry assignment to continue through His only begotten Son, Christ Jesus, with His divine and human natures, to make spiritual children, birth in them a new, sinless, holy, righteous, born again spirit; and then train them as disciples by transforming their souls, so, they are obedient servants as Father God's Kingdom Ambassadors and Kingdom Soldiers to continue taking back the earth, world system, and the fallen people that resulted in the sin committed by Adam and Eve in the Garden of Eden. Apostle Paul was sent to bring Gentiles into the Kingdom of God as well as the Jews, and the only way for both Jews and Gentiles to reconcile with God is to have the proper sincere heart belief and mouth confession of the Lord Jesus, as the Messiah, to receive everlasting life and permanent reconciliation with Father God through the death, resurrection, ascension, and enthronement of Christ Jesus, the Son of the living God for the purpose of being bondservants of the King and His Kingdom.

With Apostle Paul speaking to the Jews and Gentiles alike, he said in Romans 10:9-21, "That if thou shalt confess with thy mouth the Lord Jesus, and shalt believe in thine heart that God hath raised Him from the dead, thou shalt be saved. For with the heart man believeth unto righteousness; and with the mouth confession is made unto salvation. For the scripture saith, 'Whosoever believeth on Him shall not be ashamed.' For there is no difference between the Jew and the Greek: for the same Lord over all is rich unto all that call upon Him. For whosoever shall call upon the name of the Lord shall be saved. How then shall they call on Him in whom they have not believed? And how shall they believe in Him of whom they have not heard? And how shall they hear without a preacher? And how shall they preach, except they be sent? As it is written, 'How beautiful are the feet of them that preach the gospel of peace and bring glad tidings of good things!' But they have not all obeyed the gospel. For Esaias (Isaiah) saith, 'Lord, who hath believed our report?' So then faith cometh by hearing, and hearing by the word of God. But I say, 'Have they not heard?' Yes verily, their sound went into all the earth, and their words unto the ends of the world. But I say, 'Did not Israel know?' First Moses saith, 'I will provoke you to jealousy by them that are no people, and by a foolish nation I will anger you.' But Esaias (Isaiah) is very bold, and saith, 'I was found of them that sought Me not; I was made manifest unto them that asked not after Me.' But to Israel He saith, 'All day long I have stretched forth My hands unto a disobedient and gainsaying people.'"

In Romans 10:15, referring to Isaiah 52:7, Paul said "How beautiful are the feet of them that preach the gospel of peace, and bring glad tidings of good things!" The gospel of peace is part of the gospel of the Kingdom and is the reconciliation of all people to God who accept Jesus as Savior and Lord, whether Israelite or Gentile, to become part of God's Kingdom and family. The emphasis is reconciliation and peace with God through accepting Jesus Christ as Lord and Savior, not an ancestry based upon a birth certificate.

Paul continued in Romans 10:16, by referring to Isaiah 53:1, which says, "But they have not all obeyed the gospel. For Esaias (Isaiah) saith, 'Lord, who hath believed our report?'" Paul's Romans 10 discourse is not referred to by Paul as the "gospel of salvation" but rather as the "gospel of peace." Paul said int Romans 14:17, "For the kingdom of God is not meat and drink; but righteousness, and peace, and joy in the Holy Ghost." Thus, "peace" defines the Kingdom of God. The "gospel of salvation" if taught alone without the Kingdom of God becomes man's tradition and religion redefining and restricting the dual gospel message for initial salvation. The "gospel of peace" means reconciliation with God to end the conflict between fallen mankind and God by accepting Christ Jesus as Savior and Lord and then becoming the bondservants of Christ Jesus as the appointed King in God's Kingdom. 2 Corinthians 5:18-20 says, "And all things are of God, who hath reconciled us to Himself by Jesus Christ, and hath given to us the ministry of reconciliation; To wit, that God was in Christ, reconciling the world unto Himself, not imputing their trespasses unto them; and hath committed unto us the word of reconciliation. Now then we are Ambassadors for Christ, as though God did beseech you by us: we pray you in Christ's stead, be ye reconciled to God." In this "gospel of peace" statement it is evident that Paul finishes by saying that Believers are Kingdom government spiritual Ambassadors of Christ that represent Heaven as they are citizens of Heaven (Philippians 3:20; 2 Corinthians 5:20).

Jesus primarily focused His preaching on the "gospel of the Kingdom," which was His activating message from God's perspective and point of view, which is the will of Father God. Jesus taught His disciples to pray, "Thy Kingdom come. Thy will be done in earth, as it is in Heaven" (Matthew 6:10). For God's Kingdom manifesting and God's will to be done here in earth, God calls born again repentant Believers to be servants in the Lord's Kingdom to start thinking Kingdom righteousness, who first are translated from the kingdom of darkness to the Kingdom of God's dear Son (Colossians 1:13). It is always about the Kingdom of God here on earth and the bondservants who must be saved and made holy and righteous by God to be servants to the King of the Kingdom of God.

Jesus' gospel of the Kingdom was focused on God's Kingdom as Believers' place of living the abundant life (John 10:10), but also Believers' place of being born again and afterward the Godhead's work of transformation of Believers' souls for servanthood and activation into service as Kingdom spiritual Ambassadors and Kingdom spiritual soldiers, bondservants of the King of kings. Jesus said in Matthew 6:31-33 "Therefore take no thought, saying, 'What shall we eat? or, What shall we drink? or, Wherewithal shall we be clothed?' (For after all these things do the Gentiles seek:) for your heavenly Father knoweth that ye have need of all these things. But seek ye first the Kingdom of God, and His righteousness; and all these things shall be added unto you.'" Jesus always said and did what God the Father said and did, but Jesus did not do things to be popular with people. What is it that is the will of the Lord Jesus Christ and the entire Godhead? The answer is the primary message of the gospel of the Kingdom and repentance and remission of sins to obtain born again spirits and transform Believers' souls unto righteousness and holiness to become bondservants of Christ as the new man and Believers as the Temple of the Godhead.

When the Kingdom Age comes, then Believers also will live with Jesus' humanity nature Who will sit on His Throne in the New Jerusalem after the White Throne Judgment and the Judgment Seat of Christ (Revelations, chapters 20 & 21). Repeatedly driving this point home: Jesus mandated that His disciples preach the gospel of the Kingdom and preach repentance and remission of sins because He wanted to establish the Kingdom of God here on earth and to create a new man in Christ to live in the Kingdom of God as obedient servants who obey Christ's commandment to love one another (John 13:34-35). After Jesus' death, resurrection, ascension, and enthronement, Believers are to continue His work as the Lord's bondservants. Jesus, with His dual natures, both divine and human, without any commingling, is the good Shepherd; and Believers are the sheep. Jesus' divine nature here on earth leads Believers. Psalm 23: 2-3 says, "He maketh me to lie down in green pastures: He leadeth me beside the still waters. He restoreth my soul: He leadeth me in the paths of righteousness for His name's sake." Jesus is the Head, and Believers are His body. Believers are not their own. Believers have been redeemed for a price, not with silver or gold, but with the precious blood of Jesus (1 Peter 1:18-19).

Repentance and remission of sins are merely the initial salvation in preparing fallen humans to become organic spiritual children of Jesus' resurrected humanity nature and adopted children of Father God (Isaiah 9:6; 1 Peter 1:23; Romans 8:15). Believers can live with God the Father, God the Holy Spirit, and God the Word, the Lord Jesus Christ's divine nature, live as citizens of Heaven, live in the Lord's Kingdom, and be the Lord's bondservants as kings, lords, priests, brothers, ambassadors, soldiers, body, betrothed and eventually bride and spouse (Isaiah 9:6; Hebrews 2:13; Mark 3: 35; Romans 8:15; 12:5; 1 Timothy 6:15; 2 Timothy 2: 3-4; Revelation 1:6; 5:10; 21:9).

The *Ekklesia* is a multiplicity of saved Believers with the mandate to bring the unsaved into God's Kingdom and disciple them to become spiritually mature, gifted servants as Christ's Kingdom Ambassadors and Kingdom soldiers always motivated by love (agape). Paul stated his mandate in furthering the Lord's ultimate purpose was the making of one New Man of both Israelites and Gentiles, and this is accomplished by both accepting Jesus Christ as Lord and Savior, and not based upon ancestry as Abraham's natural descendants (John 8:32-59). Paul stated in Ephesians 2:13-18, "But now in Christ Jesus ye who sometimes were far off are made nigh by the blood of Christ. For He is our peace, who hath made both (Israelites and Gentiles) one, and hath broken down the middle wall of partition between us (Israelites and Gentiles); Having abolished in His flesh the enmity, even the law of commandments contained in ordinances; for to make in Himself of twain one New Man, so making peace (with God); And that He might reconcile both (Israelites and Gentiles) unto God in one body by the cross, having slain the enmity thereby: And came and preached peace (righteous peace and joy in the Holy Spirit which defines the Kingdom of God) to you which were afar off, and to them that were nigh. For through Him we both (Israelites and Gentiles) have access by one spirit (resurrected life in the born again spirit and by God the Holy Spirit) unto the Father."

Jesus came to earth as a Suffering Servant, who gave His life as a ransom for fallen mankind for the remission of sin to further the atonement theology (Mark 10:45). Jesus was resurrected as the King with all granted authority in heaven and earth (Matthew 28:18). Jesus even washed His disciples' feet at the time of the Lord's supper to demonstrate the servanthood He expected of His disciples, and He taught His disciples that the greatest among them was the servant of all (Matthew 23:11; Mark 10:43-44; John 13: 4-10). Jesus taught His disciples servanthood by example. Believers today are taught by some leaders that the Lord serves them, but the truth is that Believers are instead bondservants of the Lord Jesus Christ. All of the Lord's apostles referred themselves as *doulos* or bondservants of the Lord Jesus Christ (Romans 1:1; James 1:1; 2 Peter 1:1; Jude 1:1; Revelation 1:1). "Bondservants" mean Believers "serve" the Lord with their spirits, souls, and bodies to perform Kingdom services as spiritual Ambassadors and spiritual Soldiers. God does supply all of Believers' financial need while being His servants according to His riches in glory by Christ Jesus (Philippians 4:19).

The gospel of the Kingdom of God focuses upon Believers as *doulos* of Christ, seeking the very heart of the Lord and entering His crucifixion and submitting to allow Christ to live His life in and through them as His Kingdom citizens, Kingdom spiritual Ambassadors, Kingdom spiritual Soldiers, and Body (Galatians 2:20). Thus, the gospel of the Kingdom and repentance and remission of sins are receiving everlasting life for the purpose of doing a spiritual *zoe* life work as bondservants of Christ after initial salvation (Ephesians 2:10; Philippians 2:12-13). The gospel of the Kingdom is not just joining a "bless me Jesus" club, even though there are many crowns to be earned and blessings to be received for those who serve the Lord as *doulos* in His mission to take back possession of the earth, the fallen people saved and reconciled back to Father God, bringing them into the Kingdom of God and family of God, and activating them into the service of the King.

God's original message to the children of Israel from Mt. Sinai was said in Exodus 19:5-6, "Now therefore, if ye will obey my voice indeed, and keep My covenant, then ye shall be a peculiar treasure unto Me above all people: for all the earth is Mine: And ye shall be unto Me a Kingdom of priests, and a holy nation. These are the words which thou shalt speak unto the children of Israel." Why did God say, "and all the earth is Mine?" It is because God is interested in informing the Israelites that the ownership of the earth and all people belong to Father God, and He wanted back the possession His people and His earth through their assistance as a Kingdom of priests and a holy nation here on earth as God's servants. This was the message of the gospel of the Kingdom that the servants unto God are commanded to bring back possession of the earth and the people to Father God. God needed transformed servant kings and priests here on earth to accomplish His will. Exodus 19: 5-6 is a similar calling to Believers who have accepted Jesus as Lord and Savior as their mission once saved is to take back possession of earth and Believers' reconciliation with God. 1 Peter 2:9-10 says, "But ye are a chosen generation, a royal priesthood, a holy nation, a peculiar people; that ye should shew forth the praises of Him who hath called you out of darkness into his marvelous light: Which in time past were not a people but are now the people of God: which had not obtained mercy, but now have obtained mercy."

What is the purpose of both passages (Exodus 19:5-6; 1 Peter 2: 9-10) with making His people a Kingdom of priests or a chosen generation, a royal priesthood, a holy nation, and a peculiar people? Revelation 1:6 says, "And hath made us kings and priests unto God and His Father; to Him be glory and **dominion** forever and ever." Taking back **dominion** of all creation and fallen mankind is the purpose of God having Kings and Priests here on earth. 1 Timothy 6:15 says that Jesus is King of kings and Lord of lords. Kings rule here on earth over the people to bring back the people to God. Lords rule over the natural world to bring back possession of the natural creation to the Creator. Palms 24:1 says, "The earth is the LORD'S, and the fullness thereof; the world, and they that dwell therein." The LORD owns everything and everyone by right of being Creator. Priests minister to preach the gospel of the Kingdom and repentance, remission of sins, and bring new disciples to the Lord to be His bondservants to do the will of God in the kingdom of God. Revelation 5:10 says, "And hast made us unto our God kings and priests: and we shall reign on the earth." Dominion, ruling, reigning, and ministering are the purposeful professions of those responding to the invitation of the gospel of the Kingdom (Matthew 24:14), and Believers also are mandated to preach repentance and remission of sins to unBelievers (Luke 24:47), and work under the tutelage of God to help transform Believers' souls to make Believers righteous, loving, wise, knowledgeable, and loyal to God and His Christ and to others as the Body of Christ and in the Kingdom of God. Remember, Heaven is a holding place until Believers who have already died return to rule and reign with Christ back here on earth (Revelation 21).

Apostle Paul said he preached the "gospel of Christ" (Romans 1:16). Therefore, the gospel that Paul preached was the same gospel that Christ preached, which is the gospel of the Kingdom and repentance for the remission of sins to be righteous Kingdom Servants (Matthew 9:35). In applying the gospel of the Kingdom, Paul referred to the "gospel of peace" (Romans 10:15; Ephesians 6:15). He also referred to the gospel of the Kingdom as being sanctioned as the "gospel of God" (Romans 1:1; 1 Thessalonians 2:8-9). Paul insisted on keeping the Hebrew Law out of the gospel message, so Paul preached the "gospel of grace" as part of the gospel of the Kingdom and the grace that brings initial salvation (Acts 20:24; Ephesians 2:8-9). All these statements by Paul are about the gospel that Jesus preached, which primarily was both the gospel of the Kingdom, along with repentance and the remission of sins.

To be sure, Paul preached and taught Jesus' gospel of the Kingdom, along with repentance and remission of sins. In Ephesus, Paul stopped his missionary travels to teach the gospel of the Kingdom of God in the synagogue for three months and in the school of Tyrannus for two years. Acts 19: 8-10 says, "And he went into the synagogue, and spake boldly for the space of three months, disputing and persuading the things concerning the kingdom of God. But when divers were hardened, and believed not, but spake evil of that way before the multitude, he departed from them, and separated the disciples, disputing daily in the school of one Tyrannus. And this continued by the space of two years; so that all they which dwelt in Asia heard the word of the Lord Jesus, both Jews and Greeks (about Jesus' gospel of the Kingdom)." Paul felt led by the Holy Spirit to get the Believers seeing and entering the Kingdom of God and the realization that the saints are citizens of the Kingdom of Heaven with the responsibility of being Kingdom spiritual Ambassadors and Kingdom spiritual Soldiers here on earth. Getting the Jews to stop believing in the Hebrew religion and start believing as citizens of Heaven took a while, but citizenship of Heaven, and being a child in the household with God, along with being joint heirs with Christ, is much, much, better than being a member of a religion.

Towards the end of his life, Paul professed that as Jesus had commanded, he preached the gospel of the Kingdom of God and repentance for the remission of sins. In Acts 20:25, Paul said, "And now, behold, I know that ye all, among whom I have gone preaching the Kingdom of God, shall see my face no more."

Afterwards, Paul was arrested and was taken to Rome as a prisoner. The Emperor of Rome provided Paul with an apartment, water, food, under house arrest, but was allowed to see visitors daily. Living in this apartment for two years waiting for the date of trial, knowing that he would be beheaded, Paul preached and testified of the gospel of the Kingdom of God to Gentiles, Jews, and even to the Roman Guards. Acts 28:23, 30-31 says, "And when they had appointed him a day (for trial), there came many to him into his lodging; to whom he expounded and testified the kingdom of God, persuading them concerning Jesus, both out of the law of Moses, and out of the prophets, from morning till evening… And Paul dwelt two whole years in his own hired house, and received all that came in unto him, preaching the kingdom of God, and teaching those things which concern the Lord Jesus Christ, with all confidence, no man forbidding him."

Paul also wrote about the Kingdom of Christ and of God (Romans 14:17; 1Corinthians 15:50; Ephesians 5:5). Being saved with everlasting life, reconciled to God, and going to Heaven are important benefits, but there is so much more in the gospel of the Kingdom once you become a citizen of Heaven through being born again. Indeed, Ministers should explain to unsaved people that they receive everlasting life and will go to Heaven for a season but will return to the earth to rule and reign with Christ eternally if they accept Jesus as Lord and Savior. Ministers should let these new Believers also know that everlasting life and going to Heaven are the benefits, but they also are saved to serve Jesus as Lord and Savior as His Kingdom bondservants, especially as Kingdom spiritual Ambassadors and Kingdom spiritual Soldiers here on earth while they are alive. Leaders need to inform new Believers that the gospel of the Kingdom includes everlasting life as a benefit, so Believers have zoe life abundantly for the purpose of taking dominion of the creation and making disciples of all nations, while ruling and reigning as kings, lords, and priests as under rulers of Jesus' humanity nature and the Godhead here on earth. Paul warned the Believers not to listen to sermons of another gospel, so he certainly would not preach another gospel that Jesus, Himself, did not preach (2 Corinthians 11:4; Galatians 1:6-10; Revelation 5:10).

THE FOUNDATION OF THE *EKKLESIA* IS GOD'S KINGDOM SPIRITUAL GOVERNMENT AND KINGDOM SPIRITUAL MILITARY

Psalm 11:3-6 says, "If the foundations are destroyed, what can the righteous do? The Lord is in His holy temple, the Lord's throne is in Heaven; His eyes behold; His eyelids test the sons of men. The Lord tests the righteous, but the wicked and the one who loves violence His soul hates. Upon the wicked He will rain coals; fire and brimstone and a burning wind shall be the portion of their cup." The foundations of your personal beliefs system are in your heart, in your soul, and are constantly being scrutinized by the Godhead along with Christ's humanity nature through his omnipresent divine nature because Jesus wants a ".... glorious *Ekklesia*, not having spot or wrinkle or any such thing, but that she should be holy and without blemish" (Ephesians 5:27).

Paul did not say a "glorious teaching center or worship center" but a "glorious *Ekklesia*," referring to His Believers as the *Ekklesia* functioning as Kingdom spiritual Ambassadors and Kingdom spiritual Soldiers of the Lord, with the anointing and leading of the Holy Spirit. Paul understood that he held a Kingdom government office. Paul spoke to secular government leaders of the Grecian city states as a citizen of Heaven (Philippians 3:20) and as an Ambassador of Christ (2 Corinthians 5:20), with the message that a greater Kingdom where Jesus is King is the true governing body on earth *established* by God Almighty (Acts 17:6-8); and the evil government of the prince of this world system is a counterfeit (John 12:31; Ephesians 2:2).

Not only as the Ambassador of Christ in His Kingdom government, but Paul also knew that he was a General in God's Kingdom spiritual army. Paul wrote in 2 Corinthians 10: 4 that Believers should use spiritual weapons in their warfare against the kingdom of darkness that currently has the world system in evil spiritual military siege. Paul also wrote in Ephesians 6:10-18 that Believers wrestle not with flesh and blood, but against principalities, powers, rulers of the darkness of this world, and spiritual wickedness in high places, so the Lord's Kingdom spiritual Soldiers must put on the full armor of God to be victorious against the military stronghold of the kingdom of darkness. Finally, Paul wrote in 2 Timothy 2:3-4 for Believers to endure hardship as good Soldiers, not to get entangled with the affairs of this world and neglect their duties as Soldiers fighting for the *Ekklesia,* and their battle against the kingdom of darkness.

Therefore, Apostle Paul knew that he was in both the Lord's Kingdom spiritual government and the Lord's Kingdom spiritual military while he preached and taught the gospel of the Kingdom, along with repentance and remission of sins because of Jesus' suffering, death on the Roman Cross, and resurrection from the dead in three days. Paul knew that the first order of God's mandate was to enlist new Believers into God's Kingdom spiritual government and Kingdom spiritual military forces, where they had to be spiritually discipled and matured. Paul understood that the Lord's goal was taking possessory authority of the world system for the Kingdom of God, not just for only individual salvation with the gift of everlasting life and going to Heaven, as much as salvation is important as well. The good news of the gospel of the Kingdom is not only that people who accept Jesus as Lord and Savior receive everlasting life and go to Heaven for a season, but also that the Lord Jesus Christ, through His *Ekklesia,* conquers and takes over the world system from the kingdom of darkness and hands it over to its rightful owner, Father God, and that Believers will rule and reign with Christ as submitted kings and priests over all the other kingdoms of this world when Jesus returns and sets up His Throne in Jerusalem and starts the Kingdom Age (Revelation 5:10; Revelation chapters 20 & 21).

Ephesians 2:19-22 says, "Now therefore ye are no more strangers and foreigners, but fellow citizens with the saints, and of the household of God; and are built upon the foundation of the Apostles and Prophets, Jesus Christ Himself being the Chief Corner Stone; in Whom all the building fitly framed together groweth unto a holy Temple in the Lord, in whom ye also are built together for a habitation of God through the Spirit." So, another revelation by Paul is that Believers become the Temple of God, and God the Father, God the Word, and God the Holy Spirit make their abode inside Believers once they are born again (John 14:16-17,23; 1 Corinthians 6:19; 1 Corinthians 3:16; Ephesians 2:21).

Ephesians 2:19-22 informs Believers they are citizens of Heaven, officials in the Kingdom of God, and members of the household of God. Believers are children of Father God's family by adoption through the redemptive work of Christ Jesus (Romans 8:15-16). Believers are the habitation here on earth that becomes God's earthly Temple (John 14:17, 23; 1 Corinthians 6:19; 1 Corinthians 3:16; Ephesians 2:21). Believers accept that the *Ekklesia* is built on the foundation of the Apostles and Prophets (Ephesians 2:20).

The function of both the Apostles and Prophets are as guardians of the foundation of the *Ekklesia*. Prophets are not that concerned about "timing" of the fulfillment of a prophetic word. If Prophets know that a word is from God, then they say it for the edification of the individual or the Body of Christ as a whole. On the other hand, the function of the Apostles is to know the season for the fulfillment of the prophetic word and how to move in the spiritual flow of that prophetic word to accomplish the will of God. Therefore, Apostles and Prophets minister together to build, repair, and maintain the true foundational beliefs of the Body of Christ. The foundational beliefs of Believers in Christ Jesus are acquired knowledge from the foundational truths taught by the Apostles and Prophets daily following Jesus, the Apostle and High Priest of Believers' profession (Hebrews 3:1).

If Believers have a calling as an Ephesians 4:11 Apostle or Prophet, then their focus is to be a guardian, a watchman, a corrector, and a protector of the *Ekklesia*. The foundational mandates from the Lord to the *Ekklesia* is making disciples of all nations who then will enlist in the Lord's Kingdom spiritual government as spiritual Ambassadors and in the Lord's Kingdom spiritual army of resolute spiritual Soldiers standing strong against the kingdom of darkness. The foundational beliefs of the *Ekklesia* also include the ministering the benefits of the gospel of the Kingdom that are everlasting life, going to Heaven for a season, the blessings of fellowship in loving Kingdom community with other Believers, and ruling and reigning with Jesus' humanity nature in the future as kings, lords, priests, brothers, Body of Christ, *Ekklesia*, and Christ Jesus humanity nature's Betrothed, and ultimately His Bride and Spouse.

WHAT GOSPEL AND MESSAGE DID JESUS PREACH?

In truth, Jesus preached mostly the gospel of the Kingdom, as His mission to benefit God was to bring the Kingdom of heaven to earth (Matthew 6:10, 33). However, to be good citizens of Heaven, Believers had to be born again before seeing the Kingdom of God (John 3:3). Concerning the preaching of repentance and remission of sins, Jesus also said in Luke 24:47-49, "And that repentance and remission of sins should be preached in His name among all nations, beginning at Jerusalem. And ye are witnesses of these things. And, behold, I send the promise of My Father upon you: but tarry ye in the city of Jerusalem, until ye be endued with power from on high." Jesus said in Matthew 24:14, "And this gospel of the Kingdom shall be preached in all the world for a witness unto all nations; and then shall the end come." This dual message is memorialized in Colossians 1:13-14, which says, "Who hath delivered us from the power of darkness, and hath translated us into the kingdom of his dear Son: (14) In Whom we have redemption through his blood, even the forgiveness of sins." Thus, the gospel of the Kingdom and repentance and remission of sins are commanded to be preached mutually (not always at the same time, but equal time). The leaders in the Church have failed to preach the gospel of the kingdom in conjunction with preaching repentance and remission of sins. Jesus said in Matthew 4:17, "From that time Jesus began to preach, and to say, 'Repent (of sins): for the Kingdom of Heaven is at hand.'" John the Baptist said in Matthew 3:3, "Repent ye (of sins): for the kingdom of heaven is at hand." John the Baptist said in John 1:29, "…Behold the Lamb of God, which taketh away the sin of the world." Luke 23:38 speaks at the time of Jesus crucifixion, saying, "And a superscription also was written over Him in letters of Greek, and Latin, and Hebrew, THIS IS THE KING OF THE JEWS." Examining the scriptures, one can see that Jesus commanded to be preached both a gospel of the Kingdom and the message of repentance and forgiveness of sins for all who are born again by accepting Him as Lord and Savior.

Thus, what is readily apparent is there is the mandate to preach the gospel of the inaugurated Kingdom of God and the mandate to preach the repentance and remission of sins to make better citizens and bondservants of the Kingdom of God. Why are both important? It is because God wants His Kingdom to come to earth, and God wants Believers to be bondservants, who are righteous, holy, express *agape* love, and are the light and salt of the earth.

The Kingdom of God is different than the Kingdoms of this world. Jesus said in Mark 10: 42-45, "But Jesus called them to Him, and saith unto them, 'Ye know that they which are accounted to rule over the Gentiles exercise lordship over them; and their great ones exercise authority upon them. But so shall it not be among you: but whosoever will be great among you, shall be your minister: And whosoever of you will be the chiefest, shall be servant of all. For even the Son of Man came not to be ministered unto, but to minister, and to give His life a ransom for many."

Jesus gave His disciples a new commandment in John 13:34-35, "A new commandment I give unto you, 'That ye love one another; as I have loved you, that ye also love one another.' By this shall all men know that ye are My disciples, if ye have love one to another." To become loving (*agapao*), Believers have to become righteous and holy in their souls. *Agape* love comes from God and is the powerful force in God's Kingdom. Righteousness and holiness in God's Kingdom are mandatory. This is not an outward dress code, nor a religious pretentiousness of holiness. 1 Peter 1:15-16 says, "But as He which hath called you is holy, so be ye holy in all manner of conversation; (16) Because it is written, 'Be ye holy; for I am holy.'" Christ's commandment is to be loving servants to other Believers while seeking first the Kingdom of God and His righteousness is what God wants to see and hear.

Although your born again spirit is incorruptible, righteous, holy, perfect and does not sin and entitles Believers to everlasting life (John 3:16; 1 Peter 1:23; Ephesians 4:24; Hebrews 12:23; and 1 John 3:19), your soul is not born again and must become transformed, spiritual, and righteous (Romans 12:2; Romans 8:5-8; 2 Timothy 3:12; 3 John 2). Life as a Believer must always be ready to repent of sins and seek forgiveness, as this is the continuance process of the transformation and cleansing of the Believer's soul. 1 John 1:8-10 says, "If we say that we have no sin, we deceive ourselves, and the truth is not in us. (9) If we confess our sins, He is faithful and just to forgive us our sins, and to cleanse us from all unrighteousness. (10) If we say that we have not sinned, we make Him a liar, and His word is not in us." Staying in the Kingdom of God and under His reign and rule has the benefits here on earth of God's provision and health and a Kingdom where temptation is not present as it is in the world.

When Jesus appeared before Pilate, their conversation was all about the Kingdom of Caesar that Pilate represented and the Kingdom of God that Jesus represented. John 18: 33, 36 says, "Then Pilate entered into the judgment hall again, and called Jesus, and said unto him, 'Art thou the King of the Jews?'... Jesus answered, 'My kingdom is not **of this world**: if My kingdom were of this world (and follow the pattern of the worldly kingdoms like Caesar's Kingdom), then would My servants fight, that I should not be delivered to the Jews: but now is My kingdom not **from** hence (the world).'" Historically, John 18:36 has been interpreted what Jesus was saying was that the Kingdom of God was in Heaven and not here on earth, but looking at the Greek, that is not what Jesus was saying. Throughout the gospels, Jesus said that the Kingdom of God was already here on earth and that Believers should seek first the Kingdom of God and His righteousness (Matthew 6:33). However, Jesus' kingdom is not just in Heaven or outside of the natural world. The Greek for "of this world" is *ek tou kosmou touton. Ek* means "out of" or "from," so Jesus was saying that His Kingdom is "from" Heaven not just in Heaven. Thus, Jesus is speaking of God's Kingdom that indeed is in the natural world here on earth even though it is from Heaven and is spiritual and thus invisible. There is an ultimate showdown between the Kingdom of God, which takes over the kingdoms of this world. Revelation 11:15 says, "...The kingdoms of this world are become the kingdoms of our Lord, and of His Christ; and He shall reign forever and ever." Jesus' crucifixion on the Cross was the fulfillment of John 3:16, as it was the greatest act of love by Jesus. Servanthood and love are the two primary motivations of Believers who are spiritually transformed from living and communing in the Kingdom of God. In John 15:13, Jesus said, "Greater love hath no man than this, that a man lay down his life for his friends."

What did Jesus primarily preach, along with instructing His disciples to preach? Matthew 4:23 says, "And Jesus went about all Galilee, teaching in their synagogues, and preaching the gospel of the kingdom, and healing all manner of sickness and all manner of disease among the people." Luke 8:1 says, "And it came to pass afterward, that He went throughout every city and village, preaching and shewing the glad tidings (good news) of the Kingdom of God: and the twelve were with Him." Luke 9:2 says, "And He sent them (disciples) to preach the Kingdom of God, and to heal the sick." Luke 9:60 says, "Jesus said unto him, 'Let the dead bury their dead: but go thou and preach the Kingdom of God.'" Jesus sent out and instructed His disciples in Luke 10:9, saying "And heal the sick that are therein, and say unto them, 'The Kingdom of God is come nigh unto you.'" Luke 12:23 says, "Fear not, little flock; for it is your Father's good pleasure to give you the Kingdom." Jesus said in Luke 17:20-21, "And when He was demanded of the Pharisees, when the Kingdom of God should come, He answered them and said, 'The kingdom of God cometh not with observation. Neither shall they say, Lo here! or, lo there! for, behold, the Kingdom of God is within you.'"

Jesus said in Mark 1:15, "The time is fulfilled, and the kingdom of God is at hand: repent ye and believe the gospel (that Jesus preached)." Jesus said in Mark 16:15, "Go ye into all the world, and preach the gospel (that Jesus preached) to every creature." On the Mount of Ascension, Jesus instructed His disciples in Matthew 28:18-20, "All power (authority) is given unto Me in Heaven and in earth. Go ye therefore, and teach (make disciples of) all nations, baptizing them in the name of the Father, and of the Son, and of the Holy Ghost: Teaching them to observe all things whatsoever I have commanded you: and, lo, I am with you always, *even* unto the end of the world." Jesus defined the gospel He wanted preached as the "gospel of the Kingdom," but He also commanded His disciples to preach repentance and remission of sins. Since Jesus is the mandated Head of the *Ekklesia* with all authority in Heaven and earth, then why haven't the leaders in Church preached Jesus' mandated "gospel of the Kingdom?" The reason is the old religious order of both Catholic and Protestant, have established a religious Priesthood/Laity dichotomous old religious order system that allows the leadership to be a "religious profession" that pays them for their services from the tithes and offerings that come in from the laity. Yet, the Lord addressing the *Ekklesia* in Ephesus said in Revelation 2:6, "But this thou hast, that thou hatest the deeds of the Nicolaitans, which I also hate." The Nicolaitans were those who hate the laity and set up a false Priesthood/Laity system, when the Lord called all Believers to be His Kings and Priests (Revelation 1:6; 1 Peter 2:9). The Ephesian 4:11 gift ministers were to make leaders in the body of Christ, not spectators. All Believers are called to the work of the Ministry (Ephesians 4:12). The false Priesthood/Laity system robs the Believers of their crowns and rewards. The current old religious order is full of mostly unemployed Believers who have been taught an anti-work theology which overworks the Pastors. The Pastor is not to have the congregation to sign up for unemployment but to focus on the perfection of the saints for the work of the ministry for the edifying of the body of Christ. (Ephesians 4:13).

Being born again and being forgiven of sins is very important. Yet, it is readily apparent that receiving everlasting life and going to Heaven are benefits of the gospel of the Kingdom and are important to make Jesus' disciples righteous and holy to be bondservants who practice love in fellowship. Thus, the Kingdom and the atonement theology are both important works of activating disciples into Kingdom ministry mandated by the gospel of the Kingdom. What did Jesus primarily preach? It was the gospel of the kingdom. This is apparent in Luke 22: 25-30 when Jesus had to stop the striving between His disciples who were arguing who would be the greatest in the Kingdom of God where Jesus was King. "And He said unto them, 'The kings of the Gentiles exercise lordship over them; and they that exercise authority upon them are called benefactors. But ye shall not be so: but he that is greatest among you, let him be as the younger; and he that is chief, as he that doth serve. For what is greater, he that sitteth at meat, or he that serveth? Is not he that sitteth at meat? But I am among you as He that serveth. Ye are they which have continued with Me in My temptations. And I appoint unto you a kingdom, as my Father hath appointed unto Me; That ye may eat and drink at My table in My Kingdom and sit on thrones judging the twelve tribes of Israel."

On the day of His Ascension, Jesus said to His disciples in Acts 1: 4-5, 8, "And, being assembled together with them, commanded them that they should not depart from Jerusalem, but wait for the promise of the Father, which, saith He, 'Ye have heard of Me. "For John truly baptized with water; but ye shall be baptized with the Holy Ghost not many days hence" … 'But ye shall receive power, after that the Holy Ghost is come upon you: and ye shall be witnesses unto me both in Jerusalem, and in all Judaea, and in Samaria, and unto the uttermost part of the earth.'"" Jesus spoke words of activation, empowerment, and mission for all Believers, not to live a sedentary life of pew sitting as your only experience in the Kingdom of God and Kingdom community of Believers. Jesus' commandment was to go into all the world as His witnesses and preach both the repentance and remission of sins and the gospel of the Kingdom, and then the end will come when He returns to rule and reign back here on earth forever when there will no longer be a kingdom of darkness.

 Here is an example of Jesus speaking about the *Ekklesia* as His Kingdom spiritual army. Matthew 16:13-19 says, "When Jesus came into the coasts of Caesarea Philippi, he asked his disciples, saying, 'Whom do men say that I the Son of man am?' And they said, 'Some say that Thou art John the Baptist: some, Elias; and others, Jeremias, or one of the prophets.' He saith unto them, 'But whom say ye that I am?' And Simon Peter answered and said, 'Thou art the Christ, the Son of the living God.' And Jesus answered and said unto him, 'Blessed art thou, Simon Barjona: for flesh and blood hath not revealed it unto thee, but My Father which is in Heaven. And I say also unto thee, 'That thou art Peter, and upon this rock I will build My *Ekklesia*; and the gates of hell shall not prevail against it. And I will give unto thee the keys of the Kingdom of Heaven: and whatsoever thou shalt bind on earth shall be bound in Heaven: and whatsoever thou shalt loose on earth shall be loosed in Heaven.'" Again, the battle is between Christ's *Ekklesia* which is the Kingdom spiritual military of Christ against the evil spiritual military of the kingdom of darkness, while Jesus builds His *Ekklesia.*

How can Matthew 16:18 be interpreted as "church" as it is practiced today when Matthew 16:19 speaks of the spiritual battle against the kingdom of darkness by the *Ekklesia* as the Kingdom spiritual military of the Lord? Again, it says, "And I will give unto thee the keys of the kingdom of Heaven: and whatsoever thou shalt bind on earth shall be bound in Heaven: and whatsoever thou shalt loose on earth shall be loosed in Heaven.'" This scripture is how to wage spiritual war against the kingdom of darkness. The word *"Ekklesia"* in Matthew 16:18 should have been translated "… upon this rock I will build my *Ekklesia* or Kingdom spiritual army; and the gates of hell shall not prevail against it."

Matthew 16:18-19 also is one of the best statements by Jesus that the *Ekklesia* is to be about the original commandment to take dominion over the entire world system ruled by the prince of this world. Since Satan is the prince of this world system, then the spiritual directive from God for the *Ekklesia* is through spiritual warfare to take possession of every profession, every business, every school, every newspaper, every media outlet, every social media, every film maker, every music production company, every government office, both locally and federally, and all aspects of every nation, and give possession back to God as the true owner and the One who rightfully should have possession of the world system. With the anointing of the Holy Spirit, each Believer is to go into the world and preach the gospel of the Kingdom with its spiritual Kingdom government Ambassadors and its spiritual Kingdom military Soldiers, which is the rightful government and army here on earth.

DO BELIEVERS' CURRENT RELIGIOUS
PRACTICES CONSTITUTE THE TRUE *EKKLESIA*?

Again, Jesus came to establish a congregation or assembly of Believers who have repented and accepted Him as their Lord and Savior and would be part of His spiritual Kingdom government and His spiritual Kingdom army, not just Believers who go and attend a praise and worship service and listen to teachings and sermons every week, without activation into their ministry calling. Every Believer is a member of a royal priesthood (1 Peter 2:9), and every Believer is God's under King and Priest (Revelation 1:6). Why are not Believers being trained as the King's rulers that take over the world system as kings, lords, and stewards of God's creation. Ephesians 4:11-12 says, "And He gave some, apostles; and some, prophets; and some, evangelists; and some, pastors and teachers; for the perfecting of the saints, for the work of the ministry, for the edifying of the Body of Christ." What was Jesus' mandate on the Mount of Ascension? Jesus said in Matthew 28:18-20, "All power (authority) is given unto Me in Heaven and in earth. Go ye therefore, and teach (make disciples of) all nations, baptizing them in the name of the Father, and of the Son, and of the Holy Ghost, teaching them to observe all things whatsoever I have commanded you: and, lo, I am with you always, even unto the end of the world." Making disciples is making Believers mature, sanctified, and better servants who minister with love, which is the primary motivation of the fruit of the Spirit, which are all expressions of *agape* love. Galatians 5:22-24 says, "But the fruit of the Spirit is love, joy, peace, longsuffering, gentleness, goodness, faith, meekness, temperance: against such there is no law. And they that are Christ's have crucified the flesh with the affections and lusts."

An Ephesians 4:11 gift ministry can be a functioning prophetic Apostle. An additional Ephesians 4:11 gift ministry can be a functioning teaching Pastor, while another gift ministry can be a functioning apostolic Evangelist. The Ephesians 4:11 gift ministries are more so as functions, rather than titles. Yet, the primary purpose of the Ephesians 4:11 gift ministries is to function in a manner to create leaders in the Body of Christ to build up the *Ekklesia,* not followers of those in the Ephesians 4:11 gift ministries. The purpose of each Ephesians 4:11 gift ministry's function is, "For the perfecting of the saints, for the work of the ministry, for the edifying of the Body of Christ: Till we all come in the unity of the faith, and of the knowledge of the Son of God, unto a perfect man, unto the measure of the stature of the fullness of Christ" (Ephesians 4:12-13). Are the practices of the leadership in the *Ekklesia* today producing followers of the Ephesians 4:11 leaders, or as bondservants of Christ, who should be activated into ministry to fulfill Jesus' great mission in Matthew 24:14, Matthew 28:18-20, Mark 16:15, Luke 24:47-49, and Acts 1:8?

EKKLISIA SHOULD NOT HAVE BEEN
INTERPRETED BY ENGLISH WRITERS AS CHURCH

In Matthew 16:18, in the Greek, Jesus did not say He would build His *Kuriakos* (Strongs reference G2960, Church), but rather His *Ekklesia* (Strongs G1577, military assembly). *Ekklesia* is used more than 120 times in the King James Version of the Bible. The word "Church" is derived from the Greek word *Kuriakos*, (Strongs reference G2960), which is derived from the Greek word *"Kurios"* (Strongs G2962). *Kurios* means "supreme in authority, that is, (as a noun) controller; by implication God, Lord, Master, Sir." Thus, the Greek word *Kuriakos* means belonging to one's Lord or Master as a bondservant, and this is what "church" means. The word came from the Teutonic word *"kirk, kirch,"* from where we get the word "church." The word *"Kuriakos"* appears only in 1 Corinthians 11:20 which modifies the Greek word for the Lord's (*Kuriakos*) supper and in Revelation 1:10 which modifies the Greek word for the Lord's (*Kuriakos*) day.

Wikipedia describes the word *"kirk"* "(a)s a common noun, *kirk* (meaning 'church') is found in Scots, Scottish English, Ulster-Scots and some English dialects, attested as a noun from the 14th century onwards, but as an element in place names much earlier. *Kirk* and *church*, are derived from the Koine Greek, *kyriakon dōma* meaning Lord's house, which was borrowed into the Germanic languages in late antiquity, possibly in the course of the Gothic missions. (Only a connection with the idiosyncrasies of Gothic explains how a Greek neuter noun became a Germanic feminine.) Whereas *church* displays Old English palatalization, *kirk* is a loan word from Old Norse and thus has the original mainland Germanic consonants. Compare cognates: Icelandic & Faroese *kirkja*; Swedish *kyrka*; Norwegian (Nynorsk) *kyrkje*; and Danish *kirke*; German *kirche*, Dutch *kerk*; West Frisian *tsjerke*; and borrowed into non-Germanic languages: Estonian *kirik* and Finnish *kirkko*."

.

Thus, the English word "church" did not come from the Greek word *Ekklesia* but from the Scottish word *kirk*. In Acts 19: 37 the Greek word correctly translated as "churches" is *"hierosulos."* In the same discourse, in Acts 19:34-41 the word *Ekklesia* three times was translated as "government assembly." Here the secular council meeting, called an *Ekklesia*, was formed to determine what to do with Paul and his co-workers for preaching the gospel of the Kingdom in their city. The secular rulers in the city were threatened because these Believers were introducing a new Kingdom rule in their city. Also, the Roman Senate was called an *Ekklesia*, and Jesus took this Greek word and applied it to His body of Believers. In fact, in the Roman Empire any group of citizens who were "called out" to do a work for the government was called an *Ekklesia*.

To further the confusion is the misinterpretation of the word *Ekklesia* as the "church building." Historically, this falsehood came around 313 A.D. from a decree handed down from the Roman Emperor, Maximian, who had persecuted the Believers. Constantine was in war against Maximian, and Maximian understood that Constantine was supportive of those in the Christian faith. Before Maximian lost power, he issued a decree in an unsuccessful attempt to gain Constantine's favor and peace by decreeing that Believers could build the *Ekklesia* or "house of God" in the

Western part of the Roman Empire. Thus, from that day forward, the "house of God" started being referred to as the "church." Most leaders do say the true Body of Christ is the Believers, not a building, but normally their whole energy financially is supporting the building and those who work in the building as employees. Throughout the Western European and the Eastern countries are majestic religious buildings, which show the belief that the building is considered the "church." Even in the U.S. Pastors or Ministers refer to the building out of tradition as the "church." After a while, most Believers refer to attending "church" as going to a "church building" at a given location. They entirely miss the concept of the true *Ekklesia*. The leaders have not corrected the historical mistake of not seeing that the *Ekklesia* is a spiritual Kingdom assembly of Ambassadors and a spiritual Kingdom assembly of Soldiers that are empowered to take possession of the world system and hand it back to God through Christ, while at the same time preaching repentance and the remission of sins.

The term *Ekklesia* also referred to the Athenian popular "military assembly." Any male citizen with two years of military service was qualified for membership. This "military assembly" was responsible for declaring war, discussing military strategies, and had the right to vote for the Supreme Military Commander and other government officials. This *Ekklesia* as a military assembly was borrowed by Jesus for His Kingdom spiritual military army, He called *Ekklesia*.

The *Ekklesia* is a Kingdom spiritual military that all Believers are mandated to join as Soldiers. Like Israel today, all citizens of the Kingdom are spiritual Soldiers. 2 Timothy 2: 3-4 says, "Thou therefore endure hardness, as a good soldier of Jesus Christ. No man that warreth entangleth himself with the affairs of this life; that he may please Him who hath chosen him to be a soldier."

Paul saw Believers as Kingdom spiritual Soldiers commanded to conduct spiritual warfare against the evil army of the kingdom of darkness. 2 Corinthians 10: 3-5 says, "For though we walk in the flesh, we do not war after the flesh: (For the weapons of our warfare are not carnal, but mighty through God to the pulling down of strong holds;) Casting down imaginations, and every high thing that exalteth itself against the knowledge of God and bringing into captivity every thought to the obedience of Christ."

A stronghold is a military term. Warfare is a battle. Weapons are instruments of war. Yet, these are spiritual, not carnal; and the military of the Kingdom and the battles are all spiritual conflicts but resulting in natural freedom as well from the kingdom of darkness and the kingdoms of this world system. Believers' weapons are spiritual words of their testimonies, pleading the Cross of Calvary, pleading the precious spilt blood of Jesus, pleading the Name of Jesus, and speaking the *rhema* word of the Lord. Believers have the authority to pray, to bind and loosen, to decree a thing with faith as led by the Holy Spirit, and to judge a matter whether it is of God or not.

THE CALLED-OUT ONES

Once born again Believers become members of the *Ekklesia*, they are the "called out ones" who are drafted into the Lord's Kingdom spiritual military as Soldiers and appointed as members of the Lord's Kingdom Spiritual government assembly as Ambassadors under the ultimate authority of Christ Jesus. The members of the *Ekklesia* are the "called out ones" who are called out of the world to serve the King of kings, the Lord of lords, and High Priest after the order of

Melchizedek. Members of the *Ekklesia* are like those members of Congress who are called out of their states and are placed in the seat of government in Washington D.C. Members of the *Ekklesia* are also like military Soldiers who are called out from their homes to join the army and are trained and deployed to another state or another country.

In the Hebrew, Israelite, and Jewish culture, the "called out ones" were those chosen to judge a matter, and they sat at the gates of the city to make decrees and decide matters of commerce and ownership of property. Normally, there were ten Israelite adult men chosen to be the governmental authority at the gates of a city. In the Hebrew religion, they must have ten Jewish adult men to open a synagogue in a city, which is called a *minyan*. The number ten was derived from the first verse of Psalm 82, which says, "God standeth in the congregation (*edah*) of the mighty; He judgeth among the gods." The Hebrew word for "congregation" or "assembly" is *edah*, which word was also applied to the ten spies who in the days of Moses came back from the promise land with a negative report. Numbers 14:27 says, "How long shall I bear with this evil congregation (*edah*), which murmur against Me? I have heard the murmurings of the children of Israel, which they murmur against Me." Because the Hebrew word for "congregation" or "assembly" is *edah*, which word was applied to the ten spies returning to the camp with a negative or evil report after their forty day's journeys in the promise land, the Israelites followed their advice and immediately did not enter into the promise land but spent forty years in the wilderness. God judged the judgment of ten spies. Numbers 14:34 says, "After the number of the days in which ye searched the land, even forty days, each day for a year, shall ye bear your iniquities, even forty years, and ye shall know My breach of promise." Thus, historically, a congregation in a synagogue must consist of ten Hebrew or Israelite adult men who could judge wisely. The ten Israelite adult men chosen to be the governmental authority at the gates of a city, and even the ten Hebrew spies who judged the condition of the promise land as being full of giants, was the tradition that became the basis for requiring ten men in a city to form a synagogue or *minyan*.

Members of the *Ekklesia* are gifted with the spirit of wisdom from Heaven in making decisions about matters here on earth, and their heavenly wisdom is pure, peaceable, gentle, full of mercy, and bearing good fruit (James 3:17). This heavenly wisdom is the kind of wisdom that Solomon had. The governmental called out ones were not to use the fallen wisdom of this world in making their decisions, which is demonic (James 3:15).

The *Ekklesia's* primary goal is the restoration of the possession of the world system back into the hands of Father God. Therefore, the Bible is not just a book of moral laws and principles to be used as guidelines to live, but also is used to instruct the activating and maturing of the souls of the Body of Christ as Kingdom spiritual Ambassadors and Kingdom spiritual Soldiers, while being citizens of Heaven. 2 Corinthians 5:20 says, "Now then we are Ambassadors for Christ, as though God did beseech you by us: we pray you in Christ's stead, be ye reconciled to God." An Ambassador is someone who resides or works in a foreign country as a representative of his own country. Philippians 3:20 says, "For our citizenship is in Heaven, from which we also eagerly wait for the Savior, the Lord Jesus Christ."

Jesus loves "nations" and hates "global empires" because the latter is a counterfeit to the Kingdom of God, as the Kingdom of God is the only spiritual government allowed to take over the entire world. Revelation 11:15 says, "The kingdoms of this world are become the kingdoms of our Lord, and of His Christ; and He shall reign forever and ever." Acts 17: 26 says, "And hath made of one blood all Nations of men for to dwell on all the face of the earth, and hath determined the times before appointed, and the bounds (boundaries) of their habitation." God appointed and established "nations" not "global empires."

The true *Ekklesia* requires financing, and God anoints those who are called out from worldly businesses and are anointed to be about God the Father's business (Luke 2:49). God's Kingdom Business Servants have the gift of giving pronounced in Romans 12:8 to be used to bring in the necessary finances for a major outpouring of the Holy Spirit on all flesh, which will be a worldwide end time *Ekklesia* in Revival (Joel 2:28).

THE OLD RELIGIOUS ORDER STRUCTURE
HAS DONE GOOD WORKS, BUT NOT TOTALLY GOD'S WILL

In balance, there are large old religious order structures that have outreach programs in their communities, and they do give to missionaries around the world. This is better than just setting up lecture halls with attendance group pressure on the Believers and calling it the fulfillment of the Believers' servanthood for the Kingdom of God. There are outreaches of some old religious order structures that send Believers into the streets to evangelize the lost with only the message of repentance for the remission of sins without preaching the gospel of the Kingdom. Also, are the new Believers sent to an old wineskin religious order or a new, loving, dynamic *Ekklesia* fellowship that practices intimate Kingdom community relationships with the Lord and other Believers, who are activated with spiritual gifts?

Are the new Believers discipled with the word of God to become Biblitarians? Will they be joining a true *Ekklesia* as Kingdom spiritual Ambassadors and Kingdom spiritual soldiers? Will they be discipled to seek first the Kingdom of God and His righteousness? Will new Believers be instructed in family and nation salvation, as well as individual salvation as essential for living as servants in the Kingdom of God? Will new Believers be led into the practices and beliefs of an anemic old religious order system that centers its focus and activities within a building instead of using modern media methods of training disciples with Kingdom management principles that will be brought into the marketplace, homes, schools, industries, and governments to further the Kingdom dominion mandate?

God's Kingdom rule is that complex things are built on simple things well done that fit together for a greater purpose. God's Kingdom goal is that individual Believers have their souls spiritually transformed and engifted for the greater benefit and good of the Kingdom community and body of Christ. The outreach work in the Kingdom community and the supporting of missionaries, although good, may not be focused on taking dominion of the world system in each local Kingdom community and the nation and giving it back to Father God. Localized outreaches are the first mission field for establishing the Kingdom of God, and then outreaches continue there to the state level, to the national level, from there to the entire world. Again, Acts 1:8 says, "But ye shall receive power, after that the Holy Ghost is come upon you: and ye shall be witnesses unto me BOTH in Jerusalem, and in all Judaea, and in Samaria, and unto the uttermost part of the earth." Local Jerusalem is 50% of work in seeking disciples, while Judea, Samaria, and uttermost part of the world are combined as the other 50% of work in seeking disciples. The same ministry focus is throughout the *Ekklesia* locations, wherever located, and this takes daily contact. Even in "Judea, Samaria, and uttermost part of the world," God's purpose is the same as in Jerusalem.

It is always about educating Believers with the truth and activating the local body of Believers as Kingdom spiritual Ambassadors and Kingdom spiritual Soldiers, and this goal can only be reached through intimacy with and submission to the Godhead and fellowship with other Believers in Kingdom.

To its credit, the old religious order structure has good praise and worship music and songs in history. However, if you have been in old religious meetings for ten, fifteen, or thirty years, you have heard most of the sermons more than once, although often there is a new twist as to how the scriptures and truths are taught. Yet, neither the praise and worship, nor the sermons, are instructing and directing the Believers to take back possession of the means of production, the economy, the government, or other power centers of society and dedicate them to God the Father. God is King over His creation because He is the Creator. A King governs, and a Lord maintains ownership authority over the land and animals and everything that is on His Kingdom land. The earth is the Lord's (Psalms 24:1). Psalms 22:28 says, "For the kingdom is the LORD'S: and He is the Governor among the nations."

THE *EKKLESIA* IS TO CARRY OUT JESUS' "SON OF MAN" AUTHORITY AND MISSION

Daniel 7:13-14 says, "I saw in the night visions, and, behold, one like the Son of Man came with the clouds of Heaven, and came to the Ancient of days, and they brought him near before Him. And there was given Him dominion, and glory, and a kingdom, that all people, nations, and languages, should serve Him: His dominion is an everlasting dominion, which shall not pass away, and his kingdom that which shall not be destroyed....But the Saints of the Most High shall take the kingdom, and possess the kingdom forever, even forever and ever."

The "Ancient of Days" is Father God, Who gave the Messiah the prerogative and lifted Him up as the "Son of Man," of the first order, which means He is the highest spiritual finite Being as the only begotten Son of God in the divine order over all creation. Jesus is the Hebrew phrase, *"Bar Enash,"* which means Son of Man, Who has the Name that is above every other name (Philippians 2: 9-11). Jesus fulfilled this prophecy in His earthly ministry, along with His death, resurrection, ascension, and current intercessory ministry in Heaven where His humanity nature sits on the Throne of God. When Jesus mentioned Himself as the "Son of Man" in the four Gospels, His purpose was to accept His authority from the "Ancient of Days" and transfer that authority to Believers (Matthew 28:18). Jesus shared that authority with the Saints of the Most High to empower and authorize them to exercise faith to restore possession of the earth and the world system back to the "Ancient of Days," God the Father, by building an *Ekklesia* which is an assembly of Kingdom Ambassadors and Kingdom Soldiers and dutiful, loving servant's of God's Kingdom.

The primary reason why Believers as members of the family of God are redeemed and are being transformed in their souls is to exercise the authority given by God the Father to Christ Jesus, the Son of Man, and which authority is shared with Believers as the Lord's disciples (Matthew 28:18-20). Believers have the responsibility to make disciples of Christ's spiritual government and military first in their city, state, nation, and then to other countries. As the Lord's Kingdom spiritual government and Kingdom spiritual soldiers, Believers have the delegated authority from Christ Jesus to carry and preach the word of the Kingdom (Matthew 13:19) while here on the earth with the goal of taking dominion over all things here on earth to bring back possession to

God the Father of His creation and reconciling Believers through redemption and forgiveness of sins bought by the shed blood of Jesus on the Roman Cross. Everything that fell with Adam, Christ restored and gave them as blessings to Believers as members of the *Ekklesia* of the Son of Man. This requires Believers to assume their Kingdom governmental spiritual authority and responsibility as Ambassadors and as Kingdom Soldiers as the *Ekklesia* of Christ.

God wants Believers to come into agreement with Him to shift all things in each nation and family to become part of God's Kingdom here on earth where God the Father manifests His will here on earth to establish His spiritual Kingdom. The enemy does not want God's will to be done to manifest the Son of Man's Kingdom possessory authority here on earth. The Lord's Kingdom spiritual Soldiers must stand to protect the ground that the saints of the Most High received through Christ Jesus' grant of authority.

JESUS CHRIST WAS SKILLED AS A BUSINESS SERVANT, AS A CARPENTER, WHO BECAME HEAD OF THE *EKKLESIA*

Believers should be discipled *en mass* to manifest the Kingdom of God wherever they have influence every day of the week as an alternative lifestyle than the world has. When I go into a business, where there are Believer owners, it is often difficult to discern the difference between their business practices than unBelievers' business practices in the world. Why not release the Kingdom of God out of the four walls of an old religious order building and bring it into the world where people work, interact, congregate, and live throughout the week? Why not have employees read one chapter of Proverbs and five chapters of Psalms per day, with everyone participating in the reading at the workplace during special times in the morning before work begins? God's Business Servants and employees should pray for other employees, help other employees with their work-related tasks, and visit employees who are sick, and bring food for their meals? If you are a true Believer, then you will be practicing the commandment to love one another in a practical way, not just mere lip service (John 13:34-35). God's Business Servants and employees could set up a monthly contribution by all employees and owners to give a monetary gift each month to a needy family or a cause that everyone agrees to be a donor to those in need? This must be voluntary, though. God's Business Owners should help and teach employees how to establish personal budgets, buy a car, purchase a home, abolish debt, and give with pure hearts to the local *Ekklesia*. So, with the permission of the client or customer, release all the employees to pray for them as the Holy Spirit leads them. This would be evangelism in the workplace. This work will be about God the Father's business to redeem the lost and mature the souls of those who are now born again and redeemed.

If there are fellow employees that are unBelievers, it is paramount for Believers to be ready to share the true gospel of the Kingdom and repentance and remission of sins with them when they are ready. Believer employees must let unBelievers know that not only will they have forgiveness of sins and receive everlasting life, but they will receive a Kingdom community of loving Believers in fellowship who will be their support and friends during all seasons and times of their lives. Let new Believers know they will be part of God's Kingdom spiritual government here on earth right now where God's truth and love rules and let them know they will be a part of God's Kingdom spiritual military that always wins in the long run because "...we know that all things work together for good to them that love God, to them who are the called according to His purpose" (Romans 8:28). Let the new Believers know they will have genuine fellowship where they will not be lonely anymore while truth and love permeate the conversations.

Missionaries should equip the Believers in other nations to preach the gospel of the Kingdom of God, along with repentance and the remission of sins, both brought about by Jesus' death on the cruel Roman Cross. Missionaries should instruct Believers to manifest the *Ekklesia* in their own nations with the goal of discipling Kingdom servants with the primary commandment to love one another, which will enhance the entire society with the manifested spiritual government and spiritual army of the Kingdom of God. Why not teach Believers in the *Ekklesia* the mandate of God to be self-disciplined, morally principled, and spiritually mature in their souls; but especially to introduce them as citizens of Heaven and the Kingdom with responsibility to be spiritual Kingdom Ambassadors and spiritual Kingdom Soldiers in a loving, life changing way? When this happens, Believers will transform the society, and the unsaved will find the Kingdom of God irresistible. The born again spiritual citizens of Heaven living in the natural country will need less oversight from their civil, secular governments because they are living by God's biblical principles of always submitting to the authority of the King and the power of the Holy Spirit.

God wants to send business servants as citizens of God's Kingdom and the Lord's *Ekklesia* into the marketplace with the biblical principles of economics and that the workplace is for the maturing of Believers through the daily incremental problem solving that is encountered in business by using biblical principles instead of worldly principles.

BELIEVERS ALSO INHERIT A FAMILY, KINGDOM, INTIMATE RELATIONSHIP WITH THE LORD, AND AN ETERNAL PURPOSE

Believers do not inherit just everlasting life and the right to go and live in Heaven for a season; rather, in addition they inherit a family, a Kingdom, an intimate relationship with God, and God's eternal Kingdom purpose that will be their place of provision and give them a bright and fulfilling future (Jeremiah 29:11). Matthew 25:32-34 says, "And before Him shall be gathered all nations: and He shall separate them one from another, as a Shepherd divideth his sheep from the goats: And He shall set the sheep on his right hand, but the goats on the left. Then shall the King say unto them on his right hand, 'Come, ye blessed of my Father, inherit the kingdom prepared for you from the foundation of the world."

The *Ekklesia* is a Kingdom of Believers, who have received salvation because of Jesus dying on the cruel Cross, and as part of the New Man in Christ are spiritual Ambassadors and spiritual Soldiers with the purpose to take back possession of the earth, the world system, the natural creation, and reconcile the fallen people back to God here on earth. This dominion mandate once was assigned to Adam and Eve and their posterity before their fall.

Believers' born again spirits are citizens of Heaven (Philippians 3:20), and are called out to be Kingdom spiritual Soldiers and Kingdom spiritual Ambassadors to be servants in the Kingdom of God and do the will of God here on earth as it is in Heaven. Yet, the gospel of the Kingdom message also is that new Believers are born again into the household of God and are citizens of Heaven (Ephesians 2:19). As members of the Second Man, New Man, Christ Jesus (1 Corinthians 15:47; 2 Corinthians 5:17), Believers are mandated to take dominion of the world system and the physical creation that is in Believers' sphere of influence to allow God to transfer them into the Kingdom of God's dear Son. Believers are trained with God's knowledge, understanding, and wisdom when doing God's Kingdom spiritual work while performing services in the businesses, the professions, the schools, the debates, the marketplaces, the film and music industries, the newspapers, the television networks, the radio stations, the Internet, the social media, all forms of communication, and even while performing services in the world secular governments. Government workers do not have to give up their faith while working for the secular government. Secular government Believers can share their faith with others at the workplace. In fact, under the 1964 Civil Rights Act, in the event a certain action of an employer goes against an employee's "religious beliefs," then the employer must make reasonable adjustments and accommodations for the employee that does not violate the employee's faith.

Those who are trying to win back possession of the earth and reconciling fallen mankind back to God, on behalf of the Kingdom of God must have freedom to do so. The word "freedom" is really two words. "Free" means "liberty" and "dom" means "dominion." Thus, freedom means the liberty to take dominion of your God-ordained place in His Kingdom while here on earth. It means the freedom to proclaim salvation by calling upon the name of Jesus and believing that He died and rose from the dead (Romans 10:9-10).

Notwithstanding, victory only comes after the battle is won, so every Believer volunteers as a Soldier in God's Kingdom spiritual Army. Every Believer is encouraged to put on the whole armor of God (Ephesians 6:10-18). Jesus wants to give Believers liberty, but the devil wants to keep Believers in bondage in their souls by remaining carnal by continuously feeding the soul with the stimuli from the natural world instead of the spiritual stimuli from the Kingdom of God brought to the soul by the born again spirit being led by the Holy Spirit. John 8:31-33 says, "Then said Jesus to those Jews which believed on Him, 'If ye continue in My word, then are ye My disciples indeed; and ye shall know the truth, and the truth shall make you free.' They answered him, 'We be Abraham's seed, and were never in bondage to any man: how sayest thou, 'Ye shall be made free?'" Thus, being "free" is a Kingdom citizenship word, as someone not in bondage to things of this world. A Believer that works in bringing possession of the world system and people back to God, under the authority of Jesus, as anointed with power by the Holy Spirit, will be liberated from bondage. Galatians 5:1 says, "Stand fast therefore in the liberty wherewith Christ hath made us free and be not entangled again with the yoke of bondage." Romans 8:2 says, "For the law of the spirit of life in Christ Jesus hath made me free from the law of sin and death." Liberty is only experienced when Believers are free from the clutches or bondage of sin and the seeking of things in the natural world instead of the spiritual things in the Kingdom of God.

1 John 3:9 says, "Whosoever is born of God doth not commit sin; for his seed remaineth in him: and he cannot sin, because he is born of God." A Believer's born again spirit was born of God. A Believer's soul was not born again, so the soul must go through the daily incremental ministry as God the Father prunes away the flesh's influence in your soul (John 15:2). God the Word washes and sanctifies the soul by washing away the flesh in the soul by the water of the word of God (Ephesians 5:26). God the Holy Spirit mortifies (starves) the deeds of the flesh in the soul (Romans 8:13).

1 John 5:4 says, "For whatsoever is born of God overcometh the world: and this is the victory that overcometh the world, even our faith." Jesus said in Revelation 21:7, "He that overcometh shall inherit all things; and I will be his God (Jesus' divine nature), and he shall be My son

(born again spirits from the Seed of Jesus' humanity nature)." The Greek word translated "over-cometh" is *nikao*, which means "to conquer, prevail, or vanquish the enemy in battle and take the spoils after winning." A Believer is entitled to the spoils of war after winning spiritual battles against the kingdom of darkness. The extent of a Believer's spiritual inheritance depends upon the Believer working with faith in God's spiritual Kingdom government and Kingdom spiritual army to take possession of the world system currently under the authority of the evil spiritual prince of this world, the devil, and deliver it back to Father God.

Believers are not to just preach only the benefits of personal salvation that gives new Believers everlasting life, but also must preach the good news of the gospel of the Kingdom that constitutes the ministry of reconciliation. 2 Corinthians 5:18-19 says, "And all things are of God, who hath reconciled us to Himself by Jesus Christ, and hath given to us the ministry of reconciliation; to wit, that God was in Christ, reconciling the world unto Himself, not imputing their trespasses unto them; and hath committed unto us the word of reconciliation." The confession and belief of Romans 10: 9-10,13 are not only salvation promises, but, also new creation promises brought by Jesus' resurrection. The gospel of the Kingdom also has to be preached that is an activating message of Believers. Romans 10:9 says to become a new Believer one must believe that Jesus was resurrected from the dead. Christ's resurrection from the dead was the commencement of the new creation. From Christ's resurrected spirit is the source of Believer's born again spirit.

In Acts 20:24 Paul said he preach the gospel of grace, which is part of the gospel of the Kingdom, which means unmerited favor to being chosen to be God's Kingdom spiritual government as an Ambassador and Kingdom spiritual military as a Soldier and a member of God's family. Being in the Kingdom's spiritual military does not mean declaring war, taking up natural weapons, and shooting natural enemies; but it does mean the Kingdom spiritual Soldiers are vigilant in prayer against the spiritual kingdom of darkness, studies God's word, and acquires the knowledge, understanding, and wisdom about spiritually engaging in businesses, professions, secular governments, schools, and therein participating in transplanting the Kingdom biblitarian principles in that field, while seeking first the Kingdom of God and His righteousness as the foundation of the society of the nation.

The Ephesians 4:11 Ministers are chosen to equip the Believers for the work of the ministry of the Body of Christ in preaching and manifesting the Kingdom of God (Ephesians 4:12). In every place a Believer works, interacts with others, and lives, there should be the manifestation of all aspects of the *Ekklesia* with a Believer doing the work of the Kingdom with faith that pleases God (Hebrews 11:6). If a Believer is part of the overcomers who is chosen to manifest the true *Ekklesia* here on earth, then the Believer's employer and fellow employees will be enriched spiritually and naturally as the moral, economic, and biblitarian principles of God are being applied in the business and the marketplace that come up against the god of mammon, God's purposes are being accomplished; the Lord's loving *Ekklesia* is in fellowship; the Kingdom of God and His righteousness are being sought, and the Believer is being obedient to take back to Father God the possession of the area over which the Believer has authority and is assigned by the Holy Spirit while the Believer's soul is being spiritually transformed as the New Man in Christ as God's holy and righteous Temple.

Believers are to be equipped by the Ephesians 4:11 Ministers who function as apostles, prophets, evangelists, pastors, and teachers to equip and mature Believers in their minds, emotions, and hearts of their souls. Ephesians 4:11-13 says, "And he gave some, apostles; and some, prophets; and some, evangelists; and some, pastors and teachers; for the perfecting of the saints, for the work of the ministry, for the edifying of the Body of Christ: till we all come in the unity of the faith, and of the knowledge of the Son of God, unto a perfect Man, unto the measure of the stature of the fullness of Christ."

Thus, how long do the Ephesians 4:11 Ministers who function as apostles, prophets, evangelists, pastors, and teachers minister this all important assignment? The Ephesians 4:11 functioning ministers are needed "Till we all come in the unity of the faith, and of the knowledge of the Son of God, unto a perfect man, unto the measure of the stature of the fullness of Christ." The *Ekklesia* desperately is still in need of the Ephesians 4:11 functioning office ministries. These Ephesians 4:11 office ministries are functions and not titles, and they are chosen by the condition of their hearts and not just their natural education, skills, and spiritual engiftments. God deals strictly with Ephesians 4:11 office ministers to maintain their humility, purity, righteousness, and good character. There should be no division between the Ephesians 4:11 office ministries. Their knowledge of the word of God should have priority in their lives. They should strive to be of the measure of the stature of the fullness of Christ. All that they do in ministry cannot be for self-aggrandizement, for becoming famous, for obtaining wealth, or for building their own large old religious order fellowship instead of a Kingdom community fellowship that equips the Believers into ministry as Jesus' under kings, lords, and priests. They must have purity of hearts without the lust of the flesh, the lust of the eyes, or the pride of life (1 John 2:15-17).

Ephesians 4:11 office ministers especially need to forgive those who commit sin and lead them back to the Lord and place them back into the fellowship with other Believers. When another leader falls into sin, forgive the brother and sister and work fervently in prayer, in genuine loving fellowship, and with faithfulness not to abandon him or her in order to bring the Lord's servant back on the path of righteousness and in ministry; "For the gifts and the calling of God are without repentance" (Romans 11:29).

Galatians 6:1-2 says, "Brethren, if a man be overtaken in a fault, ye which are spiritual, restore such a one in the spirit of meekness; considering thyself, lest thou also be tempted. Bear ye one another's burdens, and so fulfill the law of Christ." All ministry services must be done with *agape* love, along with the ministry of reconciliation as the goal and purpose (2 Corinthians 5:18). Occasionally, the leaders become legalistic without love and shoot the wounded. Being Christ like is being forgiving. Abraham interceded on behalf of the sinners in Sodom, Gomorrah, and Zoar to save the sinners if there be only ten righteous men in Sodom. Genesis 18: 23, 32 says, "And Abraham drew near, and said, 'Wilt thou also destroy the righteous with the wicked?' And he said, 'Oh let not the Lord be angry, and I will speak yet but this once: Peradventure ten shall be found there. And he said, I will not destroy it for ten's sake." Unfortunately, there were not ten righteous in the cities, but the Lord saw that Abraham had the heart to save sinners just like God's only begotten Son that was to come in the fullness of time (Galatians 4:4). Jesus forgave sinners and did not judge, and in His instruction as to how to pray, He said in Matthew 6:14-15, "For if ye forgive men their trespasses, your heavenly Father will also forgive you: But if ye forgive not men their trespasses, neither will your Father forgive your trespasses." To forgive someone of their sins is a gracious act of agape love and is part of the mandate in John 13:34-35 to love one another.

In Luke 15:11-32 is the Kingdom parable of the Prodigal Son, where the father forgave his son because the son came to his senses, and he returned home; and the father welcomed him and restored his stature as a member of the family once again. In the same way, God waits for the unsaved and the saved that come to realize they have sinned, ask for forgiveness, and Father God welcomes them back into the family when they do. It is the willingness for the penitent to change his heart and ask for forgiveness that changes one's behavior that is central to the idea of forgiveness. Peter asked Jesus how many times he had to forgive a trespassing brother? Jesus responded in Matthew 18: 20-21, "Then came Peter to him, and said, Lord, how oft shall my brother sin against me, and I forgive him? Till seven times? Jesus saith unto him, 'I say not unto thee, Until seven times: but, until seventy times seven.'"

In John 8:1-11, the scribes and Pharisees brought to Jesus a woman caught in the very act of adultery. Jesus forgave the sinning woman and convicted all those of their own sins who wanted to stone her, who did not ask forgiveness of sins but just dropped their stones and walked away. Jesus concluded in John 8:10-11, "… 'Woman, where are those thine accusers? Hath no man condemned thee?' She said, 'No man, Lord.' And Jesus said unto her, 'Neither do I condemn thee: go, and sin no more.'" Finally, the greatest example of the continuous need to have a heart to forgive and restore the relationship of sinners with the Father. While being crucified on the Cross, Jesus said in Luke 23:34, "Father, forgive them; for they know not what they do."

Every Believer is a King and Priest under the authority of Christ (1 Peter 2:9; Revelation 1:6; 5:10). Even in the secular world, the law enforces the confidentiality of a Penitent confession to his Priest or Pastor from using the contents of the confession as evidence for prosecution. The Priest or Pastor must keep confessions of sin confidential. Unfortunately, sometimes the lead Pastor may send out a Facebook message, an email, or even type the incident on Google or other electronic communication describing the failure of a leader to shame him under the guise of their intolerance for sin in the old religious order leadership. The Senior Pastor leader terminates the subordinate leader, gives no or little severance pay, and dismisses him from office instead of accepting his confession and setting up conditions of restoration to return to his gifts and calling upon proper counseling and pastoral loving covering. Instead, the Board of Elders or Senior Pastor says, "We wish him and his family well, and are praying for them." However, this fallen leader in the old religious order may never find a job, may have his car repossessed, home foreclosed, and his children and wife suffer shame and are shunned with him, losing all their Christian friends, and losing the joy of fellowship because they are no longer welcomed in the community of Believers as if they have leprosy. This is done as the leading Minister and the governing Board become instruments of condemnation through ruining the lives of the man or woman of God and the family through public shame, scorn and condemnation. Forget about the fact the man or woman of God was a hard-working servant of the Lord in building the congregation, was a dedicated associate pastor for five, ten, or twenty years, but now has no means in the secular world to obtain a job to support himself or his family as they were accustomed. This is a horrible indictment against the Body of Christ leadership who do this. There are denominations that still believe if a Pastor goes through divorce, he or she is disqualified from ministry.

Satan promotes religious leadership to do his work and foster the Kingdom of darkness when they fall. Religious leaders preach and teach about loving one another but some of them only want to exalt, promote, and further religious infrastructure they have built and see any sinner in leadership a threat that the ministry will get a black eye; so, they have little or no compassion even for the penitent sinner confessing sin and asking forgiveness. 1 John 1:8-9 says, "If we say that we have no sin, we deceive ourselves, and the truth is not in us. If we confess our sins, He is faithful and just to forgive us our sins, and to cleanse us from all unrighteousness." The Lord is faithful and just to forgive Believers of their sins, but often the old religious order leaders are not faithful and just to forgive Believers who also are leaders of their sins, standing on their reasoning of protecting the ministry. Forgiveness of sins and loving people back by the ministry of reconciliation to become faithful servants in God's Kingdom ministering in love is foundational in the *Ekklesia*. The ministry is people, not real estate. You must not love a building or a religious structure.

God's spiritual Kingdom Soldiers keep themselves ready to engage in spiritual warfare against the kingdom of darkness. What does Jesus' divine nature command Believers to do? He commands Believers to allow the Holy Spirit to lead them while taking dominion and returning possession of all facets of the world system and the creation back to God the Father. Jesus came with His dual natures not only to save but also to establish God the Father's Kingdom spiritual Government to govern here on earth and to recruit, train, and lead a Kingdom spiritual Army to conduct spiritual warfare against the spiritual enemy of God. This voluntary faith with works of Kingdom government and military service by Believers are full time professions, even while Believers work in the natural professions in the world. Wherever a member of the *Ekklesia*, and as a citizen of Heaven, goes while he lives here on earth, the Kingdom government and military authority go with him.

Thus, the *Ekklesia* is the spiritual Kingdom governing assembly here on earth, and the *Ekklesia* is also the assembly of Soldiers ready for battle and are deciding where the next battle is to be waged. There are only a few leaders in the Body of Christ today discipling members to take dominion of the businesses, schools, governments, film and music industry, radio programs, Internet, social media, court system, and the news media. Once God sees His leaders ready, He will provide the finances to conduct the warfare at strategic locations. Jesus has given Believers authority to bind and loosen to fight spiritual warfare (Matthew 16:19).

Believers are not supposed to be just continuously going to a building to listen to praise and worship music and sitting in pews listening to sermons week after week, month after month, and year after year as the sum total of their Kingdom responsibilities as citizens of Heaven and as the Lord's *Ekklesia* here on earth. Even though this activity might be good for a season, it is not God's best because it does not activate Believers into the work of the ministry but makes Believers passive spectators. It is not being about the Father's business of performing the dominion mandate given to His *Ekklesia* or in promoting the ministry of reconciliation through atonement theology by Jesus' suffering and death on the Cross and resurrection.

Most Believers in the *Ekklesia* fear the enemy in the kingdom of darkness, as they believe they are protected automatically from attack by God; so, they do not engage in spiritual warfare, which emboldens the enemy to attack more. James 4:7 says, "Submit yourselves therefore to God. Resist the devil, and he will flee from you." Believers must strategically resist the kingdom of darkness in the world by resisting its mores, customs, traditions, norms, and ways of life that are contrary to Kingdom biblitarian principles.

Other Believers have been in religious bondage by the ecclesiastical positions they have in their congregation; and when the Revival Liberators come, they may choose not to leave the security of the old religious order structure. These Believers have developed a security like those in the concentration camps at the end of WWII who would not walk through the gates that led to freedom. I am not saying the old religious order structure is like a concentration camp. I am speaking about Believers' habitual motivation to seek familiarity and avoid change and deny the need for spiritual warfare. Some Believers also are uncomfortable with God's spiritual drill sergeants and do not want to learn and practice spiritual warfare. Many Believers think there is no requirement of work after initial salvation, even though Scriptures say otherwise (Ephesians 2:10; Philippians 2:12-13; James 2: 17-18). Thus, the Leaders fail to activate the members of the *Ekklesia* to work with faith, performing the dominion mandate to live their lives subduing and taking dominion in their sphere of influence in the marketplace and taking over the world system with God's Kingdom spiritual government and Kingdom spiritual military for the glory of the Godhead that lives inside them. Again, the gospel of the Kingdom must be preached along with the preaching of repentance for the remission of sins as new Believers call upon the name of the Lord.

Some denominations teach their congregations not to be involved in any secular government as they believe in the Doctrine of Separation of Church and State, as decided in 1947 in the U.S. Supreme Court case of *Everson v. Board of Education*. However, what the secular, worldly government under the authority of the prince of this world diabolically was trying to separate the children of God from their disciplining Father, God Almighty. What the true spiritual government of the Kingdom of God requires is promotion of God and His Kingdom but not religion in government. God has the true government, which will spread its rulership in every aspect of the society and culture of people making up a given nation. God is a disciplining Father Who does not allow the secular government Politicians and Bureaucrats to separate Him from disciplining His children to mature them and make them faithful, resolute, and obedient Kingdom spiritual Ambassadors and Kingdom spiritual Soldiers for advancement of the Kingdom of God.

God empowers Believers with His calling, Spirit, and anointing to participate in God's spiritual Kingdom government assembly and to become members of His spiritual Kingdom army to fight the good fight of faith (1 Timothy 6:12). Be one of the spiritual Believers that exercise authority as the Lord's Kingdom Ambassadors and disciplined Soldiers in their jobs, schools, businesses, social clubs, and preach the gospel of the Kingdom, preach repentance for the remission of sins, become born again, so you can see the Kingdom of God, and be born of the spirit and water to enter the kingdom of God. Believers are given the wisdom from above instead of the earthly wisdom of this world which is demonic (James 3:13-18). Believers must learn how to do spiritual warfare. They must learn how to be intercessors on behalf of people they meet in the marketplace. Believers must seek first the Kingdom of God and His righteousness, and seek biblitarian knowledge, understanding, and wisdom to share with others and apply in the workplace to prove God's biblitarian ways and principles bring profit while maturing Believers at the same time. Do not tell unBelievers they have to come to a building on Sunday to obtain prayer; instead, pray for them while the Holy Spirit's presence is manifesting, and you exercise delegated Kingdom authority from Christ as Ambassadors and Soldiers of Christ's *Ekklesia.*

THE DEVIL DECEIVES THE BODY OF CHRIST REGARDING
THE TRUE MEANING AND PURPOSE OF THE *EKKLESIA*

As the body of the *Ekklesia,* Believers are to fight against the global economic elites run by the spirit of the Antichrist. Believers are not to accept the delicate morsels of food from the false prophets' tables. The Kingdom of God takes dominion over the authoritarians in the world system, either to replace those authoritarians or influence them to accept Jesus Christ as Lord and Savior and join the *Ekklesia*, Body of Christ, the Kingdom, and family of God.

Anything that makes Believers stray from the original mandate to subdue and take dominion of the world system, but not the people, and all that exists on the earth in each nation is of the Antichrist and under the authority of the devil. Satan has the title of the "god of this world" as he is the head of all false religions (Luke 4:6; 1 John 5:19; 2 Corinthians 4:4; Galatians 1:4; 2 Thessalonians 2:3-4). Satan also is called as "the prince of this world" who runs the economic system and worldly governments (John 12:31; 14:30; 16:11). Additionally, Satan is referred to as "the prince of the power of the air," which refers to him as the king over evil spirits and with authority over the air space, television waves, radio waves, and internet (Ephesians 2:2). Satan is the "spirit of Antichrist," which is a reference to him as the "opponent of Christ," the one who is the leader of false doctrines, who is the force behind the one world counterfeit Globalists, Humanists, and Atheists, and thus of the spirit of the Antichrist (1 John 2:18-22; 4:1-4; 2 John 7). There are several other names for Satan, and it is important that Believers know the enemy of their souls.

Believers have confessed their sins, repented, and called upon the name of Jesus (Romans 10:13) to be born again and become citizens of Heaven not just to become members of an anemic "religion," but rather they have been invited to enter an intimate relationship with the Lord Jesus Christ and the entire Godhead in the Kingdom and family of God. The word "religion" is part of the world system, and false religions are ruled by the god of this world, Satan. Satan is the head of all the religions of the world. Jesus told the Jewish religious leaders opposing Him in John 8:44 they were of the devil. However, todays old religious orders are not false, but just anemic. They are lukewarm. They are the Laodicean old religious order. To their credit many old religious order Pastors and Leaders want the presence of the move of the Holy Spirit. They want revival.

The devil's strategy is to spread false religious or lukewarm ideas through misapplying scriptures to disqualify women Believers and divorced Believers from being Ephesians 4:11office ministers, which if accepted in a denomination would disqualify over fifty percent of the ministers. It is also the devil's strategy to bring every member of the Body of Christ into limitation thinking and to have them stay in bondage to the fallen world's principles that are under the law of sin and death (Romans 8:2). With God, all things that further Believers' covenantal relationship with God are possible (Matthew 19:26). The devil will try to convince Believers to go back to Egypt (representative of the world system) instead of going to their promise land (representative of the Kingdom of God). He will put in Believers enough doubt in God's desire to help them, so they must traverse in the wilderness for a season for lack of faith in God because they clearly cannot hear the voice of God. The devil will bring up each Believer's past to limit their faith, as faith is required to live a victorious life (Hebrews 11:6).

The devil will try to cause corruption in Believers' natural world until they accept what the devil falsely says from his spiritual realm as a fact, but not the truth. Yet, God has the answers to change lives for the better. The devil entices Believers to acknowledge and say, "I am sick.", "I am poor.", "I am unimportant.", or "I don't want to change."

In Matthew 4:4, Jesus said to the devil, "It is written, 'Man shall not live by bread alone (or by things in the natural world), but by every word (*rhema*) that proceeds from the mouth of God (from the spiritual world).'" What the devil says does not bring sustenance and life, but rather, what Jesus says brings spirit and life (John 6:63). Matthew 4:4 says, "every *rhema* word" not "some of the *rhema* words" that proceed out of the mouth of God. You must receive and accept the whole counsel of God and not listen to the devil's limiting words. The devil is not biblically correct because he twists scriptures to promote his kingdom of darkness agenda. The devil is proficient in studying the Bible, but he lies about what it says and means. The devil always lies John 8:44 says, "Ye are of your father the devil, and the lusts of your father ye will do. He was a murderer from the beginning, and abode not in the truth, because there is no truth in him. When he speaketh a lie, he speaketh of his own: for he is a liar, and the father of it." 2 Peter 1:4 says, "Whereby are given unto us exceeding great and precious promises: that by these ye might be partakers of the divine nature, having escaped the corruption that is in the world through lust." How do Believers escape corruption when it is all around them? Believers merely sow new seeds of righteousness when they see corruption sown. Believers sow what they want to reap. Galatians 6:8 says, "For he that soweth to his flesh shall of the flesh reap corruption; but he that soweth to the Spirit shall of the Spirit reap life everlasting." In other words, Believers activate the law of sowing and reaping.

God did not need any allies to kick the devil and the fallen Angels out of the third Heaven. God does not need any help to stop the devil from interfering with God's plans to wind up the *Ekklesia* Age and commence the Kingdom Age where Jesus sits on His Throne in the New Jerusalem and takes over the natural kingdoms of this world (Revelation 11:15). In the meantime, during the *Ekklesia* Age, the Ephesians 4:11 Ministers' assignments from the Lord are to equip the Believers for the work of the ministry as Kingdom spiritual Ambassadors and Kingdom spiritual Soldiers who have been given the ministry of reconciliation. The Believers' job is to spiritually rule and purposefully fight for the taking of dominion in every area of the culture by the leading of the Holy Spirit and transferring possession of the earth and fallen world system back to the Father. Although continuous stating of God's purpose may sound redundant, this truth must be repeated over and over to free Believers trapped in religious tradition and anemic theology.

Personally, Believers' statures in the world will change when Believers' eyes are opened to see the Lord's true *Ekklesia* and when Believers' ears are opened to hear the Lord's *rhema* voice to authorize, empower, and activate Believers as citizens and members of the Lord's Kingdom and *Ekklesia*. As Believers' souls are transformed by the renewing of their minds, emotions, and hearts through the washing by the water of the word of God (Romans 12:2; Ephesians 5:26), they will readily enlist in God's spiritual Kingdom army and will accept the position as spiritual Kingdom government ministers, with the gift of administration (1 Corinthians 12:5). This truth will embolden Believers to proclaim the gospel of the Kingdom, speak with divine wisdom, and become true disciples of Christ in their souls with the purpose of manifesting the Kingdom of God in them and through them wherever they go to work and to meet people. This is what it means to be a Minister of the Lord in God's end time Revival *Ekklesia*.

Faith without works to promote God's spiritual Kingdom government and spiritual Kingdom military does not bring God's *zoe* life (James 2:17). In order to reach the "promise land", the Believer has to become a working citizen in the Lord's spiritual Kingdom government and His spiritual army. The Believer might have to traverse through a wilderness for a season to purge the Egyptian worldly kingdom and its economic system based upon buying and selling out of the Believer's mind, emotions, and heart. The Believer's soul must put off the old man in Adam and put on the new man in Christ (Ephesians 2:15; 4:24; Colossians 3:10).

The Believer is mandated to seek first the spiritual Kingdom of God and His righteousness and no longer seek the stimuli from the natural kingdoms of this world (Matthew 6:33). The Believer's mental and emotional habits of thinking and emoting made the Believer look at the world stimuli in a certain way. When all that the Believer sees is Egypt, the Believer is basically relegating his life like the Israelites who were enslaved working in Pharaoh's mud and straw brick yard. Until the transformation of the Believer's soul, the Believer is in bondage to the things of the world. Once a Believer has a born again spirit, and the Believer's soul has started being transformed by the Godhead, God will give the Believer a new vision of the Lord's *Ekklesia* and the Kingdom of God and that the Believer is a Royal spiritual Ambassador and Royal spiritual Soldier in God's Kingdom. The Godhead will continue until the process of transforming the Believer's soul is complete. God the Word will remove the influence of the flesh in the soul by washing of water by the *rhema* word (Ephesians 5:26). God the Father will prune away the Believer's fleshy desires in the soul (John 15:2), and God the Holy Spirit will mortify the deeds of the flesh in the Believer's soul (Romans 8:13). The Believer's soul will be transformed spiritually as the Believer travels in a life-long journey of becoming an obedient spiritual child of Christ and as an adopted child of Father God (Isaiah 9:6; Romans 8:15).

"Destiny" comes from the word, "destination." Believers must know their God-given destination in order to live out their destinies as is planned by God with Kingdom life reality (Jeremiah 29:11). Jesus said in John 10:10, "The thief does not come except to steal, and to kill, and to destroy. I have come that they may have life, and that they may have it more abundantly."

In John, chapter 9, Jesus had healed a man blind from birth on the Sabbath, which was a form of work and against the traditional oral laws of Sabbath as taught by the Pharisees and the Rabbis. The Pharisees taught that if a man is born blind, then either he or his parents participated in on-going sin of iniquity. Jesus spat on the ground, made some clay, and rubbed the moistened clay in the eyes of the blind man. Then Jesus told the blind man to "Go, wash in the pool of Siloam" (John 9:7). When confronted by some of the Pharisees for healing on the Sabbath, Jesus told them they were the ones who were blind and living in sin. Thus, in context, the "thief" referred to by Jesus in John 10:10 was a demonic religious spirit who uses religious beliefs, instead of truth, to come to steal, kill, and destroy your faith and your natural health and wealth by you accepting religion instead of abundant spiritual life in God's Kingdom. Also, for a person to be healed in the pool of Siloam, an Angel had to appear and stir the water. However, here was the Son of God, who is greater than an Angel, who told the blind man to go and wash the mud off his eyes, and the blind man did not have to wait at the pool of Siloam for an Angel to appear to heal him. By His instructions to the blind man, Jesus by His actions were informing the Pharisees that He had more authority from God than them, as He was the Messiah; He rules over Angels (Matthew 26:53; 28:18), and He was Lord of the Sabbath, which means He owned the Sabbath Day (Matthew 9:38; Luke 10:2).

The devil's kingdom of darkness will try to make Believers ineffective by making Believers religious. Religion makes Believers in a certain denomination say things that are dead. Faith and

Godly fellowship make Believers say things that are alive to in turn bring *zoe* life to others.

The Lord Jesus Christ and the entire Godhead use an outward expression of an inward grace. God commands that His *Ekklesia* Leadership activate the entire Body of Christ in this next great move of His Spirit. It is estimated that eighty percent of Believers in the *Ekklesia* are doing nothing except coming to praise and worship the Lord and sitting and listening to sermons one night during the week and Saturday or Sunday morning. Ten percent of Believers work in ministry, and the estimated other ninety percent of Believers have a mouth that speaks, but they do nothing. God has given Believers a time and opportunity to gain experience up, and He no longer wants leaders to be nursemaids or babysitters for the immature. The Lord does not want leaders to make followers after themselves. The Lord insists they make mature leaders in Christ that submit to allow Christ to live His life in them and through them as He takes dominion over the Believers' sphere of influence in the workplace, school place, media place, movie place, radio place, in the court place, and even in the secular government place.

The Holy Spirit is going to touch each Believer, and anoint each Believer, so each Believer can touch others with that anointing. The devil's kingdom of darkness comes to steal, kill, destroy, distort, and derail Believers off the track that leads to their spiritual destination and make their work here on earth "mission impossible" instead of "mission accomplished."

Sometimes, the attacks are not from the devil but from other Believers, who promote their religious traditions that interfere with the movement of the Holy Spirit. Many Believers do anything to find the answer of who it is who is causing a particular test or attack, but they seldom look upward and ask God, "Lord, is this a 'character refining test' from You?" The answer is in Psalm 11:4-5, "...His eyelids test the sons of men. The Lord tests the righteous..."

The trials and tests endured by Believers are for their illumination and transformation of their souls into faithful pilgrims on their spiritual journey in the Kingdom of God. God commands His *Ekklesia* Leadership to obey the Kingdom Mandate to take the gospel of the Kingdom locally and throughout the world and into the marketplace and every place that people live and interact together and bring God's Kingdom rule there while ministering salvation to the lost and spiritual maturity to those who already are Believers.

THE FOCUS OF THE *EKKLESIA* TODAY

I will not apologize for being and decisively repetitive regarding the purpose of the *Ekklesia* being citizens of the Kingdom spiritual government as Ambassadors and Kingdom spiritual army as Soldiers. Believers must hear this over and over to come out of their denominational religious traditions of man and accept this truth from the word of God into their souls to decide to be effective, obedient servants in Christ's true *Ekklesia*. Are Ephesians 4:11 office Ministers still needed today? Yes! More than ever, but *Ekklesia* Leaders must activate Believers to serve the King in His Kingdom, not an old religious order structure.

The focus of the *Ekklesia* today should not be bigger barns with larger seating capacities to listen to praise and worship music and sermons week after week, month after month, and year after year. God desires that the *Ekklesia* enter praise and worship and be educated on biblical truths and principles and have faith that works by love (Galatians 5:6) as an integral part of the Kingdom community gatherings. The historical fact is that praise, worship, and sermons alone for over 1800 years have failed to activate the *Ekklesia* to subdue and to take dominion of all aspects of the world system, the society and the culture in each nation and deliver them back to Father God. The historical fact is that praise, worship, and sermons have not stopped the Supreme Court from handing down decisions that took prayer out of schools, legalized abortion on demand, and legalized sins in the nation as constitutional rights and a new false morality that makes legal what God says in His word as unlawful.

Where was the *Ekklesia* when the Supreme Court took prayer out of schools? Where was the *Ekklesia* when the Supreme Court made abortion on demand a Constitutional right? The truth is that members of the *Ekklesia* were not activated into Ministry. The *Ekklesia* was placed on rest and relaxation for over 1800 years in a dichotomous old religious order structure improperly teaching there is a separation of the Priesthood from the Laity. Jesus said in Revelation 2: 6, "But this thou hast, that thou hatest the deeds of the Nicolaitans, which I also hate." Nicolaitans mean leadership's hatred of the laity.

In the meantime, the prince of this world has worked hard to become the leader of the world system in every nation, and he has bribed with money, promised power, legalized sins of the flesh, and guaranteed prestige in the fallen world by fallen men and women deceived to be the devil's servants to do his evil will here on earth. Rulership of the earth is in the hands of the devil, and it is time for the Lord's *Ekklesia* to come out of its slumber and take possessory authority of the world system for the manifestation of the Kingdom of God.

It is time for the *Ekklesia* to reject the old religious traditions of man and wake up and see and join the Lord's Kingdom spiritual government and the Lord's Kingdom spiritual army. 1 Thessalonians 5:4-8 admonishes: "But ye, brethren, are not in darkness, that that day should overtake you as a thief. Ye are all the children of light, and the children of the day: we are not of the night, nor of darkness. Therefore, let us not sleep, as do others; but let us watch and be sober. For they that sleep in the night; and they that be drunken are drunken in the night. But let us, who are of the day, be sober, putting on the breastplate of faith and love; and for a helmet, the hope of salvation." Similarly, Proverbs 6:9-10 says, "How long will you slumber, O sluggard? When will you rise from your sleep? A little sleep, a little slumber, a little folding of the hands to sleep."

The *Ekklesia's* focus on the kingdom of God is manifold. Initially, the focus must be bringing the unsaved to accept Jesus as Lord, be born again, and enter into the Kingdom of God, into the household of God, and into fellowship with other members of the Body of Christ. Then, the focus immediately must be to start maturing the souls of new disciples into how to make spiritually wise decisions through first hearing God's voice and then obeying the leading of the Holy Spirit to divide the profane from the holy. Purging the carnal nature out of Believers' souls can take decades, but the process of spiritual maturation in the soul is best caught rather than taught. For new Believers to accept spiritual authority over them, God chooses to place him or her in situations and relationships designed to experience the Kingdom dynamics of God's spiritual Kingdom government authority and God's spiritual Kingdom military authority. The best place for the Believer's maturation often is at work during the week, under an owner who pastors his or her business. Thus, if possible, new Believers need to find jobs where other Believers also are employed. If the Believers are blessed in their souls with a born again spiritually mature boss, who will take the young Believers and disciple them at the workplace through the incremental daily problem-solving experience on the job, this is one of the fastest and surest ways to equip, mature, and transform the new Believers' souls. The more spiritual encounters are experienced in the workplace, the more the new Believers can draw on the experience in future spiritual interactions. Jesus said in Luke 2:49 that He had to be about His Father's business, and Father God uses business as His school for maturing His children and doing His will here on earth as it is in heaven.

Again, 1 Peter 2:9 says, "But ye are a chosen generation, a royal priesthood, a holy nation, a peculiar people; that ye should shew forth the praises of him who hath called you out of darkness into his marvelous light." A holy Priesthood working in the Kingdom of God can stand in the presence of God and can bring the Kingdom of God to a lost, dying, decadent world system under the control of the kingdom of darkness. God called out Israel of old as a Kingdom of Priests and a holy nation (Exodus 19:6). Israel fell short by neglecting God's holy requirements and commandments. In order to fulfill the desires of His heart, God sent His only begotten Son to live a holy, sinless life here on earth, to preach the Kingdom of God, and an atonement theology of repentance and remission of sins, to confirm His authority as King of the Kingdom with healings, signs, and wonders, die on a cruel Roman Cross, and be resurrected to redeem both Jews and Gentiles to qualify as citizens of Heaven, God's *Ekklesia* of Kingdom spiritual Ambassadors and Kingdom spiritual Soldiers, all for God's purpose of establishing His Kingdom here on earth and making Believers loving servant kings, lords, and a holy priesthood after the order of Melchizedek to spread the spiritual reality of salvation and the Kingdom of God to every nation.

God's holy priesthood must not mix what God has purposely separated that He specifically commands in His word. He is an absolute holy God who calls His people to live a separated life, free from all mixtures, sins, abominations, and compromises. One of the meanings of the Hebrew word for "holy" is *kadosh*, which means "separate." "… The service of the priesthood is a gift" (Numbers 18:7).

Malachi 2:6-7 says, "The law of truth was in his mouth, and iniquity was not found in his lips: he walked with me in peace and equity and did turn many away from iniquity. For the Priest's lips should keep knowledge, and they should seek the law at his mouth: for he is the messenger of the LORD of hosts." Similarly, Ezekiel 44:23 addresses Priests, "And they shall teach my people the difference between the holy and profane and cause them to discern between the unclean and the clean." Instead of staying pure in writing what God said, the Israelite Priests did not distinguish that which was spoken by God from the doctrines and traditions written by learned men, and not God, was part of the children of Israel's disobedience.

Addressing religious leaders, Jesus analyzed this problem in Mark 7:9,13, "Full well ye reject the commandment of God, that ye may keep your own tradition… Making the word of God of none effect through your tradition, which ye have delivered: and many such like things do ye." Religious traditions are at best man-created distortions of God's truths in interpreting His word.

The focus by leaders also must be on maturing Believers souls, so they can experience true fellowship for intimacy with the Lord and each other. God's mercies endure forever, and He wants His servants to be merciful and loving towards one another. The focus of the *Ekklesia* toward the body of Christ also is to feed the hungry, provide clothing to those in need, visit and pray for the sick and care for them, and minister to those in prison that they may experience liberty when they return to society. The ministry of Matthew 25:34-45 relegates the duty not to the secular government, but rather the duty is relegated to Believers, individually, and in groups, as this is mandated by the Lord, as pure hearted giving makes good servants for the body of Christ that are in need.

Thus, in addition to being Kingdom spiritual Ambassadors and Kingdom spiritual Soldiers, the focus of the *Ekklesia* is also to engage in true, spiritual, loving fellowship with other Believers. When the members of the *Ekklesia* come together, the focus must be spiritual and must be to experience the presence of the Lord's divine nature in their midst. Again, Matthew 18:20 says, "For where two or three are gathered together in my name, there am I in the midst of them." The additional focus must be transformation of Believers' souls to make them loving servants that are humble, submissive to God, and that have the wisdom from studying God's word. The focus of the leadership in the *Ekklesia* is to make mature, loving, wise, gift operating leaders, not followers of man; and then sending these spiritually mature leaders as Kingdom spiritual Ambassadors and Kingdom spiritual Soldiers with the mandate to subdue and to take dominion of the area of influence they have in the marketplace, government, media, theatres, book writing, radio and T.V. broadcasting, professions, teaching, and every other area of the nation. Jesus said the goal or His mandate is to make disciples, not mere converts of all people in every nation (Matthew 28:19).

Testimonies in the fellowship gathering should focus on how during the week a member of the *Ekklesia* fulfilled his or her mission around his or her influence that the Holy Spirit assigned him or her. It could be testimony of leading an unsaved person to the Lord at the Believer's place of employment. It could be the testimony of a Believing mother in teaching her children the principles in the Bible, and how play time had become biblical training time. Proverbs 22:6 mandates, "Train up a child in the way he should go: and when he is old, he will not depart from it." All work in the Kingdom by the *Ekklesia* is particularly important to the Lord and all efforts of focusing life transactions on God's Kingdom mandate is doing the will of God.

The foundational focus of the *Ekklesia* is to seek first the Kingdom of God and His righteousness and all the blessings of God will be added to the Believer, personally, to the Believer's family, to the Believer's fellowship Kingdom community, and then to the Believer's nation. God wants His children to not be blinded by the falsehoods of the prince of this world, the devil; so, God wants His children to see with spiritual eyes the bankrupt fallen world under the sway of the devil and hear with spiritual ears God's voice to be His Kingdom servants and do His will here on earth as it is in Heaven. When the *Ekklesia* seeks first the Kingdom of God and His righteousness, the *Ekklesia* will be experiencing the Lord's Kingdom and the presence of the Lord's divine nature as King of His Kingdom. The purposeful work of the *Ekklesia* is Kingdom spiritual governmental service and Kingdom spiritual military service, while transforming and maturing their own and other Believer's souls while caring for other Believers' needs, studying God's word, worshiping and praising the Lord, praying throughout the day, and seeking the intimate loving relationship with God and with other Believers in spirit and truth.

Now with this discussion of the word *Ekklesia* with its true meaning, especially when the Revival comes, Believers are mandated to preach the gospel of the Kingdom, along with repentance and the remission of sins; and this will include that the *Ekklesia* is a spiritual Kingdom government assembly of Ambassadors and a spiritual Kingdom army of Soldiers that are members of the family of God and will engage in intimate and *agape* loving fellowship in a spiritual Kingdom community with other Believers.

The Restoration of All Things to The Ekklesia in Revival

The Restoration of All Things
to the *Ekklesia* in Revival

BELIEVERS ARE THE *EKKLESIA* IN REVIVAL
UPON WHOM THE ENDS OF THE AGES HAVE COME

There is patience by, and some flexibility, with the Holy Spirit. Whenever He moves, He uses either Angels or human Believers with all their imperfections. If humans are so imperfect why does God choose Believers to be His ministers here on earth? God from the beginning purposed and entered covenant with His only begotten Son to activate obedient Believers to establish and manifest God's heavenly Kingdom here on earth. Jesus Christ is 100% human as His humanity nature and 100% God the Word as His divine nature. Jesus is one Person with two natures, not two persons. God used His only begotten Son, with a divine nature and humanity nature to bring His Kingdom that is in Heaven to the earth and promote His only begotten Son's humanity nature and divine nature with all authority to rule and reign over the entire spiritual and physical created universes and humanity throughout eternity (Matthew 28:18). Jesus' humanity nature sits on a throne in Heaven, while His omnipresent divine nature is in Heaven and here on earth to live inside Believers and to be in their presence (Matthew 18:20; 28:20; John 14:23). Jesus' divine nature, God the Word is omnipresent and is throughout the entire spiritual and natural universes. Since God the Word, including God the Holy Spirit, and God the Father, lives inside Believers as His temple, then the Creator is transcendent, omnipotent, omnipresent, immutable, omniscient, covenant making and covenant keeping, all-loving, all-merciful, all-grace, all-just, and Sustainer of the spiritual and natural worlds. Jesus' divine nature, God the Word is always indivisible and inseverable, but distinguishable, unconfused, and separable from Jesus' humanity nature. Since Jesus' divine nature is God the Word and omnipresent, then He is indivisible and inseverable from His humanity nature who now sits on a throne in heaven. Yet, Ephesians 2:6 says, "And hath raised us up together, and made us sit together in heavenly places in Christ Jesus." The mystery is that God the Word indivisibly and inseverable connected with His humanity nature lives inside of us, as He is God. Believers are God's Temple, so what God the Word's experience is with Jesus' humanity nature, God the Word can share with us. 1 Corinthians 6:17 says, "But he that is joined unto the Lord is one spirit."

As part of the Kingdom of God restoration plan here on earth, redemption with a new born again spirit, and transformation of the soul, make obedient and spiritual Kingdom citizens. God brought new birth to Christ's born again children through an incorruptible Seed of Christ Jesus' resurrected humanity nature by the power of His divine nature, God the Word, as the new Second Man (1 Peter 1:23; 1 Corinthians 15:47). Believers are in Christ as new creatures and no longer in Adam (2 Corinthians 5:17; Romans 6:4-8; 1 Corinthians 15:22). Believers' new born again spirits are spiritual children of Christ Jesus' resurrected humanity nature (Isaiah 9:6; Hebrews 2:13; 1 Peter 1:23), and Believers became the children of Father God by adoption when they accepted Jesus as Savior and Lord (Romans 8:15). Luke 20:36 says, "Nor can they die anymore, for they are equal to the angels and are sons of God, being sons of the resurrection." John 11:25 says, "Jesus said unto her, 'I am the resurrection, and the life: he that believeth in Me, though he were dead, yet shall he live.'" Since Jesus' humanity nature is the Resurrection, then the sons of the Resurrection are sons of Christ Jesus' humanity nature.

In order to make Believers qualified, orchestrate events, cause things to happen, and start the new movement by and of the Holy Spirit takes commitment and time. The miracle of the virgin birth still required Mary to carry baby Jesus in her womb for nine months before the Savior was born. Later, Jesus had to grow up, and as a baby, youth, and man, He suffered the things common to man. Hebrew 5:8-9 say, "Though He was a (the) Son, yet He learned obedience by the things which He suffered. And having been perfected (matured), He became the Author of everlasting salvation to all who obey Him."

To the same extent, when the Holy Spirit moves, it may be hard to recognize the divine nature of the movement because imperfect Believers in their partially transformed souls are involved. God often uses odd experiences and imperfect Believers in His Church Revivals.

Yet, God has promised to pour out His Spirit on all people in these end times (Joel 2:28). Believers today could be those end time saints, and all covenant surplus anointing of our forefathers of the faith shall be poured out upon God's end time Believers. 1 Corinthians 10:11 says, "Now all these things happened to them as examples, and they were written for our admonition, upon whom the ends of the ages have come."

There was a new beginning of physical creation when the purpose of establishing the Kingdom of God here on earth was good in the sight of God (Genesis 1). Since there was a good beginning there necessarily will be a good ending for God's covenant Believers who will rule and reign with Christ Jesus when the Kingdom of God is manifested here on earth in full measure (Revelation 5:10; chapter 21). God will pour out His potential power in these end times through His sons and daughters, whom have been born again from and in Christ Jesus. Those who allow Christ to live in and minister through them will speak and move with the anointing and power of the Holy Spirit (Galatians 2:20). Those who will remain in their "religious strongholds" will not have manifested through them the end time covenant glory basket of God's anointing and power.

Acts 3:21 says, "Whom Heaven must receive until the times of restoration of all things which God has spoken by the mouth of His holy prophets since the world began." God's prophets declared the coming of the Messiah and the establishment of an everlasting throne and Kingdom, built upon the fulfillment of the covenant the Lord of hosts that He promised to King David. The prophet Nathan prophesied to David in 2 Samuel 7:16, "And thine house and thy kingdom shall be established for ever before thee: thy throne shall be established forever." Afterwards, King David offered a thanksgiving prayer in 2 Samuel 7:26, which says, "And let Thy name be magnified forever, saying, 'The LORD (Jehovah) of hosts (angelic army) is the God over Israel.' And let the house of Thy servant David be established before Thee." 2 Samuel 7:26 emphasizes that the Lord with a host of angels will vanquish the evil kingdom of darkness and fulfill the promise to Abraham and David's Seed (Galatians 3:16; Romans 1:3) to establish an everlasting throne. Jesus' humanity nature is from the lineage of Abraham, Isaac, Jacob, Tribe of Judah, the Family of David, King David; and Jesus, who was resurrected from the dead (2 Timothy 2:8), sits on the everlasting throne and has been given the Throne of David (Luke 1:32). Overcoming Believers will sit with Jesus' humanity nature on His throne. In Revelation 3:21, Jesus said, "To him that overcometh will I grant to sit with me in My throne, even as I also overcame, and am set down with my Father in His throne."

Prior to Christ's return for His Bride, all things will be restored to the Church, with the Ephesians 4:11 Ministers activating the saints of the Lord for the work of the ministry in seeking and establishing the everlasting Kingdom of God throughout the world as prophesied to David of old in 2 Samuel 7:16. The world becomes the new Garden of God, manifesting the goodness of God in the Kingdom of God. Believers are Ambassadors of the Lord's Kingdom government that was a prophetic promise to David of an everlasting Throne. David's throne was prophetic of the greater Throne of Christ over the Kingdom of God, which will manifest in its fullness when Christ's resurrected humanity nature, having been joined always with His divine nature, God the Word, returns to earth in the New Jerusalem to rule and reign in the Kingdom Age to come, and Believers will be the dwelling place of our Triune Godhead (Revelation 21:3). Believers are kings and priests of Christ (Revelation 1:6), and Believers will rule and reign with Christ under His supreme rulership throughout eternity (Revelation 5:10). "…The kingdoms of this world are become the kingdoms of our Lord, and of His Christ; and He shall reign for ever and ever" (Revelation 11:15).

"The restoration of all things" consists of all the surplus spiritual grace, anointing, mercy, supernatural strength, gifts, protection, authority, power, office ministries, miracles, and provision that all the Old Testament and New Testament Ministers had bestowed upon them by God in His Kingdom.

Believers do not know the day of the return of Christ's humanity nature back to earth to set up His eternal throne in the New Jerusalem. Yet, Believers should be ready for His return. So, look into a mirror and see yourself as one of those chosen by God in these end times to wrap up the Church Age and to rule and reign with authority with Christ in His Kingdom here on earth in the present time. As far as fallen man's estimation of Believers, Believers do not look like they have much worth in the natural. Yet, God did not choose the wise nor the prudent (1 Corinthians 1:19), but He chose those with child like innocent hearts (Mark 10:15). There is a difference between being on the one hand childish and on the other hand innocent in the heart who believe in God the Father, God the Word/Son, and God the Holy Spirit. Stay humble and teachable. Maintain a broken spirit and contrite heart before the Lord. This will keep Believers ready for the move of the Holy Spirit for the end time generation if it comes in current Believers' lifetime. In the meantime, as Believers of the Lord, "Be sober, be vigilant; because your adversary the devil, as a roaring lion, walketh about, seeking whom he may devour" (1 Peter 5:8).

JOEL PROPHESIED THREE STAGES OF PROGRESSIVE REVIVAL
THROUGH WHICH GOD'S SURPLUS BLESSINGS WILL BE
POURED OUT ON THE *EKKLESIA* IN REVIVAL

FIRST STAGE OF REVIVAL: The First Stage of Revival in Joel 2 is the activation of the end time Revival *Ekklesia* by the sincere repentance of Believers *en masse.*

Joel 2:11-18 says, "And the LORD shall utter His voice before his army: for His camp is very great: for He is strong that executeth His word: for the day of the LORD is great and very terrible; and who can abide it? Therefore, also now, saith the LORD, 'Turn ye even to Me with all your heart, and with fasting, and with weeping, and with mourning. And rend your hearts, and not your garments, and turn unto the LORD your God: for He is gracious and merciful, slow to anger, and of great kindness, and repenteth Him of the evil. Who knoweth if He will return and repent, and leave a blessing behind Him; even a meat offering and a drink offering unto the LORD your God?' Blow the trumpet in Zion, sanctify a fast, call a solemn assembly: Gather the people, sanctify the congregation, assemble the elders, gather the children, and those that suck the breasts: let the bridegroom go forth of his chamber, and the bride out of her closet. Let the priests, the ministers of the LORD, weep between the porch and the altar, and let them say, 'spare Thy people, O LORD, and give not Thine heritage to reproach, that the heathen should rule over them.' Wherefore should they say among the people, 'Where is their God?' Then will the LORD be jealous for His land and pity His people."

Having Pure Hearts and Broken Spirits

Psalm 51:10 says, "Create in me a clean heart, O God, and renew a steadfast spirit within me." Psalm 51:17 says, "The sacrifices of God are a broken spirit, a broken and contrite heart these, O God, you will not despise." Matthew 5:8 says, "Blessed are the pure in heart, for they shall see God."

Circumcision of Hearts in Believers' Souls.

Romans 2:29 says, "But he is a Jew who is one inwardly; and circumcision is that of the heart, in the spirit, not in the letter; whose praise is not from men but from God."

Matthew 6:21 says, "For where your treasure is, there your heart will be also." The circumcised heart is an undivided heart where the Lord Jesus Christ is the Believer's greatest treasure.

Joshua and the army of the Israelites fought God's enemies all around the Promise Land. However, before allowing the Israelites to enter God's Promise Land, Joshua was commanded by the Lord to circumcise a whole generation of God's people, which Joshua obeyed (Joshua 5:2 3).

If we are going to enter God's end time blessings and promises, we must allow Christ to circumcise our hearts. Colossians 2:11 says, "In Him you were also circumcised with the circumcision made without hands by putting off the body of the sins of the flesh, by the circumcision of Christ."

Sanctified, Set Apart, Faithful, and Separated for the Lord's work in the end time Revival *Ekklesia.*

Psalm 4:3 says, "But know that the Lord has set apart for Himself him who is godly." 1 Thessalonians 4:3-4 says, "For this is the will of God, your sanctification; that you should abstain from sexual immorality; that each of you should know how to possess his own vessel in sanctification and honor."

SECOND STAGE OF REVIVAL: The Second Stage of *Ekklesia* Revival in Joel 2 is the Revival of God's Business Servants with the gift of giving (Romans 12:8), who have the anointing to spoil the wealth of the wicked to bring the necessary wealth to finance the end time Church Revival, which is the Third Stage of *Ekklesia* Revival in Joel 2.

Joel 2:19-27 says, "Yea, the LORD will answer and say unto his people, 'Behold, I will send you corn, and wine, and oil, and ye shall be satisfied therewith: and I will no longer make you a reproach among the heathen. But I will remove far off from you the northern army and will drive him into a land barren and desolate, with his face toward the east sea, and his hinder part toward the utmost sea, and his stink shall come up, and his ill savour shall come up, because he hath done great things. Fear not, O land; be glad and rejoice: for the LORD will do great things. Be not afraid, ye beasts of the field: for the pastures of the wilderness do spring, for the tree beareth her fruit, the fig tree and the vine do yield their strength. Be glad then, ye children of Zion, and rejoice in the LORD your God: for He hath given you the former rain moderately, and he will cause to come down for you the rain, the former rain, and the latter rain in the first month. And the (threshing) floors shall be full of wheat, and the vats shall overflow with wine and oil. And I will restore to you the years that the locust hath eaten, the cankerworm, and the caterpillar, and the palmerworm, my great army which I sent among you. And ye shall eat in plenty, and be satisfied, and praise the name of the LORD your God, that hath dealt wondrously with you. And My people shall never be ashamed. And ye shall know that I am in the midst of Israel, And that I am the LORD your God, and none else: and My people shall never be ashamed.'"

Corn, grain, or wheat is symbolic of God's people. Matthew 3:12 says, "His winnowing fan is in His hand, and He will thoroughly clean out His threshing floor, and gather His wheat into the barn, but He will burn up the chaff with unquenchable fire." The threshing floor brings forth the purity in Believers' souls.

Galatians 5:24 says, "And they that are Christ's have crucified the flesh with the affections and lusts." Jesus Christ's humanity nature never sinned while here during His earthly walk, but still His humanity nature had to learn obedience by the things he suffered (Hebrew 5: 8-9). How much more must Believers have to "suffer" or be "threshed" at the hands of the Godhead to learn obedience in our souls since Believers, unlike Jesus, have and still do commit sin in their souls?

The Lord God says in Joel 2 that God's end time Believers will not be reproached if they stay in God's threshing floor and remain humble before the Lord. Believers must allow humbleness and contriteness of their hearts in their souls. Yet, being threshed by the Lord God all the time seems uncomfortable, but the growth that comes by this threshing to remove the chaff in Believers' souls is needed to transform Believers into benevolent, compassionate, fruit bearing under rulers of the Lord. Referencing Job 5:17, Hebrews 12:5-6 says, "And ye have forgotten the exhortation which speaketh unto you as unto children, My son, despise not thou the chastening of the Lord, nor faint when thou art rebuked of him: For whom the Lord loveth He chasteneth, and scourgeth every son whom He receiveth."

The Wine refers to the vintage maturity process of God's *rhema* Word going from the fruit to the matured wine in a Believer's life. Wine starts with crushing of the grapes. The vintage is made as a Believer is cleansed, matured, and transformed in the soul by the pruning away the carnality in the soul by God the Father (John 15:2), by the washing away the dirty flesh in the soul by the *rhema* Word by God the Word (Ephesians 5:26), and the mortifying of the deeds of the flesh by God the Holy Spirit (Romans 8:13). Wine comes from the fruit of the Vine being crushed, and then the juice is set aside and allowed to mature into fine wine. Even though Believers are the branches connected to the Vine and do bear the fruit (John 15:4-5), the good fruit still must be crushed to make the new wine. During the crushing, a single grape is not allowed to float to the top in its independence but is blended in the Kingdom community of crushed grapes, which together create the fine wine. One single grape cannot by itself minister all that other Believers need, as it is a mixture with every member having their carnal lives crushed to develop a unique spiritual flavor of the Kingdom community of grapes.

Those Business Servants and wealthy Believers who have the Romans 12:8 gift of giving normally will go through a more serious "crushing process" to accept and follow the economic biblitarian principles of God operating in their businesses and finances that will cause the vintage anointing to flow. The Business Servants need to deal with the god of mammon and get rid of the sour grapes in their lives. After the grapes are crushed, wine becomes better as it is matured. The vintage anointing comes forth in the prophetic words spoken to others desiring to hear from the Lord.

God's Business Servants must see their businesses as their place of ministry, and they must accept the calling of God in their lives. The Holy Spirit is using the work in business to train disciples through the application of biblitarian principles in the daily solving of business problems. Disciples will be transformed as they have a spiritual experience in seeking the Kingdom of God and an intimate relationship with Christ Jesus all day long. Changing an employee as one grape into blending with other grapes that are being crushed in their souls into wine is the process of maturation of God's disciples in business. Thus, in God's eyes, the primary function of business ministry is discipleship unto maturation of each Believer who is an employee in the business, along with the business owner instead of just making profit. Timothy 2:2 says, "And the things that you have heard from me among many witnesses, commit these to faithful men who will be able to teach others also." This Second Stage of *Ekklesia* Revival in Joel 2 will cause a drastic change from the world's idea of the only purpose of the business is to make profits when Christ's purpose is to be about His Father's business of making disciples of Christ (Luke 2:49). The way of making business plans, providing goods and services, and establishing new programs and methods of management of businesses are going to change when the end time Revival *Ekklesia* manifests throughout the nation and the world.

Often, it is the hardest thing for a Believer to be prepared by God to manage money correctly, without covetousness, greed, or to "play God" with the money to control others without being led by the Holy Spirit in the investment and spending activities. A vintage Believer is a spiritually matured Believer, where the Godhead prunes, washes, and mortifies the influence of the flesh in the soul. The vintage Believer is not emotionally involved with the money earned in a sinful way. The vintage Believer's knowledge, understanding, and wisdom in the spirit will become the vintage wine for others to drink. It is the new wine miracle anointing to allow the workplace to be a venue of ministry of maturing the Believers who are employees to become mature disciples of Christ through the incremental problem solving in the business by using God's principles of economics and ethics.

The Oil represents the unity in the Body of Christ by the Holy Spirit. Psalm 133:1-2 says, "Behold, how good and how pleasant it is for brethren to dwell together in unity! It is like the precious oil upon the head, that ran down upon the beard, even Aaron's beard that went down to the skirts of his garments."

Again, Joel 2:23 says, "For He hath given you the former rain moderately, and He will cause to come down for you the rain, the former rain, and the latter rain in the first month."

The former rain is the suffering of Christ for Believers' forgiveness of sins and removing the new Believer from being in Adam, while the latter rain is the resurrection of Christ for Believers to become members of the Second Man as new creatures in Christ (Romans 6:11; 1 Corinthians 15:47; 2 Corinthians 5:17).

Paul said in Philippians 3:10, "That I may know Him and the power of His resurrection (latter rain) and the fellowship of His sufferings (former rain) being conformed to His death." Christ Jesus sits in intercession for Believers that are still here on earth. During His intercession, Christ Jesus professes His sufferings while alive to God the Father and brings the covenant He has with God the Father as consideration for God the Father to recompense, heal, and provide blessings to Believers.

1 Peter 2:21-24 says "For to this you were called, because Christ also suffered for us, leaving us an example, that you should follow His steps: 'Who Committed no sin, nor was deceit found in His mouth;' Who, when He was reviled, did not revile in return; when He suffered, He did not threaten, but committed Himself to Him Who judges righteously; Who Himself bore our sins in His own body on the tree, that we, having died to sins, might live for righteousness by Whose stripes you were healed. For you were like sheep going astray, but have now returned to the Shepherd and Overseer of your souls."

Christ's suffering has numerous benefits, and Christ's intercession as an Advocate for Believers are a great blessing (1 John 2:1). The Kingdom mandate and life of the resurrection will cause Believers to seek the whole heart of God; and they will discover that God's heart is to establish God's holy nation, chosen people, and royal priesthood in His kingdom of adopted sons and daughters. This is the manifested restoration of the spiritual reality of the end time *Ekklesia* in Revival. Revival begins the great restoration of the mystery of Christ as King of His Kingdom and Lord over all creation will illuminate Believers. When this authority anointing is manifested in and on Believers, the physical world that has been taken from Believers shall be multiplied back to them because they are under rulers of Christ Jesus as kings, lords, and priests (1 Timothy 6:16; Revelation 1:6).

Zechariah 1:18-21 says, "Then I raised my eyes and looked, and there were four horns (authorities), and I said to the angel who talked with me, 'What are these?' So he answered me, 'These are the horns (authorities) that have scattered Judah, Israel, and Jerusalem.' Then the Lord showed me four craftsmen (God's Business Servants). And I said, 'What are these coming to do?' So he said, 'These are the horns that scattered Judah (Believers of the Lion of Judah today -- See Galatians 3:28-29; 6:15), so that no one could lift up his head; but the craftsmen (God's Business Servants) are coming to terrify them, to cast out the horns (authorities) of the nations that lifted up their horn (authorities) against the land of Judah to scatter it.'" The land of Judah, where Believers live, is the land of the Lord's Kingdom and rightfully can be any nation where the Believers of Christ constitute most people, and this would apply to the United States which is the nation where the greatest percentage of Believers live. The Tribe of Judah as Christ is spread throughout the earth.

Apostles, Prophets, Evangelist, Pastors, and Teachers are not restricted to the four walls of auditoriums or buildings where Believers gather to practice their traditional religious beliefs, learn God's word, and worship. God's Business Servants are called into business with a special anointing to bring finances to the work of the Lord, especially during the outpouring of the Holy Spirit. In fact, the above scriptural passage in Zachariah says that God's craftsmen, which are Business Servants, will be used to attack the authorities (horns) of the nations which are persecuting the Believers, which will include during the end time *Ekklesia* in Revival. God's business Ephesians 4:11 Ministers are also called to bring discipleship training to their employees through the daily incremental work and applying biblical principles of economics and servanthood in God's Kingdom.

God owns the silver and gold and gives Believers power to obtain wealth to fulfill God's purposes of establishing His Kingdom as a *Ekklesia* in Revival. Haggai 2:6-9 says, "For thus says the Lord of hosts: 'Once more (it is a little while) I will shake Heaven and earth, the sea and dry land; and I will shake all nations, and they shall come to the Desire of All Nations, and I will fill this temple with glory,' says the Lord of hosts. 'The silver is Mine, and the gold is Mine,' says the Lord of hosts. 'The glory of this latter temple shall be greater than the former,' says the Lord of hosts. 'And in this place, I will give peace,' says the Lord of hosts."

Therefore, God owns all the wealth in the world, but the devil has possession of it in his stolen domain. The gold and silver are coming to the *Ekklesia* through the anointed Business Servants of God who will be used for a Godly purpose, particularly to finance the Joel 2 Third Stage of *Ekklesia* Revival.

Deuteronomy 8:17-20 says, "Then you say in your heart, 'My power and the might of my hand have gained me this wealth.' "And you shall remember the Lord your God, for it is He who gives you power (Hebrew - *Koach* - meaning capacity, ability, encompassing physical, spiritual, and soulishly) to get wealth, that He may establish His covenant which He swore to your fathers, as it is this day. Then it shall be, if you by any means forget the Lord your God, and follow other gods, and serve them and worship them, I testify against you this day that you shall surely perish. As the nations which the Lord destroys before you, so you shall perish, because you would not be obedient to the voice of the Lord your God."

The word "wealth" includes the material blessings promised by God through the patriarchs and their descendants, including Believers of today as spiritual sons and daughters of the Jewish Messiah, which make Believers the true spiritual Jews and spiritual Israel (Romans 2:28-29; 9:6-8; Galatians 3:28-29). The Lord of hosts gives God's Business Servants the power to get wealth to establish, verify, and live in the covenant blessings of God. The purpose of the Revival of finances is for the financing of the end time *Ekklesia* in Revival. The word "wealth" also includes prospering in health (3 John 2), peace, joy, friendships, along with finances. It also includes the divine knowledge, understanding, and wisdom to receive God's wealth to conduct God's purposes He has called Business Servants to fulfill. Therefore, God's wealth is always a means to an end and never an end.

Believers who are God's Business Servants must obey God's prophetic call to be about the Father's business and come up against the authorities that have come to scatter the land of Judah (Zechariah 1:18-21). God the Father is a business God (Luke 2:49).

2 Chronicles 20:20 says, "And they rose early in the morning, and went forth into the wilderness of Tekoa: and as they went forth, Jehoshaphat stood and said, 'Hear me, O Judah, and ye inhabitants of Jerusalem; believe in the Lord your God, so shall ye be established; believe His prophets, so shall ye prosper.'" Amos 3:7 says, "Surely the Lord God does nothing unless He reveals His secret to His servants the prophets."

God's Business Servants must establish and manage their businesses on the solid foundation of God's word and not based on the world's humanistic or capitalistic practices focused purely upon profit.

Romans 12:1-2 says, "I beseech you therefore, brethren, by the mercies of God, that you present your bodies a living sacrifice, holy, acceptable to God, which is your reasonable service. And be not conformed to this world: but be ye transformed by the renewing of your mind, that ye may prove what is that good, and acceptable, and perfect, will of God."

Luke 6:48-49 says, "He is like a man which built a house, and digged deep, and laid the foundation on a rock: and when the flood arose, the stream beat vehemently upon that house, and could not shake it: for it was founded upon a rock. But he that heareth, and doeth not, is like a man that without a foundation built an house upon the earth; against which the stream did beat vehemently, and immediately it fell; and the ruin of that house was great."

God's Business Servants in the Second Stage of *Ekklesia* Revival of Joel 2 will have the anointing to spoil the wealth of the wicked and bring it into the hands of the righteous to finance the end time outpouring on all flesh by the Holy Spirit (Proverbs 13:22). God's Business Servants have the anointing to spoil and should come to the resolve to build the business according to God's pattern, the resolve to establish and expand God's kingdom and the Body of Christ, the resolve to conduct the business according to God's Word, and the resolve to become God's Business Servants working with Godly biblitarian principles.

Proverbs 13:22 says, "But the wealth of the sinner is stored up for the righteous." Similarly, Ecclesiastes 2:26 says, "For God gives wisdom and knowledge and joy to a man who is good in His sight; but to the sinner He gives the work of gathering and collecting, that he may give to him who is good before God...."

Riches are the toughest things to handle with humility and obedience to God. The god of mammon has the power to corrupt like no other tempter and temptation. The god of mammon is the highest principality under Satan's rule in the kingdom of darkness. Therefore, Jesus referred to mammon or money as a master. You cannot serve two masters; you cannot serve God and mammon (Matthew 6:24). Satan is the god of this world. 2 Corinthians 4: 4 says, "In whom the god of this world (*aion*-- age) hath blinded the minds of them which believeth not..." Pride, avarice, jealousy, envy, greed, and covetousness blind people who run after the god of mammon. Those anointed to spoil the wealth of the wicked for establishment of the Kingdom of God must realize that they are coming up against the strongest demonic spirit in the world. The Believer in business must walk, live, and be always led by the Holy Spirit, especially during business hours. The ministry is no place for the feeble or the widows and orphans. The fallen business world is a dog-eat-dog world of deception where most everyone in the world system is motivated by greed, avarice, covetousness, and the love of money. It takes an extraordinarily strong Believer to have this ministry call in business to oversee the things that the principality of mammon wants to have control in the world. However, Socialistic and Humanistic government Politicians and Bureaucrats make the people lazy by ensuring people cradle to grave financial support. Also, Socialistic and Humanistic government Politicians and Bureaucrats want to make everyone in the nation equal financially, whether they worked to earn the money or not. Under a Socialistic and Humanistic government, Believers' goals and dreams are not rewarded for their demanding work, acquiring a good education, avoiding debt, trying to capture a market share, and practicing long-term biblitarian conservative economics as opposed to short term profits.

It is quite easy to get puffed up when one gets into a position of recognized power in secular business, and even if given a position of authority in the Kingdom of God based upon his or her natural leadership qualities or the size of his or her bank account or estate assets.

Riches can be a hindrance and idol that interferes with a Believer's ministry. It's okay to have riches, but riches without the submission to God may bring much sorrow. Yet, God can give you riches without sorrow to do the will of God (Proverbs 10:22). Psalms 62:10 says, "....if riches increase set not your heart upon them."

It is amazingly easy to get puffed up when one is rich in the world, and when one is giving much to a ministry with the bad motive of being recognized or controlling. It is also dangerous to bring worldly wisdom in making decisions in the *Ekklesia*, as Believers mistakenly will equate the wisdom from above and the wisdom that is worldly as the same, which it is not.

However, it is difficult for one to handle these three areas of seemingly worldly success, so one should repent and get one's life right with God in these three areas. Do not seek one's own glory in the Revival *Ekklesia* as it will be dangerous.

Finally, all things done in Joel's Second Stage of *Ekklesia* Revival involving finances must be done by the leading of the Holy Spirit, not by worldly or carnal abilities. Zechariah 4:6 says, "So he answered and said to me: 'This is the word of the Lord to Zerubbabel: "Not by might nor by power, but by My Spirit," says the Lord of hosts.'"

Joel's prophecy in Joel 2 of a Second Stage of *Ekklesia* Revival concerning the spoiling the wealth of the wicked is a spiritual and supernatural movement by and of the Holy Spirit. Matthew 12:29 says, "Or how can one enter a strong man's house and plunder his goods, unless he first binds the strong man? And then he will plunder his house." The Greek word for "plunder" is "*dia harpazo*" which is in the same family as the Greek word "*harpazo*" where leaders translate into the word "rapture" of the Church in 1 Thessalonians 4:17. Therefore, the anointed Business Servants of God will see the Holy Spirit transfer of the wealth out of the hands of the wicked into the hands of the righteous (Proverbs 13:22). Glory to God!

A good example of a supernatural acquisition of sudden wealth by being obedient to the instructions of the Lord is seen after Jesus used Peter's boat to preach a sermon by the Lake of Gennesaret. "When He had stopped speaking, He said to Simon, 'Launch out into the deep and let down your nets for a catch.' But Simon answered and said to Him, 'Master, we have toiled all night and caught nothing; nevertheless, at Your (rhema) word I will let down the net.' And when they had done this, they caught a great number of fish, and their net was breaking. So they signaled to their partners in the other boat to come and help them. And they came and filled both the boats, so that they began to sink. When Simon Peter saw it, he fell down at Jesus' knees, saying, 'Depart from me, for I am a sinful man, O Lord!' For he and all who were with him were astonished at the catch of fish which they had taken" (Luke 5: 4-9).

The key to the Fishermen's supernatural financial success that day was Peter's submission to the word of the Lord: "Nevertheless, at Your (*rhema*) word I will let down the net." The Fishermen had enough money from the one catch to leave their fishing businesses and follow Jesus. The financial miracle not only freed them financially but was truly a miracle relevant to them personally. It would be like the Lord coming and saying, "What is your yearly business income?" You respond, "About $250,000 gross per year." Jesus releases the Business Servant from his business and says, "Well, I am going to cause three and one-half years of income to immediately come into your business, so your absence from your business doing ministry with Me will not cause you or your family financial harm." How many of God's Business Servants, anointed to spoil the wealth of the wicked, would say? "I will follow You, Lord starting this day!" This is what happened to the soon to be Apostles-- Peter, Andrew, James, and John.

When God's Business Servants hear the voice of the Lord to direct him or her into the pathway of taking in the spoils to finance the kingdom work, then the supernatural *dia harpazo* starts happening. Learning to be led by the Holy Spirit concerning all business decisions is a prerequisite to being used as a Kingdom Minister of Finances in this Second Stage of Revival of the end time Revival *Ekklesia*.

THIRD STAGE OF REVIVAL: The Third Stage of *Ekklesia* Revival in Joel 2 is the revival of the end time *Ekklesia* through the outpouring of the Holy Spirit on all people, with signs, wonders, and spiritual gifts in operation and a great flood of new Believers coming into the Revival *Ekklesia*.

Joel 2: 28-32 says, "And it shall come to pass afterward, that I will pour out My spirit upon all flesh; and your sons and your daughters shall prophesy, your old men shall dream dreams, your young men shall see visions. And also upon the servants and upon the handmaids in those days will I pour out My spirit. And I will show wonders in the Heavens and in the earth, blood, and fire, and pillars of smoke. The sun shall be turned into darkness, and the moon into blood, before the great and the terrible day of the LORD comes. And it shall come to pass, that whosoever shall call on the name of the LORD shall be delivered: for in mount Zion and in Jerusalem shall be deliverance, as the LORD hath said, and in the remnant whom the LORD shall call."

These passages of Scripture relate to every age, the Church Age, the Millennium Age, and the Tribulation Age before the beginning of the Kingdom Age. Regardless of the Age involved, God still shows His mercy and anoints His Believers with the Holy Spirit and with power to fulfill God's purposes of doing good and healing all those who are oppressed by the devil (Acts 10:38).

The sign of the end times for the *Ekklesia* in Revival is clearer when more specific prophetic words are spoken by God's holy prophets. When the blood of Jesus takes spiritual voice within a Prophet, the blood of Jesus is speaking from the Mercy Seat in the spiritual Kingdom of God to His servants the prophets here on earth (Amos 3:7). The voice of Christ's Blood within the

Prophet speaking forth in prophecy is the sign that the end time outpouring of the Holy Spirit is near. Believers need to be ready to submit and obtain a hearing ear to hear the voice of the Holy Spirit leading, comforting, teaching, and sending Believers to given places to preach the gospel of the Kingdom and preach repentance and remission of sins. The Believers in the end time *Ekklesia* in Revival have been given the privilege of being the oracles of God to allow Christ's blood to speak through them, and to move with God's spiritual authority and power as God's end time *Ekklesia*.

The outpouring of the Spirit of God through every Kingdom community around the world begins the restoration of all things as God reveals the truth of, and the manifestation of, His heavenly Kingdom here on earth through His end time Revival *Ekklesia* for the glory of the Lord and the entire Godhead.

The Breadbasket of Surplus Kingdom Blessings for the Revival Ekklesia

CHAPTER FOUR

The Breadbasket of Surplus
Kingdom Blessings
For The Revival *Ekklesia*

"THAT OF ALL WHICH HE HATH GIVEN ME I SHOULD LOSE
NOTHING, BUT SHOULD RAISE IT UP AGAIN AT THE LAST DAY"

John 6:5-13 says, "When Jesus then lifted up His eyes, and saw a great company come unto Him, He saith unto Philip, 'Whence shall we buy bread, that these may eat?' And this He said to prove him: for He Himself knew what He would do. Philip answered Him, 'Two hundred pennyworth of bread is not sufficient for them, that every one of them may take a little.' One of his disciples, Andrew, Simon Peter's brother, saith unto Him, 'There is a lad here, which hath five barley loaves, and two small fishes: but what are they among so many?' And Jesus said, 'Make the men sit down.' Now there was much grass in the place. So the men sat down, in number about five thousand. And Jesus took the loaves; and when He had given thanks, He distributed to the disciples, and the disciples to them that were set down; and likewise of the fishes as much as they would. When they were filled, He said unto his disciples, 'Gather up the fragments that remain, that nothing be lost.' Therefore they gathered them together, and filled twelve baskets with the fragments of the five barley loaves, which remained over and above unto them that had eaten." The fragments were the surplus Kingdom miracle because the authority of the Kingdom is dominion authority over the physical creation. Jesus walked on water. Jesus spoke to the wind to stop. Jesus raised the dead. Jesus spoke and people were healed. Jesus commanded the preaching of the gospel of the Kingdom and repentance and the remission of sins. Jesus had total command over the physical creation because He lived in the Kingdom of God and was totally under submission to God the Father and never did anything that He did not first hear God the Father say or see God the Father do.

Now here is the relevant statement by Jesus in the same passage of Scripture. John 6:38-39 says, "For I came down from Heaven, not to do Mine own will, but the will of Him that sent Me. And this is the Father's will which hath sent Me, that of all which He hath given me I should lose nothing, but should raise it up again at the last day."

In furtherance of this biblical principle, Jesus' divine nature is equipping His end time Church through the Holy Spirit, so when the multiplication of anointing and power in His Kingdom brought by the Holy Spirit comes, nothing will be lost. There were twelve baskets containing the surplus from the miracle of multiplication: one for each Apostle in training. Although Scripture is unclear, each of the twelve disciples probably carried a basket of food to the boy's home, to teach the boy the principle that rewards follow the sowing into the work of the Lord.

Jesus started out with filling a basket of food for each of His twelve disciples to hand out the miracle food to the people, and they ended up with twelve baskets full of surplus anointing. This means that the people fed on the prayer of Jesus, as none of the food was lost or used up. John 17:20-21 says, "Neither pray I for these alone, but for them also which shall believe on me through their word. That they all may be one; as thou, Father, art in Me, and I in Thee, that they also may be one in Us; that the world may believe that Thou hast sent Me."

What are the spiritual blessings which Believers have with and through Christ Jesus, and as adopted children of God, which are for these last days? Is it more than everlasting life? God the Father, Jesus' divine nature, and the Holy Spirit have spiritually engifted, empowered, and blessed Believers; so that Believers will be well equipped to be Christ's Kingdom spiritual Ambassadors and His Kingdom spiritual Soldiers here on earth. There are administrative gifts from God the Word (1 Corinthians 12: 5; Ephesians 4:11). There are operation gifts from God the Father (1 Corinthians 12: 6; Romans 12:6-8). There are manifestation gifts from God the Holy Spirit (1 Corinthians 12:7-10). All these gifts will be highly visible during the end-time Revival.

As examples; Ephesians 1:3 says, "Blessed be the God and Father of our Lord Jesus Christ, Who has blessed us with every spiritual blessing in the heavenly places in Christ." Also, John 17: 5 says, "And now, O Father, glorify Me together with Yourself, with the Glory which I had with You before the world was." Similarly, Romans 8:37 says, "He who did not spare His own Son, but delivered Him up for us all, how shall He not with Him also freely give us all things?"

CHRIST JESUS WILL RAISE UP FOR THE BENEFIT OF THE END TIME REVIVAL *EKKLESIA* THE SURPLUS ANOINTING POURED OUT BY THE HOLY SPIRIT ON MEN AND WOMEN IN BIBLICAL HISTORY.

NOAH: The grace that was surplus that had been shown to Noah and his family has been thrown into the Kingdom Glory Basket for the end time Revival *Ekklesia*. Matthew 24: 37 says, "But as the days of Noah were, so also will the coming of the Son of Man be. For as in the days before the flood, they were eating and drinking, marrying and giving in marriage until the day that Noah entered the ark." Colossians 3:3 says, "For you died, and your life is hidden with Christ in God." Whenever Believers see crime and immorality in the street, they can take some of the grace surplus left over from Noah and remain hidden and protected in Christ Jesus, who is the Ark for His people, to be their protection. Also, God will warn Believers before major disaster comes as He did Noah.

ABRAHAM: The belief and obedience of Abraham were rewarded. Genesis 15:6 says, "Abraham believed God and it was accounted to him for righteousness." Hebrews 11:10 says, "For he waited for the City which has foundations whose builder and maker is God." The righteousness accounted to Abraham not only benefitted the children of Israel but also Gentiles. Abraham was blessed financially. Genesis 13:1-2 says, "Then Abram went up from Egypt, he and his wife and all that he had, and Lot with him, to the South. Abram was very rich in livestock, in silver, and in gold." Genesis 22:14 says, "And Abraham called the name of the place, 'The Lord Will Provide' (*Jehovah Jireh*); as it is said to this day, 'In the Mount of the Lord it shall be provided.'" Genesis 12:3 says, "... And in you all the families of the earth shall be blessed." Genesis 18:18 says, "And the Lord said, 'shall I hide from Abraham what I am doing, since Abraham shall surely become a great and mighty nation, and all the nations of the earth shall be blessed in him?" Genesis 22:18 says, "In your Seed all the nations of the earth shall be blessed, because you have obeyed My voice." "Your Seed" was stated in the singular in this Scripture and is a reference to Jesus Christ (Galatians 3:16). God took the faith of Abraham and threw it into the Kingdom Glory Basket for the end time *Ekklesia*. Galatians 3:29 says, "And if you are Christ's, then you are Abraham's seed, and heirs according to the promise."

ISAAC: God gave Isaac the anointing to bless all his children. This parental surplus anointing to bless the children was handed down, starting with Jacob, from generation to generation to the Spiritual Israel, who are those who have accepted Christ Jesus as Savior and Lord (Galatians 6:16). Hebrews 11:20 says, "By faith Isaac blessed Jacob and Esau concerning things to come. By Faith Jacob, when he was dying, blessed each of the sons of Joseph, and worshiped, leaning on the top of his staff." Thus, God took the surplus parental authority given to Isaac to bless children and through Christ Jesus put it in the Kingdom Breadbasket of Blessings for His end time Revival *Ekklesia* as the spiritual Israel.

JACOB: On Mount Peniel Jacob wrestled with the "Angel of the Lord," and his name was changed from Jacob, the "Supplanter," to Israel, the "Prince of God" or "He who strives with God." Jacob was transformed in his soul. The surplus anointing will cause a Believer to be transformed from carnality to spirituality as this was handed down to Jacob and through Christ Jesus Who has placed the anointing in the Kingdom Glory Basket to the end time Revival *Ekklesia*.

MOSES: Moses was given authority over the forces of nature, as when he stretched out the rod over the Red Sea and dry land appeared for the Children of Israel to cross over to safety. Exodus 14:21-22 says, "Then Moses stretched out his hand over the sea; and the Lord caused the sea to go back by a strong east wind all that night, and made the sea into dry land, and the waters were divided. So the children of Israel went into the midst of the sea on the dry ground, and the waters were a wall to them on their right hand and on their left." The authority over nature was immediately handed down to Joshua whose prayer of faith moved God to cause the earth to stop its rotation and the sun and moon appeared to stand still in the sky. This authority over nature has been given to the end time Revival Church through Christ Jesus. Luke 8:24-25 says, "And they came to Him and awoke Him, saying, 'Master, Master, we are perishing!' Then He arose and rebuked the wind and the raging of the water. And they ceased, and there was a calm. But He said to them, 'Where is your faith?' And they were afraid, and marveled, saying to one another, 'Who can this be? For He commands even the winds and water, and they obey Him!'"

AARON: Numbers 17: 8 says, "Now it came to pass on the next day that Moses went into the tabernacle of witness, and behold, the rod of Aaron, of the house of Levi, had sprouted and put forth buds, had produced blossoms and yielded ripe almonds." The rod of Aaron not only blossomed but also yielded mature, ripe almonds ready to eat. This made Aaron's authority established without question as Aaron's rod had gone beyond the requirements of the test. The surplus anointing on Aaron's rod is to stabilize, comfort and lift leadership authority, for the end time Revival *Ekklesia*. Aaron's rod also represented a cut down tree that was the tree of life instead of the tree of death. The tree of life in Revelation 22:2 was the Greek *xulon*, which related to the cross, a cut down tree that had 12 fruits, one for each month, and green leaves for the healing of the nations.

SAMSON: The strength of Samson is an anointing for supernatural feats in the natural, and the surplus anointing strength of Samson was thrown into Christ's Kingdom Basket of Surplus Blessings. There are some strong Believers that to a degree have the Samson anointing of strength, one of which is my old and good friend, Dr. Bill Henderson, who was one of the original Power Team. I personally have witnessed him breaking multiple pairs of handcuffs, breaking blocks of concrete, and tearing apart phone books. I witnessed him lifting a large roll of carpet, putting it on his shoulder, and dragging it into a house to be installed. I was helping him and could not even move the other end of the carpet. My children use to say he is like Samson of old.

DAVID: David had a singing Psalmist anointing that delivered King Saul of an evil spirit (1 Samuel 16: 23). The Psalmist's surplus anointing lifts demons off people, and Christ put this into the Kingdom Glory Basket for the end time Church's anointing. Likewise, David was anointed to hold the multiple offices of Priest, Prophet, and King, just like Jesus and members of his end time Revival *Ekklesia*. David prefigured Jesus as the Great Shepherd (John 10; 1 Peter 2:9; Revelation 1:6). David was anointed to bring the Israelites into the Spirit inspired worship and praise to God, and the surplus anointing on the Tabernacle of David shall be reestablished by the end time Revival *Ekklesia* (2 Samuel 6:17; 2 Chronicles 1:4; Acts 15:16). Likewise, Believers are seated in heavenly places in Christ who sits on the eternal throne of David (2 Samuel 7:12-13; Ephesians 2:6). The anointing of divine provision was given when David and his men ate the holy, consecrated showbread (1 Samuel 21:5-6). Jesus referred to this surplus anointing in Matthew 12:3-4, saying that He was the Lord of the Sabbath, and taught that human need should be considered over religious rituals, as Jesus never came to start a new religion, but to reestablish the Kingdom of God and to do God's will here on earth as it is in heaven (Matthew 6:10). Since only the priests were to eat the showbread in the holy place, then this authority of David was a forerunner to Christ Jesus, Who abolished the priest/laity distinction; so, that all Believers can go boldly before the throne of grace as kings and priests (Hebrews 4:16; Revelation 1:6).

SOLOMON: The divine gift of wisdom that was given to Solomon (2 Chronicles 1:7-12) was thrown into the Kingdom Glory Basket of Blessings and given to the end time Revival *Ekklesia*. James 1:5 says, "If any of you lacks wisdom let him ask of God, who gives to all liberally and without reproach, and it will be given to him." Isaiah 33:6 says, "And wisdom and knowledge shall be the stability of thy times, and strength of salvation: the fear of the LORD is his treasure." Solomon was thought to be in the natural the wisest King that ever lived, and certainly the wealthiest.

 NEHEMIAH: The anointing on Nehemiah to unite the people to quickly rebuild the wall around God's City from the "burned stones." Nehemiah 4:2 says, "...Will they complete it in a day? Will they revive the stones from the heaps of rubbish stones that are burned?" The surplus anointing to build what we occupy in the face of the enemy was given to the end time Revival *Ekklesia*. Nehemiah 4:17-18 says, "Those who built on the wall, and those who carried burdens, loaded themselves so that with one hand they worked at construction, and with the other held a weapon. Every one of the builders had his sword girded at his side as he built. And the one who sounded the trumpet was beside them." 1 Peter 2:4-5 says, "Coming to Him as to a living stone, rejected indeed by men, but chosen by God and precious, you also, as living stones, are being built up a spiritual house, a holy priesthood, to offer up spiritual sacrifices acceptable to God through Jesus Christ." John the Baptist informed the Jewish leaders in Matthew 3:11, "I indeed baptize you with water unto repentance: but He that cometh after me is mightier than I, whose shoes I am not worthy to bear: He shall baptize you with the Holy Ghost, and with fire." The anointing on Nehemiah is placed in the Kingdom Basket of Surplus Blessings for the end time Revival *Ekklesia* where Believers are the burnt stones from Jesus' baptism of cleansing fire which separates Believers from the religion of Christianity and manifests the Kingdom of God in their lives - A Kingdom of citizens of heaven who become the greater Temple of God where God indwells them (1 Corinthians 6:19; 1 Corinthians 3:16; Revelation 21:3). The end-time Revival *Ekklesia* is destined in Christ to build the wall around the Kingdom of God, as these Believers seek first the Kingdom of God and the Righteousness of God and are the true Kingdom *Ekklesia* (Matthew 16:18), the true Israel (Romans 9:6-8), the true Jew (Romans 2:28-29) and the true Jerusalem City that comes down from heaven (Revelation 21:9-27). The end time Believers will have the builder/fighter surplus anointing of Nehemiah in the Kingdom Basket of Burnt Stones that received Jesus' baptism of fire which burned out the briers and brambles of religion to receive the Kingdom of God in place of religion.

QUEEN ESTHER: Esther had the beauty of a virtuous woman, and this beauty of virtue was gathered up and thrown into the Glorious Basket of Kingdom Beauty for the end-time Revival *Ekklesia*, who becomes beautiful and glorious in its time (Ecclesiastes 3:11; Ephesians 5:27). There is a surplus anointing for beauty given to the virtuous Bride of Christ. Similarly, 1 Peter 3:1-4 says, "Wives, likewise, be submissive to your own husbands, that even if some do not obey the word, may be won by the conduct of their wives, when they observe your chaste conduct accompanied by fear. Do not let your adornment be merely outward arranging the hair, wearing gold, or putting on fine apparel rather let it be the hidden person of the heart, with the incorruptible beauty of a gentle and quiet spirit, which is very precious in the sight of God…" The word "submissive" in 1 Peter 3:1 is the same Greek word, *"hupotasso"* as stated in 1 Timothy 2:11 which means for a wife to subordinate herself willingly to her husband in an orderly manner conditioned upon his support and honor. In truth, the wife's submission in 1 Peter 3:1 is conditioned upon her receiving her husband's honor referred to in 1 Peter 3:7, which says, "Husbands, likewise, dwell with them with understanding, giving honor to the wife, as to the weaker vessel, and as being heirs together of the grace of life, that your prayers may not be hindered." Giving honor to the wife is holding them in high esteem, paying them tribute and support. The Greek word for honor is the word, *"time"* (pronounced "tee may"), which means "to esteem in the highest degree to the position of paying tribute money to them as a dignitary, whose presence is to be considered precious, spiritually beneficial and costly."

Esther risked her own life to use her influence as Queen to deliver God's people from certain disaster. "How can I endure to see the evil that shall come unto my people? Or how can I endure to see the destruction of my kindred?" (Esther 8:6). In the heroine's greatest hour, she risked her life to appear before the Persian King with the decision, "IF I PERISH, I PERISH" (Esther 4:16). They won, and Esther and her uncle, Mordecai, were granted by the King authority over 127 provinces (Esther 9:29-30). The unity of the *Ekklesia* was seen in how Esther and Mordecai worked together in prayer and fasting. The surplus of honor given to Queen Esther by the Persian King and Husband is thrown into the Kingdom Glory Basket as blessings for women in the end time Revival *Ekklesia*. This includes the honor bestowed upon virtuous women in these last days, especially the Bride of Christ in all her glory (Revelation 21:9-27).

ISAIAH: The anointed call upon Isaiah when the Seraphim took the live coal and touched the prophet's lips to cleanse his mouth to send him to the Israelites to proclaim the word of the Lord was placed in the Surplus Basket of Kingdom Blessings for the end-time Revival *Ekklesia* (Isaiah 6:5-13). On the Day of Pentecost cloven tongues as of fire sat on each of the Believers' heads in the upper room. They began to speak with other tongues (Acts 2:1-4), Isaiah's surplus anointing was the end time Revival *Ekklesia*'s baptism of the Holy Spirit, with the manifested sign of speaking in tongues. The power of the Holy Spirit was to come upon the disciples in the upper room to be anointed witnesses of the Resurrected and Ascended Christ, and His message of the gospel of the Kingdom and repentance and remission of sins throughout the known world. The speaking in other tongues was for a sign to unBelievers on the Day of Pentecost (I Corinthians 14:22). All 120 Believers, both men and women, in the upper room spoke in a tongue as a witness to the unBelievers present outside. After Peter's Sermon, about three thousand people came to the Lord, and His Kingdom, that day. The surplus anointing to speak in other tongues, the surplus anointing to manifest spiritual gifts, and the surplus anointing to witness were placed into the Glory Basket of Kingdom Redemption for the end time Revival *Ekklesia*.

JEREMIAH: The anointing on Jeremiah's life to call upon the Lord and receive the mysteries of God was given to the end time Revival *Ekklesia*. Jeremiah 33:3 says, "Call unto Me and I will answer you and show you great and mighty things which you did not know." 1 Corinthians 2:7 says, "Now we have received, not the spirit of the world, but the Spirit who is from God, that we might know the things that have been freely given to us by God." The greatest mystery is the "mystery of Godliness", which is only revealed when one enters the kingdom of God. Jesus said it was given for Believers to know the mystery of the kingdom of heaven. Matthew 13:11 says, "He answered and said unto them, because it is given unto you to know the mysteries of the kingdom of heaven, but to them it is not given." There is the mystery of God's wisdom (1 Corinthians 2:7). There is mystery of God's Will which God purposed in His heart that in the dispensation of the fullness of times He might gather in one all things in Christ, both which are in heaven, and which are on earth; even in Him (Ephesians 1:9-10). There is the mystery of God's Will to make one New Man in Christ, both Jew and Gentile, to become the habitation of the Godhead (Ephesians 2:15-22). There is the mystery of Christ and the *Ekklesia* in the Kingdom of God brought to the earth (Matthew 6:10; Ephesians 5:32). There is the mystery of the Triune Godhead as One God and Christ having dual natures, both divine as God the Word and human as the Lamb of God, Son of God, Son of Man, Last Adam, and Second Man (John 1:1, 14; 1 Corinthians 15:47; Colossians 2:2; 1 John 5:7 King James Version).

EZEKIEL: Ezekiel saw the wheel in the middle of the wheel (Ezekiel 1:16) which symbolized the surplus anointing of God calling forth the Bride, the end time Revival *Ekklesia*. Revelation 18:4 says, "And I heard another voice from Heaven saying, 'Come out of her, My people, lest you share in her sins, and lest you receive of her plagues.'" The surplus anointing given to Ezekiel was also to call forth the spiritual army of God from people brought back to life, the end time Ephesians 6 Kingdom spiritual army of God to go into the world and fight against the strongholds of Satanic forces. Ezekiel 37:9 says, "Also He said to me, 'Prophesy to the breath, prophesy, son of man, and say to the breath, 'Thus says the Lord God: "Come from the four winds, O breath, and breathe on these slain, that they may live.'"… I will put My Spirit in you, and you shall live, and I will place you in your own land. Then you shall know that I, the Lord, have spoken it and performed it.' says the Lord." The surplus anointing, putting life in God's Kingdom spiritual Army who are the "dry bones" that are currently dead spiritually caught up in the old religious order that needs the anointing and resurrection life of Christ, was thrown into the Kingdom Glory Basket to be experienced by the end time Revival *Ekklesia*.

DANIEL: When Daniel was thrown into the lions' den, God sent an Angel to shut the mouths of the lions (Daniel 6:22). The name "devil" refers to him as "tempter, accuser, slanderer, and whisperer." He tempts man and slanders man to God and God to man. This name is used about 35 times in the Bible (Matthew 4:1; 13:39; 25:41; John 8:44; Ephesians 4:27; 6:11; Hebrews 2:14;

James 4:7; Revelation 12:10). The devil roams about as a roaring lion seeking whom he may devour through temptation, accusation, slander, and whispers (1 Peter 5:8). The end time Revival *Ekklesia* was given the surplus anointing through Christ to shut the mouths of the accusers of the brethren, even those used by the devil as gossipers, revilers, backbiters, defamers, and criticizers of Believers (Revelation 12:10).

THREE HEBREW CHILDREN: Shadrach, Meshach, and Abed Nego were rescued by the Fourth Man during their fiery trial in the furnace (Daniel 3:25). Christ Jesus' divine nature was seen as the "Fourth Man" who said in Matthew 18:20 "For where two or three are gathered together in My name, I am there in the midst of them." The Fourth Man protection surplus anointing was thrown into the Kingdom Basket of Overcomers for the end time Revival *Ekklesia*. Romans 8:38-39 says, "For I am persuaded, that neither death, nor life, nor angels, nor principalities, nor powers, nor things present, nor things to come, nor height, nor depth, nor any other creature, shall be able to separate us from the love of God, which is in Christ Jesus our Lord."

HOSEA: The Bridegroom anointing is prophesied by Hosea to Christ Jesus' Betrothed to come. Hosea 2:19-20, 23 says, "I will betroth you to Me forever; yes, I will betroth you to Me in righteousness and justice, in loving kindness and mercy; I will betroth you to Me in faithfulness, and you shall know the Lord. . . Then I will sow her for Myself in the earth, and I will have mercy on her who had not obtained mercy; then I will say to those who were not My people, 'You are My people!' And they shall say, 'You are my God!'" Ephesians 5:26-27 says, "That He might sanctify and cleanse her with the washing of water by the word, that He might present her to Himself a glorious Church, not having spot or wrinkle or any such thing, but that she should be holy and without blemish." The Bridegroom anointing to perfect Christ's Bride was thrown into the Kingdom Glory Basket of Soul Transformation and given to the end time Revival *Ekklesia*. The anointing of the coming forth of the Bride of Christ is seen in Revelation 22:17, which says, "And the Spirit and the Bride say, 'Come.'"

JOEL: What Prophet Joel is to a spiritually destitute Judah, the end time Revival *Ekklesia* is to a decadent world of today, where the blood of Jesus inside each born again Believer speaks forth a prophetic voice of the good news of the Kingdom of God to all who will listen. There is an outpouring of repentance and remission of sins, in the first stage of Revival, along with the benefits of an outpouring of financial prosperity to be used to expand God's Kingdom to finance the end time Revival as the second stage of *Ekklesia* Revival, and the outpouring of God's Spirit on all flesh with the sign of prophecy proclaims by the sons and daughters of the end time Revival *Ekklesia* as the final stage of Revival. Jesus promised the outpouring of the Holy Spirit after He ascended to the throne having provided the appropriate sacrifice for redemption of those who call upon Jesus' name and are born again (John 3:3,5; 1 Peter 1:23; 14:15-18; 16:5 24; Romans 8:13). The e*n masse* pouring out of God's Spirit began at Pentecost and was proclaimed by Peter in Acts 2:16, but the Spirit has even a greater outpouring surplus anointing in His Kingdom Glory Basket of Anointing to restore all things as prophesied by all of God's holy Prophets (Amos 3:7) to wrap up the *Ekklesia* Age (Acts 3:21).

JONAH: Jonah was commanded to be God's Ambassador and go to Ninevah, which represented the world, to warn them to repent to escape God's judgment. The Ambassador surplus anointing was placed in the Kingdom Glory Basket for the end time Revival *Ekklesia* to go into all the world with the ministry of reconciliation unto repentance and remission of sins, while preaching the gospel of the Kingdom in the entire world (Matthew 24:14; Luke 24:46-49; Acts 1:8; 2 Corinthians 5:18-20). Similarly, the Jonah surplus anointing of "second chances" is given to the end time Revival *Ekklesia* because the gifts and calling of God are irrevocable (Romans 11:29). God changed Jonah's direction from disobedience to one of obedience. Sometimes, when Believers miss their sense of direction, God will put them back on course where He wants them to be, even though it may be a Whale of an experience. If Believers' hearts repent and submit, they will fulfill their destiny and arrive at their spiritual destination in these last days, especially in the Revival *Ekklesia*. God has promised to bring Believers up from the "belly of the great fish" when they suffer great anguish, and God then will give Believers resurrected life from Jesus' humanity nature brought to earth by Christ's divine nature. Christ Jesus was raised after three days from being in the "heart of the earth," and the end time Revival *Ekklesia* shall experience the fullness of the revelation of Christ's resurrected life (Jonah 1:17; 2:1-10; Matthew 12:40).

OBADIAH: The anointing on Obadiah by the Holy Spirit was to repent and confront the terrible cost of pride which prevented him from seeing the error of his ways. Likewise, Obadiah confronted the sin of Edom against Judah and said in verse 15 that "...As you have done, it shall be done to you...." The Apostle Paul reiterates this truth in Galatians 6:7, as whatever Believers sow in this life they will also reap in this life. God is a rewarder of them that diligently seek Him (Hebrews 11:6). God rewards obedient Believers at the Judgment Seat of Christ (2 Corinthians 5:10) with certain "crowns" in the life to come, including the "Crown of Life" (James 1:12), "Crown of Glory" (1 Peter 5:4), "Crown of Exultation" (2 Timothy 4:8), "Incorruptible Crown" (1 Corinthians 9:25), and "Crown of Rejoicing" (1 Thessalonians 2:19). On the other hand, those brothers who are religious and judge other brethren will find they will be judged at the Judgment Seat of Christ (Romans 14:10). Even while we are alive here on earth, Lord's divine nature seeks vengeance against the kingdom of darkness on behalf of His Believers. The end time Revival *Ekklesia* will receive the wonderful conviction of the Holy Spirit to humble themselves, as Christ humbled Himself, even to death on the Cross (Philippians 2:5-11). Humility is important for the end time Revival *Ekklesia* as Believers declare, "I have been crucified with Christ; it is no longer I who live, but Christ lives in me; and the life which I now live in the flesh I live by faith in the Son of God, who loved me and gave Himself for me" (Galatians 2:20). God will take care of the enemies of the end time Revival *Ekklesia*, and this is their blessing. The surplus anointing to repent of pride, humbly seek reconciliation of broken relationships, and seek forgiveness of the brethren of the Lord with whom strife existed is part of the Kingdom Basket of Anointing to Minister Reconciliation for the end time Revival *Ekklesia*.

MICAH: The prophetic vision given to Micah was the dominion authority through Christ Jesus to the end time Revival *Ekklesia*. Micah 4:8-9, 13 says, "And you, O tower of the flock, the stronghold of the daughter of Zion (*Ekklesia*), to you shall it come, even the former dominion (that was given to Adam before the fall) shall come, the Kingdom of the daughter of Jerusalem. Now why do you cry aloud? Is there no King (type of Jesus) in your midst? Has your counselor (type of Holy Spirit) perished? ...Arise and thresh, O daughter of Zion (discipline of the Father); for I will make your horn iron (strength given through the Lord), and I will make your hooves bronze; you shall beat in pieces many peoples; I will consecrate their gain to the Lord, and their substance to the Lord of the whole earth (transfer of wealth from the wicked to the just)." The prophet Micah prophesied in Micah 5:2 that Bethlehem would be the birthplace of the Messiah. The surplus anointing on Micah for the end time Revival *Ekklesia* was for the Bethlehem experience of being born again into the Kingdom of God to participate in the New but Final Movement of the Holy Spirit through the end time Revival *Ekklesia* in Christ to retake dominion of the earth and all things herein and transfer everything to the Kingdom of God. The authority of Christ and the power of the Holy Spirit to take dominion through the establishment of God's Kingdom here on earth were thrown into the Kingdom Surplus Basket for the end time Revival *Ekklesia*.

NAHUM: Nahum's prophetic word was that God is both a God of judgment and a God of mercy. The wicked lioness (Nineveh representing forces of evil) was defeated (Nahum 1:15), and the righteous Lion of Judah (Revelation 5:5) reigns. God's judgment against the sinful is often forgiven by His mercy toward the faithful redeemed. The Lord brings His discipline against the proud, the arrogant, and the rebellious Believers. Jesus said in Revelation 3:19, "As many as I love, I rebuke and chasten: be zealous therefore, and repent." Yet, God brings honor and comfort to the humble, devoted, faithful, and submissive. This promise of mercy, honor, and comfort for God's elect was thrown into the Kingdom Basket of Promises for the end time Revival *Ekklesia*.

HABAKKUK: The anointing for vision was given to Habakkuk and was placed in the Kingdom Basket with foresight and destiny as the result, along with the wisdom to take the steps to fulfill the vision to the end time Revival *Ekklesia*. Wherever and whatever God's vision is, God will bring His provision to fulfill it. Habakkuk 2: 2-3 says, "...Write the vision and make it plain on tablets, that he may run who reads it. For the vision is yet for an appointed time; but at the end it will speak, and it will not lie. Though it tarries, wait for it; because it will surely come, it will not tarry." Habakkuk wrote about his spiritual growth from doubt and unbelief to faith and worship of God. Habakkuk learned to hear and see the results of God's presence here on the earth and was no longer anxious about the circumstances around him. God truly has not left the earth. Jesus said in Matthew 28:20, that "... And lo, I am with you always, even to the end of the age." God's indwelling presence by making Believers His Temple is a blessing thrown into the Kingdom Glory Basket for the end time Revival *Ekklesia* (1 Corinthians 3:16; 2 Corinthians 6:16; Ephesians 2:21). 1 John 4:4 says, "He who is in you is greater than he who is in the world."

ZEPHANIAH: The vision given to Zephaniah was to see the wrath and judgment of God in the terrible Day of the Lord (Zephaniah 1:14-18). The whole earth will be consumed (Zephaniah 1:2-3). Zephaniah was shown the end time Revival *Ekklesia* a prophecy that the Day of the Lord is indeed coming when the wicked will be consigned into damnation and the righteous will receive eternal life blessings. There is a promise that God will hide and protect us when His anger is poured out on the evil of the land. Colossians 3:3 says, "For you died, and your life is hidden with Christ in God." God promises in Zephaniah 3:9, 20 that He will restore the faithful remnant and bless them with fame and praise among all the people of the earth. The hidden protection of God through Christ was placed in the Kingdom Glory Basket as an end time blessing for the Revival *Ekklesia* as the heathens' rage and sin abounds. This is a promise of God for the end time Revival *Ekklesia* as His Spirit is poured out on all flesh.

HAGGAI: The anointing on Haggai was for Holy Spirit empowered stewardship work. People in Haggai's time had returned from exile and were disinterested in building God's Temple (Haggai 1:1-5), which had been their purpose for returning to Jerusalem (Ezra 1:2-4). The people had become more concerned with building their own houses instead of the Temple of God (Haggai 1:4). God tells them to consider their ways and repent, for their efforts result in fruitlessness (Haggai 1:5-6). The people were discouraged (Haggai 2:1-9) as some had remembered the glory of Solomon's Temple. The Temple being built could not compare to the former. Haggai tells the people that the Lord says to "be strong … and work, for I am with you." Haggai prophesied in 2:7-9 that in the end time, God will "'...shake all nations, and they shall come to the Desire of All Nations (reference to Christ Jesus), and I will fill this Temple with glory,' says the Lord of Hosts. 'The silver is Mine, and the gold is Mine,' says the Lord of Hosts. 'The glory of this latter Temple shall be greater than the former,' says the Lord of Hosts, 'And in this place I will give peace,' says the Lord of Hosts." This prophecy is a reference to God's indwelling of human Temples through Christ (1 Corinthians 6:19; 1 Corinthians 3:16; 2 Corinthians 6:16; Ephesians 2:21). As the Temple of the Lord matures, she shall be transformed into the Bride of Christ adorned with the glory of Christ (Ephesians 5:26-27); then to become the most beautiful City of God (Revelation 21:9-27). The surplus anointing on Haggai's prophecy was thrown into the Kingdom Glory Basket for God's true dwelling Temple to be poured into the end time Revival *Ekklesia*.

ZECHARIAH: Zechariah's prophecy is one of the most Messianic of all the Old Testament prophetic books. The Messiah is referred to as "My Servant the Branch" (Zechariah 3:8), as "the Man whose name is the Branch," Priest and King (Zechariah 6:12-13) and as the True Shepherd (Zechariah 11:4-11). Zechariah prophesied that Jesus would be betrayed for thirty pieces of silver (Zechariah 11:12-13). He also prophesied Christ's crucifixion (Zechariah 12:10), His sufferings (Zechariah 13:7), and His Second Return for His Bride (Zechariah 14:4). The prophetic blessing most often recognized and quoted is 4: 6, "'...Not by might nor by power, but by My Spirit,' says the Lord of Hosts." The pouring out of the Spirit of God in full measure upon His people is the glorious destiny of the end time Revival *Ekklesia*. Zechariah prophesied much eschatology for the end time Revival *Ekklesia*. God will deliver His people (Zechariah Chapter 9). God will restore prosperity to His people (Zechariah Chapter 10). Zion is restored, and the Shepherd Savior will appear (Zechariah Chapter 10,13). The Day of the Lord is truly coming (Zechariah Chapter. 14). The anointing for those end time prophecies were placed in the eternal Kingdom Glory Basket of a revealed future for the end time Revival *Ekklesia*.

MALACHI: The anointing on the tithe and gifts to bring blessings to God's people to finance God's end time harvest was prophesied by Malachi and was thrown into God's Kingdom Basket of Surplus Blessings for the end time Revival *Ekklesia* (Malachi 3:11-12). Financial blessing is part of Believers' inheritance, but only through Christ Jesus and His eternal Kingdom. This includes the Jesus' Kingdom authority to rebuke and bind the forces of darkness as led by the Holy Spirit. Malachi prophesies in 4:2-3 that "But to you who fear My name the Sun of Righteousness shall arise with healing in His wings; and you shall go out and grow fat like stall fed calves. You shall trample the wicked, for they shall be ashes under the soles of your feet on the day that I do this,' says the Lord of hosts." Similarly, Malachi 4:6 foretells the blessing of reconciliation by turning the hearts of the fathers to the children and the children to the fathers. These are all in the Kingdom Glory Basket of Blessings for the end time Revival *Ekklesia*.

Even the surplus anointing poured out in the Gospels, the Epistles, and on through to Revelation of the New Testament is stored up for the greatest outpouring of the Holy Spirit into the Lord's Revival *Ekklesia* and into the world of the unsaved during this end time Revival. John 14:12-14 says, "Most assuredly, I say to you, he who Believers in Me, the works that I do he will do also; and greater works than these he will do, because I go to My Father, and whatever you ask in My name, that I will do, that the Father may be glorified in the Son. If you ask anything in My name, I will do it." Signs will follow the word preached (Mark 16:20) because they contain the signatory authority of Jesus, with His divine and humanity natures, through the anointing and power of the Holy Spirit. Even the surplus from the double portion anointing of Acts 5 has been thrown into God's Kingdom Basket of Blessings for the end time Revival *Ekklesia*.

The reason why the Holy Spirit and the Lord's divine nature, God the Word, want to pour out Their anointing on Believers in the end time Revival *Ekklesia* is because they want Believers to demonstrate Kingdom authority here on earth and find the spiritual blessings they have received and displayed them to the forces of darkness. They want to "show off" the Lord of host. The Lord's divine nature, God the Word, is present in Believers, along with God the Father and God the Holy Spirit (John 14:16-17, 23; 1 Corinthians 6:19; 1 Corinthians 3:16; Ephesians 2:21). Wherever the devil tries to keep God out, that is exactly where the Godhead will go and have Believers testify of Jesus' humanity nature as the King and Lord of the Kingdom of God, the High Priest in the order of Melchizedek, the Son of God, the Son of Man, the Last Adam, the Second Man, and the Passover Lamb of God who died on the Roman Cross but Who was resurrected on the third day and ascended on high at the right hand of God, where He sits on His throne in intercession, waiting to return to earth.

It is the anointing that breaks the yoke of the enemy (Isaiah 10:27). Those who lift up the Lord will not be ashamed. God will exalt the humble. God will make significant the insignificant. God will make a mockery of those who mock Believers who seek the Kingdom of God with faith and humble hearts. God will invade the natural with His supernatural power and bless the Believers who have invited the Holy Spirit to visit them.

The Holy Spirit is the Great Teacher who will be invited to teach God's school children. Students will demand the school display the Ten Commandments in their club rooms although the teachers are not allowed to display them in their classrooms. Student leaders will bring prayer back into public schools even though the teachers are not allowed to lead the prayer. The Lord will not be judicially decreed out, or legislated out of the schools by secular government. The Holy Spirit is moving amongst students because the devil is sending terrorists to school to kill God's children and teach false ideas that deranges their minds. God is bringing Revival to wake up students from their spiritual slumber. The presence of the Holy Spirit in the schools will be so evident that the students rejecting the gospel of the Kingdom of God with Jesus as King and Lord will have to make a conscious choice to go to hell.

The Lord wants Believers to share their end time blessings with others to entice them to accept Jesus as Savior and Lord, come into the Kingdom of God, become the children of God by adoption, are members of the household of God, and are joint heirs with Christ. God will start a Revival amongst the Islamic; and when these radical Believers accept Jesus as Savior and Lord, they will come into the Kingdom of God with total commitment to set others free who are still in religious bondage.

The Lord's divine nature here on earth is refining His mysteries. He is giving Believers further clarification of His purpose and will be here on earth during the end time Revival *Ekklesia*. The Lord's divine nature is revealing His kingdom authority. He will manifest His presence in a tangible way to His end time Revival *Ekklesia*. The Lord's divine nature is revealing a new wine skin into which to pour the Holy Spirit's new wine of Revival.

The end time Revival *Ekklesia* Believers are not satisfied in just reading about miracles in the

Bible and miracles reported in other countries. Believers want to witness and participate in these miracles. Believers want more of God's spiritual reality in their lives. They yearn and pray for loving Kingdom community relationships where the Lord's divine nature is present. They will seek maturation in other Believers' souls as their minds, emotions, and hearts transform from carnality to spirituality. The end time Revival *Ekklesia* Believers will abandon old religious order practices when the Holy Spirit fills the room and their souls with His presence and anointing. The Holy Spirit will lead Believers out of their old religious order traditions.

PLEASE JOIN WITH ME IN THIS PRAYER:

Father God, I pray that You send to your children a greater Revelation of the Lord Jesus Christ, so that all the blessings come to Your Revival *Ekklesia* as Christ becomes "all in all" and the Way, Truth, and Life personified in each Believer. Father God, I pray that in these last days all the Kingdom surplus blessings gathered up by Christ as He stated in John 6:39 be poured out onto Believers in His Revival Church by the Holy Spirit. Father God, I pray that you allow Believers to partake of the Kingdom Basket full of Kingdom surplus anointing, authority, power, and glory which will be poured out in these last days of great calling forth of the Kingdom spiritual Army of the Lord and the manifestation of His Kingdom government throughout the earth. We thank You, Jesus, that You promised that You will not allow anything to be lost. We thank You, Lord Jesus, that by the power of the Holy Spirit, You will release Your surplus of Kingdom anointing, authority, power, and glory to Your *Ekklesia* in Revival. We thank You, Father God, for allowing us to be born at the time of the manifestation of Your end time Revival *Ekklesia*. As Believers of Your end time Revival *Ekklesia*, we will be recipients of Your Kingdom surplus blessings from the beginning of time, including the faith of Abraham, the sure mercies requested by David, and the visions of the Prophets. We thank You Father God for giving us the unction of the Holy Spirit, so we may receive our share of the Kingdom spiritual blessings personified by Your presence, Lord Jesus, in Your Revival *Ekklesia*!

Revival of Jesus' Ekklesia as Seen by Matthew

Revival of Jesus'
Ekklesia as Seen by Matthew

JESUS' COMMANDMENT IS TO MAKE DISCIPLES OF ALL NATIONS AND TRAIN BELIEVERS TO PROPERLY HANDLE KINGDOM AUTHORITY.

Matthew 28:18-20 says, "All power (authority) is given unto Me in heaven and in earth. Go ye therefore, and teach (make disciples of) all nations, baptizing them in the name of the Father, and of the Son, and of the Holy Ghost: Teaching them to observe all things whatsoever I have commanded you: and, lo, I am with you always, *even* unto the end of the world."

The Greek word in this scripture passage for power ("authority") is "*exousia,*" not "*dunamis.*" "*Exousia*" means Jesus, with His divine nature and humanity nature, received from God the Father meaning for authority is Kingly supreme authority, Kingdom unlimited dominion, absolute rulership, unqualified freedom to act, total force, complete power, competency to act, omnipresence, omniscience, omnipotence on earth, all inherit rights, and ownership of the entire earth. Only Jesus, with His divine nature as the Present One and His humanity nature as the Ascended One, has the jurisdictional Kingdom authority as man's Mediator to be the Liberator, Savior, King, Lord, and High Priest of all things created, including the people whom call upon His name entrance into the Kingdom of God and for salvation, deliverance, healing, and provision by being citizens of heaven.

Does verse 19 say, make converts? No, it means, make disciples of the Kingdom of God of its King Christ Jesus. Disciples are those whose souls have been matured through discipline by God the Word (Ephesians 5:26), God the Holy Spirit (Romans 8:13), and God the Father (John 15:2) indwelling transformation and through God's assigned Ephesians 4:11 ministers for the equipping of the saints for the work of the Kingdom ministry (Ephesians 4:12).

The phrase all nations does not mean governments, politics, or bureaucracies. The Greek word for nations is *ethnos*, which means ethnic groups or nationalities or those with particular cultural traditions. It refers to the ethnicity of people whose boundaries here on earth have been established by God. Acts 17:26-27 says, "And He has made from one blood every nation of men to dwell on all the face of the earth, and has determined their pre-appointed times and the boundaries of their dwellings, so that they should seek the Lord...."

Matthew 28:20 ends with the Lord saying "...and lo, I am with you always, even to the end of the age." In the context of making disciples and teaching them... the phrase in verse 20 means that Jesus' divine nature, who is omnipresent, will be with Believers until His school of discipleship training is out. Believers will be discipled the rest of their lives as Christ's divine nature will be constantly training, maturing, and cleansing them. School is never over until Jesus' humanity nature returns to earth or they die and go to be with Him in Heaven. The Greek word for "end" in verse 20 is *sunteleia,* meaning "entire completion and specifically a consummation of a dispensation." The Greek word for "age" is *aion,* which means "*Ekklesia* age, course, eternal purpose, and continuous duration or period." Therefore, Jesus is saying that His divine nature always will be with His *Ekklesia* to disciple the Believers and to be the place of the habitation of the entire Godhead. Jesus' divine nature will always be training all Believers because there is always a higher place of obedience to His Word in which He is requiring of His children.

"Teaching them to observe all things whatsoever I have commanded you" in verse 20 is the main topic of this study. What was it that Jesus commanded Believers to teach other disciples to make them mature and useful in His Kingdom as servant citizens and obedient children? The Greek word for "commanded" is *entellomai*, which means "to enjoin, charge, command." The word is of the same family as the Greek word "*teleo*," which means "to complete, accomplish, end, expire, fulfill, finish, gone, made, make over, pay, or forever." The word used here is a Kingly term, so what did Jesus command? He told His disciples to preach the kingdom of God (Matthew 4:17), preach repentance and remission of sins (Luke 24:47), heal the sick, and then He said John 13:34-35, "A new commandment I give unto you, that ye love one another; as I have loved you, that ye also love one another. By this shall all men know that ye are my disciples, if ye have love one to another."

The Apostle Matthew, being trained as an accountant, a tax collector, prior to becoming a disciple and apostle of Jesus, was inspired to orderly put in the Gospel of Matthew five parts or places where he said Jesus completed, finished, or ended His sayings, parables, or commandments. These five areas specifically are the words He commanded to be taught by Believers to make disciples of all nations as mandated in Matthew 28:19-20. To find these five areas or places of His sayings, parables, or commandments, one may look at where Jesus had used the Greek word *teleo* to conclude that He had finished or ended His sayings, parables, or commandments in that discourse or sermon. These five areas or places of His teachings can be found in Matthew 7:28, 11:1, 13:53; 19:1 and 26:1.

SCRIPTURES IN MATTHEW WHERE JESUS "FINISHED" OR
"ENDED" HIS SAYINGS, PARABLES, OR COMMANDMENTS, AND
TEACHINGS WHICH ARE TO BE TAUGHT TO DISCIPLES OF ALL NATIONS

MATTHEW 7:28: This verse says, "And so it was, when Jesus had ended (*sunteleo*--to complete entirely, finish, fulfill, make) these sayings (*logos*-- divine expressions intended later to become the written word), that the people were astonished at His teaching...." Jesus had finished His Sermon on the Mount. Jesus' sayings are important and should be taught to new Believers to make mature disciples of them that are saved during this next great Revival as commanded by Matthew 28:18-20 and prophesized as the Third Progressive Stage of the Revival in Joel 2.

MATTHEW 5: This chapter starts out in verses 1-12 with Jesus' teachings called the "Beatitudes." In each Beatitude, a blessing is proclaimed, identifying the ones being blessed, along with an explanation of or the reason for the blessing. In verses 13-16, Jesus teaches that His disciples are the salt of the earth for seasoning and light unto the world for illuminating the glory of the Father. In verses 17-20 Jesus then taught that He did not come to abolish the law or the Prophets but to fulfill what was written in the Law and the Prophets. Jesus teaches the Jews that the law was given because Israel was the spouse of God after coming out of Egypt (Jeremiah 3:14; 31:32), but God related to them by dwelling in a natural tabernacle built according to a pattern. The Holy Spirit came upon them, not in them. However, Jesus is saying that He is bringing a Kingdom that shall be within man, giving reference to the fact that He needs to prepare and build His *Ekklesia* as the dwelling place of the Godhead. This is why Jesus teaches on issues dealing with the heart, such as in verse 22 to exhibit anger toward someone or call someone a fool being the same as murder, in verses 23 to 26 that the impure heart when you have odds against someone as affecting your gift, and in verses 27 to 30 lust toward a woman the same as committing adultery. In verses 31 and 32 Jesus introduces a higher law on marriage and declares it to be sacred and binding. In verses 33 to 37 He disdains the taking of oaths and says just let your "yes" be "yes" and "no" be "no." In verse 38 to 42 He further gives instruction to seek reconciliation, go the extra mile and avoid lawsuits. In verses 43 to 48 He concludes with the command to love your enemies, as this is the higher law. These are some of the commandments which disciples must be taught and trained to do.

MATTHEW 6: In verses 1 to 4 Jesus teaches that Believers should do their charitable deeds to please God, not men. In verses 5 to 15, Jesus introduces the model prayer. The Greek word for "*pray*" in verse 6 is *proseuchomai*, which means "to go onward with God." It means when Believers pray earnestly to be disciples of the Lord, then bring up what is in their hearts with purity, honesty, forthrightness as this will please God. Believers are not to just pray out loud in the Church just to be heard by men. Jesus continued with instructions to Believers to fast to be seen only by God and not to be religious. The best teaching by Jesus in this portion of Matthew is in verses 19 to 33. He taught Believers to lay up treasures in Heaven, not on earth, do not worship the god of mammon, and seek first the Kingdom of God and His righteousness and all other things shall be added to Believers. The Kingdom of God is Believers' place of provision, blessings, and protection.

MATTHEW 7:1-6: In verses 1 to 6, Jesus warns His disciples not to judge. In describing the goodness of His Father, He says keep asking, seeking, and knocking to God who will give Believers what they need because God is the best Father who loves Believers. In verse 12 He pronounced the "Golden Rule" to do unto others as you would have them do unto you. In verses 13 and 14 Jesus said Believers must enter by the narrow way of closeness of relationship with God. In verses 15 to 20 Jesus warns Believers of false prophets, as they are like trees with bad roots that bear bad fruit. In verses 21 to 23 Jesus says that Believers who do the will of God the Father here on earth shall enter the kingdom of Heaven. Obedience to Jesus' sayings denotes mature discipleship. In verses 24 to 29 Jesus then concludes that those Believers who hear and obey His sayings are compared to a wise man who built his house on the rock as opposed to the foolish man who built his house on the sand. When the storms came, the house built on the rock stood and the one on the sand fell.

MATTHEW 11:1: This verse says, "Now it came to pass, when Jesus finished (*teleo*) commanding His twelve disciples, that He departed from there to teach (*didasko*) and to preach in their cities." Here, again, the reference of the end of this teaching, saying or commandment is the Greek word *teleo*, which is of the same Greek family as the word "commanded" in Matthew 28:20. Matthew 11:1 directly refers to Jesus' teachings, revelations, and commandments in Matthew, chapters 8, 9 and 10.

MATTHEW 8: Verses 5 to 8 present the faith of the Centurion directly connected to authority in the Kingdom and obedience to Jesus' words. Jesus introduces His work of healing the sick as part of His office ministry. Jesus teaches His disciples the true cost of discipleship in verses 18 to

20. Jesus then instructs His disciples to use His authority over the elements, the sea, and the wind in verses 23 to 27. In verses 28 to 34 Jesus demonstrates His authority which He delegates to His disciples over the demons and the kingdom of darkness.

MATTHEW 9: In verses 1 to 8 Jesus teaches Believers that some sicknesses are result of sin in the person, but He has the power to forgive sins and heal. In verses 9 to 13, in calling Matthew, a tax collector as a disciple, Jesus teaches He came to bring mercy for sinners and that no one is disqualified to receive salvation and entry into His Kingdom. In verses 14 to 17 Jesus reveals His office as the Bridegroom and the joy of the disciples being with the Bridegroom. In verses 18 to 31 Jesus informs His disciples how faith can make one receive healing. Jesus concludes the chapter by teaching His disciples the gospel of the kingdom and demonstrating the power of the kingdom. Then Jesus offers His most relevant statement that the harvest is plentiful, but the laborers are few. He instructs His disciples to pray that the Lord of the Harvest sends forth the laborers.

MATTHEW 10: In Matthew 10 Jesus sends out His twelve disciples to minister. He gave them specific instructions to be taught to new disciples. In verses 7 and 8 Jesus tells them to preach that the Kingdom of Heaven is at hand, a reference that the Messiah has come. He said, "heal the sick, cleanse the lepers, raise the dead, cast out demons."

This mandate is still good today! As Believers are sent out to preach the gospel of the Kingdom and preach repentance and the remission of sins, the spiritual signs should follow. In verses 16 to 26 Jesus says that His disciples will be hated and persecuted for Jesus' name's sake. In verses 27 to 31 Jesus teaches Believers that one should fear God instead of man as only God can kill the soul. In verses 32 to 33 He then says as Believers confess or deny Him before men, He will do the same before His Father in Heaven. In verses 34 to 39 Jesus said that He did not come to bring peace between His *Ekklesia* and the world, but to bring division by calling out and separating His *Ekklesia* from the world. In verses 40 to 42 Jesus finally says he who receives His disciples receives Jesus and God the Father, and he who gives to a prophet, or a righteous man receives the reward from God the Father of a prophet or righteous man.

MATTHEW 13:53: This verse says, "Now it came to pass, when Jesus had finished (*teleo*) these parables, that He departed from there." Matthew 13:53 is a reference to the parabolic teachings in Matthew, chapters 11, 12 and 13.

MATTHEW 11: In verses 4 to 19 Jesus teaches Believers that His ministry can be judged by both gospel of the Kingdom and repentance and remission of sins being preached with the miracle signs following. Jesus defends John the Baptist as the greatest prophet of the Old Covenant and is the fulfillment of Malachi 4:5-6, as John the Baptist had the spirit of Elijah and was the forerunner of the Messiah. Then Jesus says that the kingdom of God suffers violence and the violent take it by force. Jesus says in verses 20 to 24 woe to the impenitent cities who reject the gospel of the kingdom and the suffering and death on the Roman Cross for the forgiveness of sins. In verses 25 to 30 Jesus says only in Him is true rest for He is gentle and humble. His yoke is easy, and His burden is light.

MATTHEW 12: Jesus instructs in verses 1 to 21 that He is Lord of the Sabbath, and all things are lawful since He is God's anointed. Jesus further teaches Believers in verses 22 to 30 that a house or kingdom divided against itself cannot stand, and those who are not with Him are against Him. In verses 31 to 32 Jesus teaches His disciples about the unpardonable sin. In verses 33 to 37 Jesus teaches Believers that a tree is known by its fruit, and out of the abundance of the heart, where there are beliefs or roots, the mouth speaks, which is where the fruit comes forth. In verses 38 to 42 Jesus tells the Pharisees and scribes that the only sign He will give them is the sign of Jonah, as the Son of Man will spend three days and rights in the heart of the earth. In verses 43 to 45 Jesus warns that when a demon is cast out and the Holy Spirit is not moved in, the demon, along with seven others, will return and the condition is worse than before. In verses 46 to 50 when Jesus' mother and brothers seek Him to come out and speak with them, Jesus says, those who do the will of His Father in Heaven are His brothers, sisters, and mother. He explains the existence of a new spiritual family.

MATTHEW 13: Each of these parables was a lesson about the kingdom of Heaven where salvation was the divine benefit but not the goal of God the Father for sending His only begotten Son to earth. Father God mandates Believers to be Kingdom spiritual Ambassadors and Kingdom spiritual Soldiers to take back possession of the earth, world system, and the people through reconciliation and salvation by the delegated Kingdom authority from the absolute authority God the Father gave to Jesus, with His divine nature and humanity nature. In verses 3 to 23 the first parable taught and explained by Jesus was the parable of the Sower, where the Word of God is sown in the hearts of people, whose hearts are defined as four different soils. The last and best soil is he who hears the word, understands it and then obeys it to bear fruit, some one-hundred-fold, some sixty-fold and some thirty-fold. In verses 24 to 30 and 37 to 43 the Lord taught and explained the parable of the wheat and tares, where the purity of conduct Believers are not to be overly concerned, as the pure hearted and religious Believers will be separated by God's angels on Judgment Day. Premature separation of the pure hearted and religious Believers will bring too much division in the *Ekklesia*.

In each of the parables about the Mustard Seed, Leaven, Hidden Treasure, Pearl of Great Price and Dragnet, Jesus always taught Believers on the Kingdom of Heaven. The kingdom of Heaven is alive, costly, precious and of eternal value, and will be like a dragnet gathering of fish on the Day of Judgment.

Every disciple must be trained, per Jesus' commandment in Matthew 28:20, concerning the nature and value of the kingdom of Heaven. Matthew used the phrase "kingdom of Heaven" in thirty verses and the "kingdom of God" in only five verses. The other Gospels speak solely of the "kingdom of God," but the reference is to God's kingdom. The Kingdom of Heaven denotes the source of the Kingdom, whereas the Kingdom of God reveals the Author of the Kingdom. Thus, the phrases are interchangeable and do not denote a conflict in the phrases used.

MATTHEW 26:1: This verse says, "Now, it came to pass, when Jesus had finished (*teleo*) all these sayings (*logos*), that He said to His disciples..." This verse is referring to Jesus' sayings in chapters 19, 20, 21, 22, 23, 24 and 25.

MATTHEW 19: In verses 2 to 12 Jesus teaches His disciples that a higher law is a marriage without divorce and commends those who have been called to live a life of a Eunuch for Heaven's sake, and Jesus uses the opportunity to teach His disciples about giving everything to the Lord in His discourse with the Rich Young Ruler. Jesus teaches the principle of a one-hundred-fold return along with everlasting life to those who enter the Kingdom and give up those things of this world. This is not a vow of poverty, but a great exchange of the things that are passing away for those that are eternal.

MATTHEW 20: In verses 1 to 16 Jesus uses the Parable of the Workers in the Vineyard to teach Believes that rewards are given by God's Kingdom standards, not the world's standards. In verses 20 to 28 Jesus deals with the competition of His disciples as to who is the greatest. Jesus teaches His disciples that the greatest is he who is the servant and who seeks to be last not first.

MATTHEW 21: In verses 1 to 11 is an enacted parable to fulfill prophecy with Jesus' Triumphal Entry. Jesus cleanses the temple calling it a house of prayer instead of a den of thieves. In verses 18 to 22 Jesus teaches His disciples the lesson of the withered fig tree. In verses 28 to 32, Jesus teaches Believers the Parable of the Two Sons. One son said he would obey but did not while the other son said he would not but repented and did the will of his father. Jesus compared the priests and elders to the son who said he would obey the father but went his way and did not. The religious ones are those who just give mere lip service, as the obedient son is the one who has a good heart. The religious "say and do not." In verse 33 to 46 Jesus then gives them the Parable of the wicked vine dressers who killed or persecuted all those sent to gather the fruit, including killing the vineyard owner's son, an obvious reference to Jesus and His Father in Heaven. Jesus tells them that the Kingdom of God will be given to another.

MATTHEW 22: In verses 1 to 14 Jesus compares the kingdom of God to a wedding feast where those originally invited would not come because they were more concerned about their farms and businesses. He then invited strangers to the feast. The references were to the Jews, who rejected the invitation, and the Gentiles, who will accept Jesus as the Bridegroom. The Pharisees, Herodians, and Sadducees in verses 15 to 46 tested Jesus, trying to entrap Him with questions: (a) Is it lawful to pay taxes to Caesar? (b) Are there marriages in the resurrection? and (c) What were the greatest commandments? Jesus was able to outwit them easily, and the religious leaders were all befuddled. However, Jesus finally asked the one question which they could not answer, and they stopped asking Him any questions after that. Jesus asked them the meaning of Psalm 110:1 where David called his prophesied Greater Grand Son, "Lord."

MATTHEW 23: In this chapter Jesus instructed His disciples to do as the scribes and Pharisees say but not as they do, "...For they say, and do not do." Jesus rebuked the Pharisees and scribes for their hypocritical self-righteousness. He criticized them for their outward practice of religiosity but as having no inner relationship with God. Jesus criticized them because they had issued countless rules and regulations in interpreting the Mosaic Law which had put heavy burdens on the people that they, themselves, do not follow. The scribes and Pharisees had erected barriers to stop the people from receiving the Truth. The scribes and Pharisees were more interested in the form instead of the substance of the Law. Finally, in verses 37 to 39 Jesus lamented over Jerusalem who He said kills the prophets and stones those who are sent to Her.

MATTHEW 24: In this chapter in verses 1 to 14 Jesus talks about the signs that will appear before His return, such as wars and rumors of wars, nation revolting or attacking other nations, famines, pestilence, and earthquakes in various places. Persecution against the Church will increase, and many false prophets will be in the land. In verse 14, the end-times will also be evident with the *Ekklesia* preaching the gospel of the kingdom and repentance and remission of sins "...in all the world as witness to all the nations, and then the end will come." In verses 15 to 31 Jesus then describes the Great Tribulation that precedes the coming of the Son of Man. In verses 32 to 44 Jesus gives the parable of the fig tree and says no one knows the day or hour of His return except the Father. Finally, Jesus warns His disciples to be faithful, and He gives them a parable of the Faithful and Evil Servants.

MATTHEW 25: Jesus continues His teaching of the futuristic expression of the kingdom of Heaven. In verses 1 to 13 He compares the kingdom to ten Virgins who are waiting for the return of the Bridegroom, five faithful who keep their lamps full of oil, representing the anointing of the Holy Spirit, and five unfaithful who fail to keep their lamps full of oil, representing the loss of the anointing of the Holy Spirit. The "virgins" represent the Church (as virgins are not lustful in the world), but some become lukewarm, religious whose excitement and heart grow cold in their waiting. They have loss the zeal of the Lord. In verses 14 to 30 Jesus instructs His disciples with the Parable of the Talents. The first servant is given five talents, which he doubles in his Master's absence. The second servant is given two talents, which he doubles in his Master's absence. However, the third servant is given only one talent, but he buries it in the ground. To the first two the Master rewards them by giving rulership over many things. The servant who hid his talent in the ground was punished and his talent taken away and given to him who had ten talents. Contrary to the belief or practice of some, there is a Godly work to be done after initial salvation.

In verses 31 to 46 Jesus instructs about the Day of Judgment, impliedly speaking about both the White Throne Judgment (Revelation 20: 11-15) and the Judgment Seat of Christ (Romans 14:10; 2 Corinthians 5:10). Those who come into the kingdom of Heaven will be judged as to whether they have ministered to those in the Body of Christ who are spiritual and physically hungry, thirsty, naked, lonely, sick or in bondage. Jesus said when you have ministered to the "least of My brethren" (referencing to those in the Body of Christ), you have ministered to Me.

THE ONLY PLACE IN THE GOSPELS WHERE JESUS INSTRUCTS
HIS DISCIPLES CONCERNING HIS *EKKLESIA* IS ALSO PART
OF THE TEACHINGS OF JESUS BY MATTHEW WHICH ARE
TO BE TAUGHT TO DISCIPLES IN THIS END TIME REVIVAL.

MATTHEW 19:1: This verse says, "Now it came to pass, when Jesus had finished (*teleo*) these sayings, that He departed from Galilee and came to the region of Judea beyond the Jordan." This was a reference to the discourse Jesus had with His disciples in Matthew, chapters 15, 16, 17, and 18.

Theses chapters are the only places in the four Gospels where Jesus specifically speaks about His *Ekklesia*, meaning "the Lord's Kingdom government assembly, the Lord's Kingdom military assembly, the called-out ones, those sent to do Kingdom service, a Kingdom community of Believers and the dwelling place of the Lord." Looking at the context of scripture, one must determine how the word *Ekklesia* is being used. The word *Ekklesia* is a government assembly and/or a military assembly in the Lord's Kingdom, which is far greater than the Church as an educational assembly as practiced today. The Roman legislature during the time of Caesar was called the *Ekklesia*. Also, in Acts 19:34-41 the word *Ekklesia* three times was translated as government assembly. In this context the secular council meeting, called an *Ekklesia*, was formed to determine what to do with Paul and his co-workers for preaching the gospel of the Kingdom and repentance and remission of sins in their city. The secular rulers in the city were threatened because these Believers were introducing a new Kingdom rule in their city, so they formed a government assembly which in the Greek they called an *Ekklesia*. On the other hand, in Matthew 16:18-19 the reference to *Ekklesia* is as a Kingdom military army doing battle against the kingdom of darkness, not a Kingdom government assembly.

Again, in Matthew 19:1 the Greek word *teleo* is used. A word of the same Greek family is used in Hebrews 12:23, which says, "...to the saints of just men made perfect." The Greek word for "perfect" in Hebrews 12:23 is "*teleioo*," which means "to grow in mental character, to complete, to accomplish, be consecrated, finished, mature, or to make perfect. The purpose of Jesus' sayings, parables, and commandments is to make perfect or mature the disciples in His Church. If disciples follow these teachings of Jesus in this end time Revival, they will be "finished spiritual adults," matured by the Godhead. God the Father prunes away the flesh's influence out of the soul (John 15: 1-3); God the Word washes away the dirty flesh out of the soul (Ephesians 5:26), and God the Holy Spirit mortifies the deeds of the flesh out of the soul (Romans 8:13-14).

However, why is the Lord perfecting His *Ekklesia*? Do Scriptures connote a specific purpose? You can find the answers in this chapter regarding the book of Matthew. Matthew was the only book of the four Gospels of Matthew, Mark, Luke, and John where Jesus specifically spoke about His *Ekklesia*. It is very important for Believers to study what Jesus said about His *Ekklesia* so that the new wine being poured out in this end time Revival will be poured into a new wineskin as made by Jesus. Jesus spent three and one-half years with His disciples here alive on earth building His new wineskin or *Ekklesia*, and His life was poured into this new wineskin by the Holy Spirit on the Day of Pentecost.

MATTHEW 15: In verses 1 to 20 Jesus teaches that the scribes and the Pharisees transgress the law because of their oral traditions. It is what comes out of the mouth that defiles a man. Any person whom God the Father has not planted will be pulled up by the roots. The religious leaders are the blind leading the blind. What defiles a man is what is in his heart.

MATTHEW 16: In verses 1 to 4 Jesus replied to the Pharisees and Sadducees who came to Him to show them a sign. Jesus rebukes them as being able to interpret signs regarding weather, but they were unable to interpret the spiritual signs of the times. In verses 5 to 12 Jesus instructs His disciples to beware of the leaven of the Pharisees and Sadducees, referring to their doctrines and practices. The Pharisees were religious in their practices in following an orderly structure of rules and regulations under the Mosaic Law, but they lacked the presence of, and relationship with, God. The Pharisees were not only the chief ruling party but also the patriotic party, faithful to the Jewish nation. They loved their religion and country and were zealous to protect it. They put their trust in religious practices. They had the Mosaic laws, including the Ten Commandments and Rabbinic teachings, but they had mere religion without the Life, Himself, the Messiah. Similarly, the Sadducees were like our present-day Modernists or Church Liberals, who did not believe in the resurrection, did not believe that the Holy Spirit inspired the word of God, did not believe that angels or spirits existed, and did not believe in the resurrection from the dead (Acts 23:8). There are many Modernists or Church Liberals today who do not believe that the Bible is the inspired word of God, do not believe that Jesus is the Son of God, do not believe that Jesus was born of a virgin, do not believe that He died on the Cross, do not believe that His blood was shed for our redemption, and do not believe that He was raised physically from the dead. The

Pharisees and Sadducees needed to know Jesus in a living way in order to know the power of God, needed to know that the Lord Jesus' divine nature is the living God the Word. Since God is living, His people must be living, as God is the God of the living, not the dead (Matthew 22:29-32). The Pharisees and Sadducees were of the old wineskin and were the leaven to be avoided.

Jesus followed with the teaching that His presence in His Church brings life, power, and purpose. In Matthew 16: 13-20 Jesus mentions the *Ekklesia*, for the first time.

Jesus first asked His disciples a question of whom men say that He is. Some of the disciples say that other people say that Jesus is John the Baptist, Elijah, Jeremiah or one of the other prophets, all, by the way, were dead men. Peter finally answered, "You are the Christ, the Son of the living God." This is the revelation, or teaching that Jesus wants His disciples to know-- that His presence and relationship with Him brings to them the living God Who is the great I Am. Yet, Peter's revelation of Jesus as the Christ is only part of the revelation which Jesus wanted His disciples to know. He also wanted them to know that they will be His Body, and He would be the Head.

Jesus said in verse 18: "And I also say to you that you are Peter (*petros*--part of the rock or small piece of rock), and on this rock (*Petra*--the foundational Chief Corner Stone) I will build (*oikodomeo*--make dwelling place) my Church (*Ekklesia*-- Kingdom government assembly or military assembly, but in this case military assembly), and the gates of Hades shall not prevail against it." Again the Greek *Ekklesia* was wrongfully translated as "church" which subdued the rank and file Believers without authority as the word "church" involves the ranking authority lording over the laity Believers. The operative word here is "also." Jesus says that Peter (*petros*) is a piece of the Rock (*Petra*). The *petros* is representative of the Body of Christ and the *Petra* is the Head of that Body. Peter had the revelation that Jesus was the Christ or Messiah, the Son of God; but Peter did not have a revelation of the Body of Christ or *Ekklesia*, Jesus was giving the second part of the revelation to His disciples that the *Ekklesia* will be outside the established religious structure that was then in existence headed up by the Pharisees and Sadducees whom He had just confronted in verses 1 to 4 and warned His disciples about in verses 5 to 12.

The word "Rock" (*Petra*) and the word "build" (*oikodomeo*) are the same words used by Jesus in Matthew 7:24, which says, "Therefore whoever hears these sayings (*logos*-- word of God) of Mine, and does (*poieo*-- obedient performance of) them, I will liken him to a wise man who built (*oikodomeo*-- make dwelling place) his house on the rock (*Petra*-- the foundation Chief Corner Stone)."

The Greek word for "does" in the verse is *poieo*, which is a word of the same family as the Greek word *prasso*, meaning "to practice doing or making an act an ongoing habit." *Poieo*, however, is a reference to the individual act of doing without delay each part of the Lord's sayings. *Poieo* is a Greek word in the same family as the word *poiema* in Ephesians 2:10, "For we are His workmanship (*poiema*), created in Christ Jesus for good works, which God prepared beforehand that we should walk in them." Thus, it is a direct reference to allow the Head, Christ Jesus, through His divine nature, to do an artistic work in you, as a Believer, in order to do a work through you to build His *Ekklesia*.

Jesus was, and is, a wise Master Builder who knows how to build the House, Tabernacle, or Temple of God. Jesus knew what He was talking about since He worked as a stone mason and a carpenter, was trained by His stepfather, Joseph, as a young boy, teenager, and during His early years of manhood prior to going into full time ministry in His thirtieth year. Jesus was a journeyman stone mason and a carpenter who discipled His half-brothers how to be good carpenters after Joseph died. He used this same journeyman-training methodology to disciple His Apostles. Jesus intends to build together Believers as citizens of Heaven to make them God's dwelling place as His *Ekklesia*.

God the Father, God the Word, and God the Holy Spirit will live in the New Wineskin where the New Wine is stored (John 14:16-17,23), with Kingdom *zoe* life, *agape* love, with *exousia* authority from the Lord, *dunamis* power of the Holy Spirit, and the *karpos* fruit of the Spirit is poured into the new *Ekklesia* structure built upon relationship with the Lord and built upon the leading of the Holy Spirit. This means God wants to *koinonia* (fellowship) with Believers, which means communicate intimately, contribute to the Believer's welfare, minister through them to touch others in the world with His love and Kingdom benevolence while having a close, interacting daily fellowship with Believers. God wants to live in Believers and live amongst them. God is building His Kingdom Temple, Tabernacle, family, house, and *Ekklesia* in such a way that the citizens in His Kingdom will also have *koinonia* with each other in the same way. Thus, when the storms come, the *Ekklesia* will not be destroyed because the Lord made it a dwelling place where Jesus is the Foundation, the Rock, and Chief Cornerstone, and Believers are the living stones as a spiritual house (1 Peter 2:4-9). Jesus' divine nature is going to build His *Ekklesia* and the gates of Hades shall not prevail against her. Jesus' divine nature is going to personally be the Great Shepherd living amongst His sheep to disciple, cleanse, and mature her as His Body and *Ekklesia* (John 10:11,14,16; Hebrews 13:20; 1 Peter 2:25; 5:4).

John 17:21-23 says, "That they all may be one; even as You, Father, are in Me and I in You, that they also may be in Us; that the world may believe that You have sent Me. And the glory which You have given Me I have given to them, that they may be one, even as We are one; I in them, and You in Me, that they may be perfected into one, that the world may know that You have sent Me and have loved them even as You have loved Me." Similarly, John 15:9-13 says, "As the Father loved Me, I also have loved you; abide in My love. If you keep My commandments, you will abide in My love, just as I have kept My Father's commandments and abide in His love. These things I have spoken to you, that My joy may remain in you, and that your joy may be full. This is My commandment, that you love one another as I have loved you. Greater love has no one than this, than to lay down one's life for his friends."

In Matthew 16:19, Jesus says, "And I will give you the keys of the kingdom of Heaven, and whatever you bind on earth will be bound in Heaven, and whatever you loose on earth will be loosed in Heaven." Jesus is giving Kingdom authority to His *Ekklesia*. There are *two keys* given by Jesus for His *Ekklesia* to use, one denoting the authority to bind the demonic spirits of darkness and the other to loosen the authority, power, fruit, anointing, and blessings from God through the Holy Spirit. The Greek word for "bind" is "*deo*," which means "to bind, knit, to tie up or wind up." The Greek word for "loose" is "*luo*," which means, "to reduce to the constituent parts." The power to bind and loose brings the *zoe* life, *agape* love, *exousia* authority, *dunamis* power, and the *karpos* fruit of the Spirit from the kingdom of Heaven to manifest as the Kingdom of God here on earth.

The Greek construction of the Scripture of "will be bound" and "will be loosed" indicates that

Jesus' divine nature will be in the Church He is building. His divine nature is the Present One, and He is the One who has activated the provisional benefits of the Cross and given them to members of His *Ekklesia*. Since Jesus' divine nature is living within Believers and dwelling amongst Believers when they gather in fellowship, and since everything Jesus does pleases God the Father, then whatever He wants done in His living tabernacle will be authorized by God the Father. Thus, Jesus' *Ekklesia* is given delegated Kingdom authority to minister with that authority that Jesus received from God the Father as stated in Matthew 28:18. The *Ekklesia* has the delegated *exousia* authority from Jesus and the *dunamis* power through the Holy Spirit to sow the earth with the Kingdom of Heaven, manifested by the very presence of the Godhead dwelling within the *Ekklesia* as His Body, Church, Tabernacle, Temple, and House.

In verses 24 to 28 Jesus instructs His disciples to deny themselves, take up their Crosses and follow Him. In order to build His Kingdom *Ekklesia* a great exchange of life must take place. Jesus insists that only He who is Life personified can manifest Himself in His Kingdom *Ekklesia*. Believers need to exchange their lives for His life. He concludes that the Son of Man is coming in His kingdom to reign forever. Jesus intends that His disciples will rule and reign with Him in His Kingdom.

MATTHEW 17: This chapter begins with the Mount of Transfiguration where Jesus manifests His eternal glory, and Moses and Elijah appear with Him in the vision for the disciples present to see. Although chapter 16 gave the disciples, especially Peter, the "revelation" of Jesus as the Head of His Body and *Ekklesia* Kingdom spiritual army, chapter 17 in verses 1 to 13 gives the three disciples (Peter, James and John) a "vision" of whom Christ is as the Greater Son of David, the Messiah, and Son of God. A vision causes a greater retention indelibly pressed into memory than a revelation. Peter ignorantly suggested to the Lord to make three tabernacles, elevating each person in the vision to an equal stature. Just six days before, Jesus had revealed to Peter the *Ekklesia* as the tabernacle or dwelling place for the Lord, and here Peter wants to establish "three" tabernacles, one for Moses, a second for Elijah and still a third for Jesus. Peter still is revering Moses and Elijah, the Law Giver and the prophet, as great men of God in the Hebrew religion and history. Jesus had already explained to Peter of a new Kingdom order, the revelation of Christ with His Church, the Head with His body. The Father interceded. While Peter was yet speaking "... a bright cloud overshadowed them; and suddenly a voice came out of the cloud, saying, 'This is My beloved Son, in whom I am well pleased. Hear Him!'" The Father was saying, "Moses and Elijah are not on an equal par with My Son, Jesus." There cannot be three tabernacles, or denominations, but only one Kingdom *Ekklesia*, one body united by one Spirit (Ephesians 4:4-6). The Father did not say to listen to Moses (the law) or Elijah (the prophets), but to listen to Him who had come to fulfill the law and the prophets.

Although Moses represented the law, and Elijah represented the prophets, there was something else significant about each of their bodies. Moses died in the land of Moab and was buried by God there in a place unknown by any man (Deuteronomy 34:5-6), and Elijah's body was carried up by God in a whirlwind (2 Kings 2:11). Thus, they had no bodies in known graves here on earth. Jesus' body is not in a grave here on earth. Jesus in His resurrected body ascended to the Third Heaven and took with Him Moses and Elijah and all those in the Bosom of Abraham or Paradise (Ephesians 4:8). However, the resurrected life of Jesus will be manifested in Believers, which Peter would be a part. Neither Moses nor Elijah could build a living tabernacle for God to have as a dwelling place. Only Jesus qualified as the Divine Carpenter from Heaven to build His living Tabernacle where the entire Godhead would dwell throughout eternity.

Jesus told His disciples not to tell anyone about the vision until the Son of Man is risen from the dead. Sensing that He is the Messiah, the disciples asked Him a point of Scripture: "Why do the scribes say that Elijah must come first?" Jesus told them that Elijah had already come, referring to John the Baptist as being in the spirit of Elijah, but the scribes did not know him. Likewise, He informed them that He was going to suffer at the hands of the leaders of the Hebrew religion because they did not recognize Him as the Messiah.

In verses 14 to 21 Jesus instructs His disciples regarding their faith and the need to die to self through prayer and fasting in order to manifest the Kingdom authority over all the demonic forces of darkness. The cause of their lack of spiritual authority was their lack of belief. In verses 22 to 23 Jesus predicts His death.

In verses 24 to 27 Jesus shows His ability to provide even the money to pay taxes. However, Jesus is still dealing with Peter's individualism. Peter is still trying to make Jesus look good in the eyes of the Hebrew religion during a discourse with the tax collectors who came to collect a temple tax. The tax collectors asked Peter, "Does your Teacher not pay the temple tax?" Peter answered quickly, "Yes!" Jesus asked Peter whether a king would require a tax to be paid by His sons or by strangers. Of course, Peter had already said the Son pays taxes to maintain the temple. Jesus was exempt from the temple taxes because He was the Son of God. Peter had declared that Jesus was the "Son of the living God," but he forgot so easily because of his religious, Hebrew upbringing. He did not bother discussing the issue of the temple tax with the Head, Jesus, nor his brothers as part of Jesus' Body, before he answered the tax collectors. Had he done so, he would have found out that they were exempt from tax on the natural temple. Notwithstanding, Jesus sends Peter alone to catch a fish, which will have a coin in it of sufficient value to pay the temple tax for Jesus (the Head) and Peter (as part of the Body), so as not to offend the authorities.

MATTHEW 18: In verses 1 to 14 Jesus answers the disciples' inquiry as to who is the greatest amongst the disciples in the kingdom of Heaven. Jesus says that unless they are converted and become like children, they will not be able to enter the kingdom of God. A child is totally dependent on his father for his sustenance. A child's primary purpose is to obey his father. A child should never do anything unless he or she first asks permission from the father. The one who humbles himself as a little child, Jesus says, is the greatest in the kingdom of Heaven. Jesus then warns not to lead the younger ones into sin. As leaders, the disciples have a serious responsibility to be true *Ekklesia* leaders in the kingdom of Heaven. Jesus instructs them to be good stewards over the sheep, and if one goes astray and sins, then it is the leader's job to go after the "young or baby Christian" and bring them back into the sheep fold. This is a major principle in the life in the *Ekklesia*.

In verses 15 to 20 Jesus further instructs His disciples as to how to deal with a sinning brother in the *Ekklesia* interaction of the Kingdom community life. When the *Ekklesia* is acting under the delegated authority of the Lord in bringing discipline, the purpose is always to restore the sinning brother, and not to wound the brother in the process. First go to the sinning brother in private; and if he will not listen, then take with you one or two other witnesses of the wrongdoing to see if he will repent. If he does not, then the brother must go before the local *Ekklesia* Kingdom community for discipline. If he still will not repent and change, then he is to be excommunicated so as not to contaminate others until he comes to his senses. Thus, authority to bind and loosen in verse 18 is a direct reference to the disciplining of a fallen brother. This is serious business to the Lord.

In verses 19 and 20, Jesus says that when two or three are gathered in His name, then He is amid them. Since He is amid them, then the favor of the Father is upon the gathering as the Father wants to bless the Son. Therefore, "if two of you agree on earth concerning anything that they ask, it will be done for them by My Father in Heaven." However, this Scripture has been misused to mean that people do not have to gather in a Kingdom community of Believers because Jesus said if two or three come together, He is in their midst. In the context this Scripture has with the topic being discussed in the previous Scripture, Jesus is referring to when people come together in an *Ekklesia* setting where the Lord's government, with Him as Head, is in function. Hebrews 10:25 makes it clear that people are not to forsake the assembling together as the *Ekklesia*.

Finally, Jesus instructs His disciples in verses 21 to 35 that the Kingdom community behavior should always be one of continuous forgiveness of each other for wrongs committed. Jesus uses the parable of a king who had forgiven his servant of ten thousand talents, the largest sum imaginable. This represents the forgiveness of the Father of our sins. The servant would not forgive a fellow servant who owed him only a hundred *denari*, a very small amount. Forgiveness is a vital element in Kingdom community living and *Ekklesia* discipline. In the context, if a brother sins or trespasses another, Jesus taught that he must be forgiven to restore him to the status of a brother. Jesus does not want divisions in His *Ekklesia*. Since we have been forgiven of so much, we should forgive those who trespass against us. Matthew 6:10 says to ask the Father to forgive us our trespasses as we forgive those whom trespass against us.

The delegated authority of the Believer by Christ Jesus to "bind and loose" can work against the Believer if he does not forgive.

The unforgiving servant was still in jail at the end of Jesus' parable. You can bind yourself up if you do not forgive others who have trespassed against you. Unforgiveness binds communication in the Kingdom community of Believers and can hurt the Revival. Thus, forgiveness is perhaps the greatest loosening force to express God's love here on earth to cultivate and enrich the Revival and to edify the *Ekklesia* and stop division.

PLEASE DIRECT YOUR HEARTS TOWARD THIS PRAYER:

"Father God, in Jesus' name, I pray that You inhabit Your people, who are the called-out ones. Lord, show me how to help You build Your *Ekklesia*, so that it will express Your glory here on earth in this Revival. Lord, teach me to be Your disciple who has turned my heart over to You. Jesus, You promised always to be with Your *Ekklesia* even unto the end of the age. Help me never to forget that I am always in Your school of discipleship. Lord, help me continue to seek after Your knowledge, understanding, and wisdom in Your word, which are spirit and life. Teach me, Lord, to be a faithful and obedient leader who will properly disciple those who come into the Kingdom of God during this end time Revival. May I never forget Your gracious gift of forgiveness. May the spirit of forgiveness bring down the walls that separate the members in Your *Ekklesia*, consisting of your Kingdom Government Assembly and Kingdom Army. Lord, help me to believe that You are indwelling Your *Ekklesia*, directing Your *Ekklesia*, and perfecting Your

Ekklesia. Lord, help me be a teacher to others of all You have commanded to be taught to Your disciples. In Jesus' name. Amen."

Christ's Resurrected Humanity Spirit and Life in the Revival Ekklesia

Christ's Resurrected Humanity Spirit and Life in the Revival Ekklesia

THE DIFFERENCE BETWEEN BAPTIZING BY THE SPIRIT AND DRINKING OF THE SPIRIT

1 Corinthians 12:13 says, "For in one Spirit (pneuma) were we all baptized (baptizo) into one Body (soma), whether Jews or Gentiles, whether bond(doulos) or free (eleutheros); and were all made to drink (potizo) of one Spirit (pneuma)."

Believers were not only baptized in one Spirit, but they also were made to drink of one Spirit. There is a difference between being baptized of the Spirit and drinking of the Spirit.

Suppose as a Believer, you have a large glass of water. If you stick your finger in the water, then your finger is baptized in the water. The water only touches the outside of your skin. The water stays separate from your finger. However, if you take the glass of water and drink its contents, then you have partaken of the water, and it gets inside of you and becomes a part of your body to quench your thirst. To be baptized in one Spirit, you are put under the water. However, if you drink the water the water becomes part of your body. The Spirit upon you is one experience, but the Spirit within you is a much more special, nourishing, and an intimate experience.

Jesus instructed His disciples in Acts 1 concerning the Holy Spirit. Acts 1:5,8 says, "For John baptized with water, but you shall be baptized in the Holy Spirit not many days from now…. But you shall receive power when the Holy Spirit comes upon you, and you shall be My witnesses both in Jerusalem and in all Judea and Samaria and unto the uttermost part of the earth." In these Scriptures, the Lord said that the Holy Spirit would come upon His disciples, and the Holy Spirit will empower them to be witnesses that Jesus is King with all authority in the spiritual and natural worlds as they preach the gospel of the Kingdom of God along with repentance and remission of sins throughout the known world.

Acts 10:38 says, "How God anointed Jesus of Nazareth with the Holy Spirit and with power: who went about doing good and healing all that were oppressed of the devil; for God was with Him." Jesus had the fullness of the Godhead within Him (Colossians 2:9). Thus, Jesus had both the Holy Spirit upon Him and the Holy Spirit, being part of the Godhead, inside Him. Being anointed by the Holy Spirit and with power is a similar experience that the Lord wants for His body of Believers to have.

WHAT DOES BEING BORN AGAIN MEAN?

Jesus said in John 3:16-18, "For God so loved the world, that He gave His only begotten Son, that whosoever believeth in Him should not perish, but have everlasting life. For God sent not His Son into the world to condemn the world; but that the world through Him might be saved. He that believeth on Him is not condemned: but He that believeth not is condemned already, because he hath not believed in the name of the only begotten Son of God."

Through the power and work of Christ's divine nature (1 Peter 1:23), Believers' born again spirits receive zoe life from Jesus' resurrected humanity nature as their organic Father (Isaiah 9:6; Hebrews 2:13). Thereby, Believers' born again spirits are joined in relationship to the Lord's humanity nature resurrected spirit by Jesus' divine nature, God the Word. This is a mystery but truth. 1 Corinthians 6:17 says, "But he who is joined to the Lord is one spirit with Him." Believers became new creatures in Christ Jesus as the Second Man (2 Corinthians 5:17; 1 Corinthians 15:47). When Believers were born from and were joined with Jesus' resurrected Spirit as one spirit, they received in their new born again spirits as the new Second Man the perfection, righteousness, and holiness of Christ's resurrected spirit of His humanity nature (Hebrews 12:23; Ephesians 4: 24; Colossians 1:22; 3:10) and the born again spirit does not sin (1 John 3:9). Believers' new born again spirits have the everlasting *zoe* life of the humanity nature of Jesus' resurrected spirit in John 3:16. Believers' new born again spirits are connected with Jesus' resurrected spirit of His humanity nature as the Last Adam and Second Man, just as Believers' souls still are connected to some degree with the soul of the first Adam until spiritual transformation is complete (Romans 12:2). Believers' souls were not born again, but they likewise are saved as far as living eternally with the Godhead. 1 Corinthians 15:45 says, "The Last Adam became a life-giving spirit." The *zoe*, everlasting, resurrected life of Christ's humanity nature which supernaturally is used to birth Believers' new born again spirits is manifested in Believers by Christ's divine nature, God the Word.

The Second Person of the Godhead is God the (*Logos*) Word (John 1:1). 1 Peter 1:23 says, "Being born again, not of corruptible seed, but of incorruptible (Seed), by the Word (*Logos*) of God, which liveth and abideth forever." This is how Christ's divine nature works with His humanity nature regarding initial salvation of new Believers. Although Believers' born again spirits are from the Seed of Christ Jesus' resurrected humanity nature, Believers are born again by the working of Jesus' divine nature, God the (*Logos*) Word, along with the power of the entire Triune Godhead. The members of the Triune Godhead work in unison as one to accomplish God's purpose. Believers' new born again spirits were born sinless by the power of God and do not sin. 1 John 3:9 says, "Whosoever is born of God doth not commit sin; for His (Christ's resurrected humanity nature) Seed remaineth in him: and he cannot sin, because he is born of God."

The soul must be transformed and put on the resurrected spirit of Christ by the Believer's soul putting on his born again spirit who are connected as one spirit with Christ as the new garment by primarily the ministry of Christ's divine nature, God the Word (John 1:1; Romans 12:2; Ephesians 4:24; 1 Corinthians 6:17). Matthew 9:16 says, "No one puts a piece of unshrunk cloth on an old garment; for the patch pulls away from the garment, and the tear is made worse."

The word "unshrunk" means "uncarded, unseamed and unwashed, unfinished, untreated wool." Believers' born again spirits are that new unshrunk cloth, and Believers' old spirit could not be attached to the New Garment of Christ without first being shrunk, carded, steamed, washed, finished, and treated. But the Believer's old unconscious spirit was not regenerated. The born again spirit was made brand new as a new creature in Christ filled with *zoe* life. Jesus is the last Adam through His death to remove Believers' sins and to become the Second Man in His resurrection (1 Corinthians 15: 45,47; Romans 6:11). Believers' born again spirits become that perfect piece of new cloth that is made ready to be attached to the New Garment of Jesus' resurrected humanity nature. But how does the soul become that new cloth that is attached to the New Garment of Christ? Believers' minds, emotions, and hearts of their souls are renewed through daily spiritual transformation from glory to glory into the image of the Lord's humanity nature by the power of Christ's divine nature (2 Corinthians 3:18). Once transformed, Believers' souls become the new cloth that is shrunk, carded, steamed, washed, finished, treated, and attached to Believers' born again spirits as the New Garment and New Man (Ephesians 4:24). Thereafter, Believers in their born again spirits enjoy intimate fellowship with Christ's divine nature and receives the Lord's resurrected everlasting life abundantly (John 10:10). Believers' souls which souls can enjoy the same intimate fellowship with Christ's divine nature to the extent that Believers' souls are spiritually transformed and have put on the new garment of the New Man, the born again spirits.

Believers' born again spirits have the perfection of Christ's spirit as part of His resurrected humanity nature, because Christ is the "Everlasting Father" of the new creation of Believers' born again spirits (Isaiah 9:6), just as Adam was the father of the old creation of fallen humanity (Romans 5:12-21). Hebrews 12:23 says, "...And to the (born again) spirits of just (*dikaios*- innocent, holy) men made perfect (*teleioo*- complete, totally mature, finished, flawless character)." Colossians 1:22 says, "Yet He has reconciled you (Believer) in His fleshly body through death, in order to present you (born again spirit) before Him holy and blameless and beyond reproach."

The Believer's born again spirit, which is the righteous and holy new man (Ephesians 4:24; Colossians 1:22; 3:10), member of the Second Man (1 Corinthians 15:47), and new creature in Christ (2 Corinthians 5:17), must come into the soul by the soul's invitation to participate in the soul's transformation. The soul needs to be spiritually transformed into the likeness of Christ, but the soul was not immediately perfected upon initial salvation as was the born again spirit. 2 Corinthians 3:18 says, "But we all, with open face beholding as in a glass the glory of the Lord (humanity nature), are changed into the same image from glory to glory, even as by the Spirit of the Lord (divine nature). A Believer's will is in the heart in the soul in the process of being spiritually transformed and submitted, not in the born again spirit which is already absolutely holy and righteous (Ephesians 4:24; Colossians 1:22; 3:10). In seeking first the Kingdom of God and His righteousness (Matthew 6:33), a Believer's will must submit to having the soul's carnality pruned by God the Father (John 15:2), the soul's carnal nature washed by the water of the *rhema* word by God the Word (Ephesians 5:26), and the soul's sinful deeds of the flesh mortified by God the Holy Spirit (Romans 8:13). Spiritual transformation in the soul will cause the Believer's soul to join in agreement with the Believer's born again spirit to live with humility before the Lord as His bondservant and to perform genuine loving service towards other Believers, while exercising spiritual gifts in Kingdom community for the edification of the Body of Christ. 3 John 2 says, "Beloved, I wish above all things that thou mayest prosper and be in health, even as thy soul prospereth." A Believer's prosperity and health are conditioned upon the Believer's soul having spiritual transformation. The word "even" in 3 John 2 means equal to or no more than or no less than the soul prospers spiritually similarly as to how the born again spirit and Christ's resurrected humanity nature are alike.

Jesus was the Firstborn from the dead as God's only begotten Son. Colossians 1:18, "And He is the head of the body, the church: Who is the beginning, the Firstborn from the dead; that in all things He might have the preeminence." Jesus' humanity nature was the only begotten Son born of God before the beginning of time and before the worlds began (John 17:5). Jesus' divine nature, as God the Word, was not born of God because He already is/was a member of the Godhead; so, the reference is to Jesus' humanity nature. Jesus' divine nature was not born and did not die as He is eternal and infinite; it was His humanity nature that was the Lamb of God that was slain on the Roman Cross while Jesus' divine nature acted as the High Priest that offered up Jesus' humanity nature as the Sacrificial Lamb. Colossians 1:18, states Jesus' humanity nature is the Firstborn from the dead. Since there was a Firstborn from the dead unto resurrected life, then there must be a second born, third born, fourth born and so on to several billionth born from the dead. Before being born again, Believers were dead in their sins (Ephesians 2: 5). So, after being born again, then each Believer's new spirit is the next in order born from the dead.

WHO IS THE FATHER OF BELIEVERS' BORN AGAIN SPIRITS?

Being born again is a reference to the birth of a new spirit in the new Believer and is not the independent regeneration of an old spirit that was dead unto his trespasses (Ephesians 2:1). Also, the born again spirit was not begotten directly by and from God the Father, as He is the Father of only One begotten Son, Jesus. Believers are adopted by God the Father, so Believers have the status of being children of God and joint heirs with Christ Jesus; but they were not begotten by God the Father as was Jesus (Romans 8:14-16). To make it clear, Believers are not God the Father's begotten second born, begotten third born, begotten fourth born, or begotten billionth born, as Christ Jesus is the only begotten of God the Father. Romans 8:15 says, "For ye have not received the spirit of bondage again to fear; but ye have received the Spirit of adoption, whereby we cry, Abba, Father." Believers are adopted children of God the Father and Believers' born again spirits are resurrected spiritually organic children of Jesus' resurrected humanity nature.

Romans 6:5-6 says, "For if we have been planted together in the likeness of his death, we shall be also in the likeness of his resurrection: Knowing this, that our old man (of the flesh in the soul) is crucified with Him, that the body of sin might be destroyed, that henceforth we should not serve sin." As the last Adam, Christ Jesus died on the Roman Cross, "blotting out the hand-writing of ordinances that was against us, which was contrary to us, and took it out of the way, nailing it to his cross" (Colossians 2:14).

Jesus' humanity nature became the Second Man upon His resurrection. Galatians 6:15 says, "For in Christ Jesus neither circumcision availeth anything, nor uncircumcision, but a new creature." By accepting the resurrection of Christ, Believers become members of the Second Man, Believers become new creatures in Christ with the resurrection life of Christ in their born again spirits, and old things pass away and behold all things become new (2 Corinthians 5:17). However, Believers were not born again in their souls, which have to be spiritually transformed by the God-head to rid Believers of the habitual desire to commit sin, even after receiving a born again spirit.

Jesus' resurrected humanity nature is the Second Man and Lord from Heaven (1 Corinthians 15:47). Jesus' resurrected humanity nature is the spiritual Father of the new creation of born again spirits of Believers (Isaiah 9:6; Hebrews 2:13), so Believers born again spirits are new creatures in Christ and do not sin (2 Corinthians 5:17; 1 John 3:9). Believers' born again spirits are the new man in Christ with resurrection life from Jesus' resurrected humanity nature, that is perfect, righteous, holy, and in the image of Christ (Hebrews 12:23; Ephesians 4:24; Colossians 3:10). Paul said in 1 Corinthians 15:45, "And so it is written, 'The first man Adam was made a living soul; the last Adam was made a quickening spirit.'" Jesus, as the last Adam and second man became a quickening spirit and the Lord from Heaven (1 Corinthians 15:45, 47). Believers are citizens of Heaven (Philippians 3:20), Ambassadors and Soldiers of the Kingdom of God (Luke 17:21; 2 Corinthians 5:20; 2 Timothy 2:3-4) and adopted children into the family of God

(Romans 8:15). Believers' born again spirits are in Christ, the Second Man and no longer in fallen First Adam (Romans 6:11). Adam had the stature as the natural father of the first man and thereafter the natural ancestor of fallen mankind. Christ Jesus' resurrected humanity nature spirit, as the Second Man, has the stature as the spiritual DNA Father of Believers' born again spirits (Isaiah 9:6; Hebrews 2:13). Believers' born again spirits are new creatures in Christ, and old things have passed away and all things became new (2 Corinthians 5:17). On the other hand, the Believer's soul did not experience being born again as a new creature in Christ because the soul still had memory of hurts, relationships, betrayals, joyful times, elations, sins, memories. So, the soul has to be transformed, and with the Believer's submission, by the Triune Godhead starts the transformation. God the Father prunes away the carnality in the soul (John 15:2). God the Word sanctifies and cleanses the flesh out of the soul by washing of water by the word (Ephesians 5:26). God the Holy Spirit mortifies or puts to death the deeds of the flesh in the soul to bring spiritual transformation.

I purposefully am repeating truths from scripture, so through repetition the relevance and illumination of these scriptural truths can become part of the belief foundation in Believers' hearts. Again, in Isaiah 9:6, the Messiah's humanity nature has the title of "The Everlasting Father." To be the "Everlasting Father," the Messiah must have "everlasting children." Referring to the Messiah in Isaiah 8:18, Hebrews 2:13, says, "And again, I will put my trust in Him. And again, 'Behold I and the children which God hath given Me.' Forasmuch then as the children are partakers of flesh and blood, He also Himself likewise took part of the same; that through death He might destroy him that had the power of death, that is, the devil." 1 John 3:8 says, "…For this purpose the Son of God was manifested, that he might destroy the works of the devil."

Being in Christ as one of the new creatures of mankind, the Believer's born again spirit is sinless, holy, perfect, pure, righteous, innocent, incorruptible, complete, fully mature, with flawless character (Hebrews 12:23; Ephesians 4:24; Colossians 3:10; 1 John 3:9). Under the leading of the Holy Spirit, the born again spirit brings from God's Kingdom into the soul godly, spiritual stimuli that also helps the soul become spiritually minded in thinking, spiritually emoting in feelings, and spiritually believing in the heart by receiving God's spiritual stimuli. The Believer's new born again spirit does not sin because it has been begotten from the perfect, sinless, Seed of the resurrected humanity nature of Jesus and is born by the power of Christ's divine nature, God the Word, along with the entire Godhead (John 1:1; 1 Peter 1:23; 1 John 3:9). In truth, although the Believer's soul received the gift of eternal life upon initial salvation and will not be thrown into the Lake of Fire at the White Throne Judgment (Revelation 20:15), the Believer's soul is not born again, is still partially in the First Adam, and has to be transformed spiritually to become an obedient servant in Christ (Romans 12:2). If the Believer's soul decides to become spiritually transformed in Christ, the soul will partake of the blessing of resurrected life that was birthed in the Believer's born again spirit. To do this, the Believer's soul must submit to being transformed as a mature spiritual member of the Body of Christ and must volunteer to be an active spiritual Kingdom Ambassador and trained spiritual Soldier in the Kingdom of God.

The Believer's soul has to submit to put on the new man (Ephesians 4:24), the Believer's born again spirit, and the soul and born again spirit must enjoy daily fellowship with each other. It is most important for the Believer's soul to come into agreement with the born again spirit. Jesus said in Matthew 18:19, "Again I say unto you, 'That if two of you shall agree on earth as touching anything that they shall ask, it shall be done for them of my Father which is in Heaven.'" In other words, when your soul comes into agreement with your born again spirit, who communes in fellowship with God and Christ, is sinless, and does not sin, then you will not ask from God something that God does not want you to have. The covenant of agreement between the transformed soul and the perfect, sinless born-again spirit through the power anointing and blessings came down to earth from heaven from God's spiritual realm.

The desire of the born again spirit to commune with the soul is because the born again spirit wants to be the new husband of the soul. The soul must divorce the body as her husband that has been her sole source of stimuli, and that worldly, carnal stimuli has corrupted the soul with sin. The soul will fall in love with the born again spirit because he has been born again by an incorruptible Seed from Jesus' resurrected humanity nature (1 Peter 1:23). The born again spirit is joined to the Lord Jesus Christ and is one spirit with Him (1 Corinthians 6:17), so the soul is able to experience Christ through the born again spirit in a practical way. Ephesians 4:24 says, "And that ye (soul where the Believer's mind, emotions, heart and will exist) put on the new (*kaimos*-freshness) man, which after God is created in righteousness (*dikaiosune*- holy, innocent) and true holiness (*hosiotes*- absolute purity)." Similarly, Colossians 3:10 says, "And have put on the new man, which is renewed in knowledge after the image of Him that created him." The new man is the Believer's born again spirit with the zoe resurrected life that was and is from the incorruptible Seed of Christ Jesus' humanity nature resurrected spirit (1 Peter 1:23). Jesus' divine nature, in assistance with the entire Godhead, will direct and help the born again spirit to come into the heart of the Believer's soul to change the foundation of beliefs in the heart to do a significant work for the soul's spiritual transformation.

Galatians 4:6 says, "And because ye are sons (of God by adoption), God hath sent forth the (born again) spirit (with new birth from) His Son (resurrected humanity nature spirit) into your hearts (in the soul), crying, 'Abba, Father.'"

As a Believer, your soul has to submit to God the Father in pruning away the branches yielding carnal fruit in your soul (John 15:2). Your soul has to submit to God the Word in the washing away the influence of your carnal flesh out of your soul and sanctifying your soul by the *rhema* word of God (Ephesians 5:26). Your soul has to submit to God the Holy Spirit who mortifies the deeds of the carnal flesh in your soul to make room for God's spiritual *zoe* life in Christ in His Kingdom (Romans 8:13). As your soul is transformed from carnality to spirituality in Christ (Romans 8:6; 12:2), then your soul can put on the new man born again spirit of true righteousness and absolute holiness in the area of the soul that has been cleansed of sins of the flesh and has truly made Jesus Lord.

Again, as a Believer, your soul can invite and put on your born again spirit as the new man, and resurrection *zoe* life will come into the soul. By the power of Christ's divine nature, your soul can put on Christ, Himself as your New Garment. Galatians 3:27 says, "As many of you as were baptized into Christ did put on Christ." The method is to be baptized by the Holy Spirit that gives you, as a Believer, anointing and power and then baptizes you with fire to burn the briers and brambles of sin out of your mind, emotions, and heart that come from the sins of the flesh, natural world, and the kingdom of darkness. Your soul maturation and transformation is a life exchanging experience that continues your entire life that makes your soul spiritually minded and renewed, spiritually emotional and stable, and spiritually submitted and obedient with Kingdom beliefs that direct your will to submit to the leading of the Holy Spirit. 1 Corinthians 2: 9 says,

"But as it is written, "Eye hath not seen, nor ear heard, neither have entered the heart of man, the things which God hath prepared for them that love Him.""

When Christ Jesus was crucified and then resurrected through the power of the Godhead (Romans 8:11), He became a life-giving *pneuma*, a fresh breath of living air (1 Corinthians 15:45). Before Pentecost, Jesus "breathed" on His disciples. John 20:21-22 says, "So Jesus said to them again, 'Peace to you! As the Father has sent Me, I also send you.' And when He had said this, He breathed on them, and said to them, 'Receive the Holy Spirit.'" Romans 8:11 says, "But if the Spirit of Him that raised up Jesus from the dead dwell in you, He that raised up Christ from the dead shall also quicken your mortal bodies by His Spirit that dwelleth in you."

The allusion in John 20:21-22 is to Genesis 2:7 where God "breathed" life into the first Adam. The first Adamic man started with a Breath of God, and the new created Second Man through Christ Jesus also started with the Breath of God the Word. In this meeting the disciples went through what Paul later describes in Romans 10:9, "That if thou shalt confess with thy mouth the Lord Jesus, and shalt believe in thine heart that God hath raised Him from the dead, thou shalt be saved." John 20:21-22 was the first time the disciples truly confessed Jesus as Lord and believed in their hearts that God raised Jesus from the dead because He had only then died on the Cross of Calvary and only then had been resurrected. The disciples now entered into salvation and received their new born again spirits. The new birth of a born again spirit experience revealed by Jesus, Paul, and Peter in John 3:3, 2 Corinthians 5:17, and 1 Peter 1:23 suddenly became reality; and the disciples' new born again spirits were holy and righteous and became part of the New Creature, the New Man, and the Second Man in Christ (2 Corinthians 5:17; 1 Corinthians 15:47; Ephesians 4:24).

Romans 8:8-13 says, "So then they that are in the flesh (in their souls) cannot please God. But ye are not in the flesh, but in the spirit, if so be that the Spirit of God (Holy Spirit) dwell in you. Now if any man have not the Spirit of Christ (born again spirit from Christ's humanity nature), he is none of His. And if Christ be in you, the body is dead because of sin; but the (new man born again) spirit is life because of righteousness. But if the Spirit (Holy Spirit) of Him (Father God) that raised up Jesus from the dead dwell in you, He that raised up Christ from the dead shall also quicken your mortal bodies by His Spirit that dwelleth in you. Therefore, brethren, we are debtors, not to the flesh, to live after the flesh. For if ye live after the flesh, ye shall die: but if ye through the Spirit (Holy Spirit) do mortify the deeds of the body, ye shall live."

Believers' born again spirits, joined with Christ Jesus' divine nature Who is imparting resurrected life from Christ's humanity nature by the authority and power of the Godhead can bring *zoe* life and healing in Believers' bodies now (1 Peter 2:24) and can bring life into Believers' new resurrected bodies in the future (1 Corinthians 15:44, 53).

As God the Word, it is easy for Jesus' divine nature to bring resurrected life of His humanity nature to indwell each Believer. Jesus is the Testator of the New Testament. Jesus died, was raised from the dead, and ascended to Heaven to sit on a throne at the right hand of God. Christ's divine nature as God the Word is present here on earth to be with Believers because His divine nature is omnipresent and is always with every Believer (Matthew 18:20; 28:20). The Holy Spirit was sent as the Executor of Jesus' New Testament and is the manifested Breath of God come to comfort and guide Believers in all truth (John 16:13; Romans 10:13). Also, the Holy Spirit as the

Executor of the New Testament has the responsibility to make sure the benefits, inheritance, and legacy of the New Testament passes to Believers who are Jesus' beneficiaries of the New Testament. When Believers are baptized into the Spirit, they put on Christ's resurrected humanity nature through the born again spirit as the New Garment, and the born again spirit takes on His image and glory of His resurrected humanity nature (2 Corinthians 3:18). Believers' born again spirits cause Believers to be clothed in the spirit of Christ's resurrected humanity nature, while Christ's divine nature receives Believers and covers them with the image and glory of Christ's resurrected humanity nature.

THE GODHEAD TAKES UP RESIDENCE INSIDE BELIEVERS

The entire Godhead takes up residence inside of each Believer. This great blessing is seen in John 14. In verse 6, Jesus says, "I am the way, the truth, and the life. No one comes to the Father except through Me." In verse 2, Jesus said, "In my Father's house are many mansions (Greek *mone*): if it were not so, I would have told you. I go to prepare a place for you." Then in verses 16 and 17, Jesus says, "And I will pray the Father, and he shall give you another Comforter, that He may abide with you forever; Even the Spirit of Truth; whom the world cannot receive, because it seeth Him not, neither knoweth Him: but ye know Him; for He dwelleth with you, and shall be in you." Then in verse 20, 23 Jesus reveals: "At that day ye shall know that I *am* in My Father, and ye in Me, and I in you…. If a man loves Me, he will keep My words: and My Father will love him, and We will come unto him, and make Our abode (*mone*) with him." The Greek word in John 14:2 translated as "mansions" is *mone,* and the same Greek word in John 14:23 for "abode or home" is *mon*e. Jesus also was implying that in that day, Believers will drink of the entire Godhead which carries and imparts Jesus' humanity nature's resurrected everlasting life. Also, Jesus was saying that Believers become the Temple, Tabernacle, and House of the Godhead here on earth (1 Corinthians 3:16; 2 Corinthians 6:16; Ephesians 2:21; 1 Peter 4:17).

The entire loving Godhead is living with the born again spirits of Believers, and nothing can separate Believers from this loving relationship. Romans 8:31-39 is our assurance, "What shall we then say to these things? If God be for us, who can be against us? He that spared not His own Son, but delivered Him up for us all, how shall He not with Him also freely give us all things? Who shall lay anything to the charge of God's elect? It is God that justifieth. Who is he that condemneth? It is Christ that died, yea rather, that is risen again, who is even at the right hand of God, who also maketh intercession for us. Who shall separate us from the love of Christ? Shall tribulation, or distress, or persecution, or famine, or nakedness, or peril, or sword? As it is written, For thy sake we are killed all the day long; we are accounted as sheep for the slaughter. Nay, in all these things we are more than conquerors through him that loved us. For I am persuaded, that neither death, nor life, nor angels, nor principalities, nor powers, nor things present, nor things to come, nor height, nor depth, nor any other creature, shall be able to separate us from the love of God, which is in Christ Jesus our Lord."

Thus, as a Believer the whole Godhead dwells within you, loves you, provides for you, heals you, and protects you. Even when you die, you have everlasting life in Christ; and your spirit and soul are sent to Heaven while your mortal body decays away into dust here on earth. Notwithstanding, you return to earth with Christ to rule and reign with Him throughout eternity (Revelation 5:10). Paul said in Philippians 1:21, "For to me to live is Christ, and to die is gain." Adam and Eve's souls, along with their posterity, were created immortal; so unbelievers will experience infernal everlasting dying without Christ (Genesis 2:7; Psalms 16:10; Ecclesiastes 12:7; Matthew 10:28; 17:1-8; 25:46; Luke 12:4-5; 16:19-31). Believers will experience everlasting life in Christ (John 3:16). The body is mortal and decades away back to dust for all humans, but Believers receive a new eternal spiritual body in the future (1Corinthians 15:44, 53).

The Godhead will only dwell with that part of the Believer that is without sin and who is perfect and holy. Consequently, the Godhead can only dwell with your perfect and sinless new born again spirit (Hebrews 12:23, 1 John 3:9; 1 Corinthians 6:17), not your soul until transformation occurs by putting on the new man (Ephesians 4:24; Colossians 3:10). Then the Godhead brings the born again spirit with Jesus' resurrected *zoe* life into the heart of the soul, so the soul's mind, emotions, and heart can enjoy resurrected life of Christ's humanity nature and be transformed spiritually, prosper in finances, and be in health. This is what Jesus meant when He said in John 10:10, "I am come that they might have life, and that they might have it more abundantly."

Christ had to undergo crucifixion, death, and resurrection in order to have a resurrected life-giving spirit to give to people who seek Him and accept Him as Savior and Lord. Jesus said in John 7:37-39 that: "If any man thirst, let him come unto Me and drink. He that believeth on Me, as the Scripture hath said, from within him shall flow rivers of living water. But this spake He of the (born again) spirit, which they that believed on Him would receive: for the (born again) spirit was not yet." The Holy Spirit was in existence, so this reference cannot be speaking of the Holy Spirit. Some scholars have interpreted this to mean that the jurisdictional authority of the Holy Spirit was not as yet since Jesus had not been crucified, resurrected, and ascended on high. However, a more personal interpretation is that it refers to Jesus' disciples obtaining new born again spirits that only could come after Jesus' humanity nature as the Lamb of God was crucified, died, and resurrected. Jesus' humanity spirit was not resurrected yet at the time Jesus was speaking in John 7:37-39. The 1 Corinthians 6:17 joining as one spirit between Jesus' resurrected humanity spirit and Believers' born again spirit could not be until Jesus' death and resurrection because the price had to be paid for the reconciliation with Father God, and until Jesus' stature as the Second Man was accomplished. Christ Jesus was crucified on the Roman Cross to rid fallen mankind who become Believers repenting of their sins and restraining spiritually the sin nature inside to kill that which was in Adam. Jesus was resurrected from the dead after three days and nights to make Jesus' humanity nature the Second Man and the Firstborn from the dead to impart the Seed of His resurrected humanity spirit to give birth to Believers' new born again spirits (1 Corinthians 15:45, 47; Colossians 1:18; 1 Peter 1:23).

As a Believer, do you want to be baptized into the resurrection of the Lord? Better yet, do you want to drink of Him? By being baptized into the Lord, you are baptized into the Body of Christ, which becomes your outward qualification. However, by drinking of Christ's divine nature, He becomes your inward satisfaction. You will never thirst again! Glory to God! Hallelujah! And because ye are sons, God hath sent forth the Spirit of his Son into your hearts, crying, Abba, Father.

THERE ARE BASICALLY FOUR KINDS OF CHRISTIAN TEACHERS TODAY WITH DIFFERENT BELIEFS THAT WILL CAUSE WEAK OR STRONG BELIEVERS COMING IN THE END TIME *EKKLESIA*

Basically, there are four kinds of Christian Leaders and Teachers, today, who function either as the old religious orders or the dynamic of the Kingdom Community Life *Ekklesia*. These four emphasize different fundamental beliefs that will cause either spiritual birth defects or spiritually healthy new Believers being born again during the end time Revival.

The first kind of Christian Teachers is called "**Modernists Believers**" who believe that a Believer should look at the life of Jesus and incorporate the principles of life that He taught in the Believer's own life. They teach that Jesus was full of love and compassion, so that is what a Believer should express in his life. The modernists of today normally do not believe in the supernatural, such as healings or the expressions of other spiritual gifts. Many do not believe in the virgin birth of Christ. Some Modernists do not believe that Jesus really died on the Cross or was resurrected. They really do not believe in a personal relationship with the Lord. Because God is good, they believe their religious beliefs will save them. Some of these people probably have become the new cloth, but have not been baptized in the Spirit, nor have drunk of the Spirit. Sadly, to say, there may be some of these religious people that are not saved and will have infernal death in the Lake of Fire, along with the other unsaved sinners with the kingdom of darkness.

The second kind of Christian Teachers is called, "**Doctrinalists Believers**" who are those who believe that Christ is the Living God; that He is our Redeemer because He died on the Cross, was raised on the third day, and ascended to Heaven where He waits to return for His old religious order. Studying the Bible and living by its doctrines and principles is of utmost importance. However, these Christians generally do not believe in the gifts of the Spirit and do not experience the present manifestation of tongues, healings, or other spiritual gifts manifestation. The focus of most of these Believers is generally restricted to the belief in the initial conversion experience and that they are going to Heaven. They become converts but not true, activated mature disciples of Christ. They see that getting saved and going to Heaven as the main points of their Christian experience and goal. Leaders spend most of their time trying to get others saved, so the initial preaching of repentance and remission of sins for initial salvation has rewards of filling the old religious order building with Believers with "easy believism" messages. Often, they rarely experience the vibrancy of the present all-encompassing life which Jesus wants to share with them in the present time here on earth. They often do not taste the living water within. They have not put on the new man, the born again spirit, as the new garment in their souls. They wrongfully teach that "For we are His workmanship, created in Christ Jesus unto good works, which God hath before ordained that we should walk in them" (Ephesians 2:10). They do not teach their followers to become Kingdom spiritual Ambassadors and Kingdom spiritual Soldiers who are mandated to fight the good fight of faith against the kingdom of darkness to take back possession of the fallen creation to God. They believe that their Christian experience is going to a building and worshiping the Lord, listening to a weekly sermon, and paying offerings; and they do have the privilege of going to Heaven when they die and rarely talk about Jesus' return to earth to set up His eternal Kingdom and Believers ruling and reigning with Him throughout eternity (Revelation 5:10).

The third kind of Christian Teachers is called "**Life Experiencing Believers**" who are those who not only seek the redemption by Christ because of the death, resurrection, and ascension of Christ's humanity nature as the Ascended One, but also the fellowship here on earth with Christ's divine nature, God the Word, as the Present One. They teach Galatians 2:20 that reveals that it is good that Believers no longer have to die because of Christ's spilt blood, but it is better that Believers no longer have to live because they have submitted and allowed Christ to live His life in them and through them to touch others spiritually. Some of these teachers add spiritual gifts to their foundational beliefs, pray for the sick, prophesy to others, and look for a sign from the Holy Spirit as evidence of His presence. Generally, these Christians constantly seek a close, personal relationship with the Lord which is good. They spend much time listening for His voice, so they can be led by the Spirit daily. They are very concerned with maturation of the soul. They are concerned with the inner life development, taking people from immaturity to maturity. These Christians have new cloth fitted into the New Garment of Christ and they have experienced the baptism of Christ yet have only tasted the thirst-quenching drink of the Spirit. They do not focus on the initial salvation by evangelizing new Believers; they are more focusing on the maturation and transformation of the souls of Believers instead of acquiring new converts. Most Life Experiencing Leaders do not activate Believers to become Kingdom spiritual Ambassadors of Christ, as Kingdom spiritual Soldiers, or as the Royal Priesthood, as if rank and file Believers are rarely mature enough to be ordained Ministers with their own congregation. If someone leaves the congregation, the leader considers it as rebellion, and grave things may happen to them without the "covering" of a Pastor. These Christian Life Experiencing Ministers seek followers of their ministry instead of activating the saints for the work of the ministry as leaders. They do not want their congregation members to go into all the world to make disciples; they want them to bring these Believers to the leadership in the old religious order for training. Believers are mandated to become followers and disciples of Christ not followers of earthy Ministers or Pastors. Believers are to experience liberty in Christ in spiritual fellowship, not be bound in natural fellowship of a leader.

The fourth kind of Christian Teachers I call "**Kingdom community Life Believers**" who are those who become the servants, the true *doulos* of the Lord, who seek Kingdom community fellowship as a lifestyle, but also practice ongoing evangelism of the lost. Kingdom community Life Leaders teach that the world is a mission field, and Believers are sent out to go into every business, school, profession, trade, home, entertainment center, and everywhere outside of a Church building to witness of Christ Jesus and make disciples. They teach that all the spiritual gifts are for today, teach that all the Ephesians 4:11 Ministers are operating today, and they teach that life in Christ is for servanthood to Him and to other Believers. They teach Believers to study their Bibles daily; to pray throughout the day, to intercede for others, to be givers that help other Believers in need as they are led by the Holy Spirit, to seek wisdom from above instead of the wisdom of this world, to become truly principled Biblitarians. They teach the plurality of gifts, the plurality of the Body of Christ, and the plurality of ministries where all Believers are members of a chosen generation, a royal priesthood, a holy nation, and a peculiar people. They teach that the job of the Ephesians 4:11 ministers is to make leaders and followers of Christ, not the followers of a particular man or woman Minister.

This fourth kind of Kingdom community Life Leaders also teach that Believers have spiritual operations by God the Father (1 Corinthians 12:6) as listed in Romans 12:6-8, have spiritual administrations by God the Word (1 Corinthians 12:5) as delineated as office gifts in Ephesians 4:11, or have spiritual manifestations by God the Holy Spirit (1 Corinthians 12:7; 8-11) as the nine ascension gifts listed in 1 Corinthians 12:8-11. Kingdom community Life Leaders teach spiritual gifts become evident by the spiritual transformation of Believers' souls and acquiring spiritual character exhibiting spiritual fruit and foundationally exhibiting *agape* love that seeks *zoe* life in the Kingdom community experience with others. Believers are shown the way to seek first the Kingdom of God and His righteousness. Kingdom community Life Leaders teach when spiritually matured, Believers truly enter the crucifixion of Christ and allow Christ to live His resurrected life through His divine nature in and through Believers to build His *Ekklesia,* which is *zoe* life in the loving fellowship between Believers (Galatians 2:20; 1 John 1:1-7). Kingdom community Life Leaders teach that mature Believers experience the highest form of resurrected *zoe* life in Christ through worshiping and serving the Lord and other Believers through Kingdom community living, which involves the studying of God's word, being in daily prayer, following the leading of the Holy Spirit, and seeking daily the loving fellowship with other Believers. Kingdom community Life Leaders teach that mature Believers are not religious, but witness to other Believers that the flesh profits nothing but the words that Jesus spoke are spirit and life (John 6:63). They teach that mature Believers see their Kingdom experience is one that can best be expressed and experienced in spiritual Kingdom community fellowship. They teach that mature Believers are not only to have a close relationship with the Lord, but they come to understand the resurrected *zoe* life from Christ's humanity nature dispensed by Christ's divine nature wants to be expressed here on earth through loving, caring relationships in spiritual Kingdom communities. Kingdom community Life Leaders teach that mature Believers know that Kingdom community fellowship is the way the Lord's divine nature is present with them (Matthew 18:20). They teach that mature Believers have attached the new cloth to the New Garment, and they have found the secret that a multi-Believer Betrothed of Christ wears the New Garment. They teach that mature Believers accept the truth that individual spiritual engiftments are for the edification of all Believers in Kingdom community fellowship, and the spiritual health of the Kingdom community of Believers is sought by all.

These Kingdom community Life Leaders teach that mature Believers follow the instructions and the lifestyle of Paul who wrote about the life in the Kingdom community as one body in Christ. Paul said in 1 Corinthians 12:26, "And whether one member suffer, all the members suffer with it; or one member be honoured, all the members rejoice with it." Paul taught that Believers have not only been baptized in the Spirit, but they have found the well in the Kingdom community lifestyle where they daily may come and drink of the Spirit and find full spiritual satisfaction. They teach that Paul revealed that *agape* love in the Kingdom community is the greatest virtue (1 Corinthians 13:13), following Jesus' New Commandment in John 13: 34-35, which says, "A new commandment I give unto you, That ye love one another; as I have loved you, that ye also love one another. By this shall all men know that ye are my disciples, if ye have (*agape*) love for one another." They teach that Paul taught that mature Believers are Kingdom spiritual Ambassadors of Christ and Kingdom spiritual Soldiers who are mandated to fight against the kingdom of darkness in the world to take back possession of the fallen creation and fallen mankind to God (2 Corinthians 5:20; 2 Timothy 2:3-4).

These Kingdom community Life Leaders teach that mature Believers instruct other Believers the mandates of Christ Jesus in Matthew 28:18-20, 16:18-19, and 18:15-20. They teach that this spiritual Kingdom lifestyle of Kingdom community fellowship is much more than going to a building sitting in a pew, standing for praise and worship, listening to a Pastor or Teacher deliver a sermon, and depositing money for support of this experience from the day of Believers' initial salvation to the day they die. How can a Believer be a servant of Christ and His Kingdom? This fourth kind of Kingdom community Life Leaders instruct Believers that life flows from Kingdom community fellowship experiences. These Kingdom community Life Leaders focus on old and new Believers that Kingdom living is a lifestyle change. These Kingdom Community Life Teachers also focus on activating Believers into fellowship ministry and their direct participation in the Joel 2 Third Progressive Revival where the Holy Spirit is poured out on all believers to bring in a massive harvest of new Believers. These Kingdom Community Life Teachers train the Believers to be ready to receive new Believers into Kingdom community fellowship. New Believers must be taught that *zoe* life flows from continuous fellowship. Although these statements may seem redundant, yet the Lord through me is trying to change the long-standing religious practices that God wants to revolutionize and rebuild the *Ekklesia* on and by a more vibrant, activating, and spiritually dynamic world Kingdom of Jesus' mature disciples. Community love where God the Word, God the Holy Spirit, and God the Father are in the midst of the Believers in fellowship should be what is seen as spiritually mature, healthy, and attractive to saved and unsaved (John 18:20). God will use this attractive, loving, caring lifestyle to draw unbelievers.

WHAT WERE JESUS' INSTRUCTIONS JUST BEFORE HIS ASCENSION?

In Jesus' final days here on earth, one would think that Jesus would have spent numerous conversations telling His disciples how to choose deacons and elders, how to take offerings, how to conduct meetings, how often to have communion, how to set up a children's ministry, how to set up a women's ministry, how to establish a prison ministry, how not to become divided into denominations, and so on if He wanted to start a new religion to set up a new religious patterned structure after tradition with a lecture hall and worship center as it is practiced today. Jesus said "go" not "stay." The gospel of the Kingdom and repentance and remission of sins are a dual activating gospel to do the Lord's work, which has the benefit of imparting everlasting life that cancels out infernal damnation and establishes what God wants here on earth as His Kingdom instead of what the kingdom of darkness wants.

Yet, when Jesus took His disciples up on the Mount to witness His Ascension, He had merely a three-verse instructional teaching in Matthew 28:18-20. The instruction to expand His *Ekklesia* and Kingdom probably took less than a couple of minutes. Jesus' instructions have not changed. These are the same instructions for the actions of the *Ekklesia* in glorious Revival. Jesus said in Matthew 16:18-19, "...I will build my church (*Ekklesia* –Kingdom government assembly and Kingdom military assembly); and the gates of hell shall not prevail against it. And I will give unto thee the keys of the kingdom of Heaven: and whatsoever thou shalt bind on earth shall be bound in Heaven: and whatsoever thou shalt loose on earth shall be loosed in Heaven."

On the Mount of Ascension, Jesus said in Matthew 28:18-20, "All authority has been given to Me in Heaven and on earth. Go therefore and make disciples of all nations, baptizing them in the Name of the Father and of the Son and of the Holy Spirit, teaching them to observe all things that I have commanded you; and lo, I am with you always, even to the end of the age."

First, Jesus established that He was granted not some authority but all authority from God the Father in both the spiritual and natural worlds, expressed as in Heaven and in earth. This established Jesus as the Supreme Leader of the universe, King of God's Kingdom, the Head of the Church, the Lord over all creation, and the Judge over all principalities, powers, rulers of the darkness of this world, and spiritual wickedness in high places.

Second, Jesus was proclaiming that He also had the authority to delegate that authority to His disciples to fulfill His Father's purpose that His Kingdom come and His Father's will be done on earth as it is in Heaven (Matthew 6:10).

Third, Jesus simply said "Go therefore and make disciples of all nations...." This portion of the Lord's instruction was simple but profound and all pervading. It is important to simplify Believers' work as much as is possible, so Believers are single minded and do not go off track and lose their focus. Making disciples does not mean making only converts. Making disciples means developing mature Believers in their souls who follow the direction of the Head of the Church, "For we are His workmanship, created in Christ Jesus unto good works, which God hath before ordained that we should walk in them" (Ephesians 2:10). Jesus' life was shared daily in fellowship with His disciples, and this is the type of fellowship that the Lord wants His Believers to share with each other (1 John 1:1-7). Jesus commands His Ephesians 4:11 ministers to make Believers mature disciples of Christ in Believers' souls by putting on the new man (Romans 6:5,11; Ephesians 4:24; Colossians 3:10) and becoming members of the Second Man as new creatures in Christ (1 Corinthians 15:47; 2 Corinthians 5:17). Jesus commands that Believers receive activation as Kingdom spiritual Ambassadors and Kingdom spiritual Soldiers. Jesus wants His *Ekklesia* to do damage to the kingdom of darkness that is the spiritual enemy of God. Jesus' divine nature, God the Word, encourages Believers to work as Kingdom Ambassadors and Kingdom Soldiers to bring back possession of the earth, possession of the world system, reconcile the lost people back to Father God, as He has the right to ownership and possession by right of being Creator, unlike the thief, usurping devil and his kingdom of darkness.

Fourth, the disciples are to be baptized in celebration of Jesus' death and resurrection in the name of the Father, Son, and Holy Spirit, where Believers become the functioning dwelling place of the Triune Godhead as His Temple (John 14: 17, 23; 1 Corinthians 6:19; 1 Corinthians 3:16; Ephesians 2:21). Baptizing disciples means to take them under water symbolizing the death of Christ and coming up out of the water symbolizing the resurrection of Christ. Believers' dwelling place is revealed as the Family of God, the Kingdom community of Believers, the Body of Christ, and the Kingdom of God. Baptism also symbolizes the translation of new Believers from the kingdoms of this world into the Kingdom of God's dear Son (Galatians 1:13). It is important that Believers stay encouraged concerning their spiritual growth unto maturity in their souls. 2 Corinthians 4:16-18 says, "For which cause we faint not; but though our outward man perish, yet the inward man is renewed day by day. For our light affliction, which is but for a moment, worketh for us a far more exceeding and eternal weight of glory; While we look not at the things which are seen, but at the things which are not seen: for the things which are seen are temporal; but the things which are not seen are eternal."

To baptize Believers in water means to put them in water. To baptize Believers into the name of the Father, Son, and Holy Spirit is to put Believers into the Family of God and in their place in the *Ekklesia* Kingdom community of Believers for growth and maturation, training in the functioning of their engiftments, with the focus of being about the ministry fulfilling the purpose of their callings. If Believers' souls grow and mature unto transformation outside of fellowship with other Believers, what good does it do for the Kingdom community, which is pluralistic in nature, in vision and in purpose? Believers commit themselves to grow into being members of the spiritual family of the Triune Godhead and the fellowship of the Believers as the functioning Body of Christ. As disciples, Believers must be baptized into the Triune Godhead, so the relationship is one, the movement is one, and the purpose is one with the Lord as Head of the *Ekklesia*, with the Believers seeking first the Kingdom of God and His righteousness and becoming activated as citizens of the Kingdom of Heaven as spiritual Kingdom Ambassadors and spiritual Kingdom Soldiers.

Fifth, the disciples are to be taught all that Jesus had commanded to make them principled, loving Biblitarians who live in Kingdom community with other Believers. Being taught means that disciples' souls are to seek being spiritually minded, emotionally stable, and willfully submissive and their hearts solidifying God's Kingdom beliefs. Being taught means Believers continuously studying the word of God, living a life of worshiping the Lord, practicing *agape* love with fellow Believers in Kingdom community, offering up daily prayer and supplication to God for each other, regularly taking communion, preaching the gospel of the Kingdom and preaching repentance and remission of sins, making disciples of all nations through evangelism, seeking first the Kingdom of God and His righteousness each day to enjoy the righteousness, peace, and joy in the Holy Spirit, and building the *Ekklesia* through His believers, who are His spiritual Ambassadors of Reconciliation in the Lord's Kingdom government and obedient spiritual Soldiers in the Lord's Kingdom army that stand strong against the enemies of God and His *Ekklesia*.

Sixth, Jesus assured His disciples that He would not leave them as orphans, so He said, "and lo, I am with you always, even to the end of the age." Whatever Believers need each day of their ministry, His divine nature will be there to teach them, help them, discipline them, and provide for them. He intends to indwell them with His divine nature as God the Word, along with the other members of the Godhead (John 14: 16-17,23). Through the Holy Spirit, He assures His disciples that He will communicate with them, while the Holy Spirit empowers and anoints them to do the work of the ministry that they are commissioned to do. Whatever they are commanded to do until Jesus' humanity nature returns to physically coronate His Kingdom here on earth in the Kingdom Age, Jesus promises that His divine nature will be here on earth, living in each and all Believers, to assure God the Father's mission will be done. Jesus Christ's divine nature is here on earth with resurrected life from Jesus' humanity nature as the Pattern, as Jesus' humanity nature only did and said what God the Father did and say (John 5:19; 12:49). Jesus Christ's resurrected life from His humanity nature is abundantly given to Believers by and through Christ's omnipresent divine nature to help and encourage Believers to be obedient to the Godhead.

Jesus is the fulfillment of the law and the prophets. After Believers' initial salvation, Jesus did not lay down a multiplicity of laws, regulations, or endless doctrines, except the new commandment to love one another (John 13:34-45). Additionally, He simply said that all authority has been given to Him, and we Believers, as His disciples, must go forth as His Kingdom Ambassadors and Soldiers as His *Ekklesia* baptizing disciples into the family of God, and training them to obey all that Jesus commanded. Jesus promised that His divine nature always will be present with Believers here on earth and indwelling inside Believers to guide, empower, and protect His disciples. Thus, with His authority, power, and presence, then Believers can do all things through Christ's divine nature who strengthens them (Philippians 4:13).

Again, Jesus is God the Word made flesh (John 1:14). As a Believer, you do not need all the rules and regulations to follow. In fact, you must enjoy, appreciate, and love the presence of the Lord Jesus' divine nature more as much as studying the written words contained in the Bible as Jesus' divine nature is indeed God the Word [John 1:1; 1 John 5:7 (King James Version)]. There is no conflict between the two, but Jesus' divine nature is not a book, not mere words, not a Greek capricious god who is living in a faraway place. Jesus' divine nature is always here on earth inside you as a Believer, teaching you, bringing life to you, using you to fulfill the purpose of building a human Temple for the Triune Godhead, to establish God's Kingdom inside you, and then through you to manifest the Kingdom of God in the world to take back possession of the world for its rightful Owner, Father God in fulfillment of prophecy and God's will.

If the Jews were better schooled and properly interpreting prophecy, they would have known the prophecy of Daniel 7:13-14, 27, which again says, "I saw in the night visions, and, behold, One like the Son of Man came with the clouds of Heaven, and came to the Ancient of Days, and they brought Him near before Him. And there was given Him dominion, and glory, and a kingdom, that all people, nations, and languages, should serve Him: His dominion is an everlasting dominion, which shall not pass away, and His kingdom that which shall not be destroyed…. And the Kingdom and dominion, and the greatness of the Kingdom under the whole Heaven, shall be given to the people of the saints of the Most High, whose Kingdom is an everlasting kingdom, and all dominions shall serve and obey Him."

Instead of the laws, regulations, creeds, and legalistic religious jargon of the scribes and Pharisees, Jesus just instructed His disciples to teach others all that He had commanded them in a living way, not as some dead letter of the law. Believers need to be consumed with entering the crucifixion of Christ to die to self and allowing Christ to live His life in and through them (Galatians 2:20). Believers need to be dependent on the Lord's authority, the Holy Spirit's power and anointing, and the presence of the entire Godhead within them to manifest the Lord's presence and God's Kingdom throughout the earth. That is the great transference that Christ delegates His authority to all His disciples, who God has chosen as Believers in Christ before the foundation of the world (Ephesians 1:4-5) and wrote Believers' names in the Lambs Book of Life before the foundation of the world (Revelation 13:8).

HOW DO BELIEVERS SUBMIT TO, DEPEND UPON, AND ENJOY THE PRESENCE OF THE LORD'S DIVINE NATURE?

How do Believers meet with the present, all-encompassing Christ's divine nature as the Present One, so that Believers experience Jesus' resurrected life of His humanity nature? Believers must first accept the truth that the Lord's divine nature, along with the entire Godhead, live inside of Believers. This is a major truth and reality (John 14: 16-17, 23) that lukewarm Believers do not comprehend and rarely experience. Often, old religious order leaders do not teach most Believers how to activate this prevailing incarnate truth in their daily living. However, the moment Believers' souls yield to the authority of God's presence in continuous fellowship with Believers' born again spirits, then the Lord's divine nature, God the Word, God the Holy Spirit, and God the Father will lead Believers and reveal to Believers minute by minute, day by day, how to live, move and have fullness of being in loving fellowship with the Lord's humanity nature, the entire Godhead, and other Believers.

Most Believers are taught religion and not Kingdom intimate and loving community fellowship because it is easier for a Leader to give people a few nuggets from the Bible and send the Believers home thinking there must be more to experience and learn in the Lord's Kingdom. Most Believers catch the knowledge of religion instead knowing Christ intimately. Most Believers are still too religious when they come together in fellowship as a Kingdom community of Believers. The presence of Jesus' divine nature must be lived out in loving spiritual fellowship in a Kingdom community of Believers where the spiritual presence of the Lord's divine nature is the primary focus of attention and not only natural and social interactions and communications.

Again, when Jesus gave His instructions to His disciples on the Mount of Ascension, there is not a single hint of anything that is religious in His directives. Not one of His statements resembles any law or regulation in Genesis, Exodus, Leviticus, Numbers, or Deuteronomy, Prophets, or the Rabbinical teachings. Everything Jesus said was from Father God and wrapped up in following the presence of the Lord's divine nature. The Lord did not tell each of His disciples what part of the world each was assigned to minister to go and make disciples, what kind of people to disciple, how to witness, what Commandments to observe, or the time His humanity nature would return. What He did instruct them in Acts 1:5, 8 was to travel and to stay in Jerusalem until the Holy Spirit comes upon them and anoints them with power to be His witnesses, "…both in Jerusalem, and in all Judaea, and in Samaria, and unto the uttermost part of the earth." This means fifty percent locally and fifty percent to the country, state, nation, and other nations.

Unfortunately, most old religious order leaders run the ministry with the attitude that the Lord Jesus is sitting on a Throne in the Third Heaven, where they want Him to stay and not interfere with the work here on earth. Yet, Jesus has an omnipresent divine nature as God the Word, and His fullness can be in all places and in all Believers at the same time. A lot of the problems encountered throughout old religious order history would not have happened had they been led by the Holy Spirit in the first place. Wrong thinking causes wrong sowing, and the result is undesired reaping (Galatians 6:7-8)

What is worthy to note is that in the gospel of Matthew and John nothing is mentioned about the Lord's factual ascension. Matthew's emphasis is about Emmanuel, God with us (Matthew 1:23). John's emphasis is God the Word becoming flesh and dwelling amongst us (John 1:14). Matthew 18:20 says, "For where two or three are gathered together in My name, I am there in the midst of them." In Matthew 28:20, Jesus says He will be with Believers always. Thus, Matthew and John both emphasize that through Jesus' divine nature He will be present being about the Father's business of first bringing into the family of God through adoption new Believers and second, taking back possession for God of the fallen people, the fallen creation, and the fallen world system that was stolen through the serpent deceiving Eve and high treason by Adam.

Jesus' humanity nature is indeed sitting at the right hand of the Father in the Third Heaven (Ephesians 2:6; Hebrew 12:2), but He is also with Believers always with His divine nature, which is omnipresent. Believers must not only see Christ Jesus as the Ascended One of His humanity nature, but also see Christ Jesus as the Present One of His divine nature who disburses and shares with Believers the resurrected life of Jesus' humanity nature. When Believers start experiencing the reality of resurrected life of the Ascended One through His divine nature as the Present One, then Believers can experience resurrected life in their souls, as they already have in their born again spirits.

It is imperative that Believers drop all religious pretenses that rob them of intimate relationship with Christ Jesus. The main thing that matters is that Believers have the resurrected life of Jesus' humanity nature as manifested by Jesus' divine nature, God the Word, as the Present One in their midst who is omniscient, omnipotent, and omnipresent. Jesus has a divine nature and humanity nature that are distinguishable, not commingled, but unified in purpose. Believers need to revise their foundational beliefs that do not conform to the biblical truth.

Through His divine nature Jesus delegates to Believers His authority, but His divine nature is present to instruct Believers how to use that delegated authority; so there is no abuse of authority, the Kingdom manifestation, and God's will being done here on earth as it is in Heaven. Believers need to learn to stay under submission as the resurrected life flows from the authority of the Ascended One sitting on His throne and through His divine nature as the Present One with the whole Godhead training disciples to baptize new disciples and teach new disciples what Jesus commanded and Kingdom Community Lifestyle. Again, Jesus Christ's divine nature is God the Word and has all the attributes as part of the Triune Godhead, and He can be everywhere and in everyone when the Joel 2 progressive Revivals begin with Jesus as the Head of the Church.

Most old religious order Believers think of Jesus' humanity nature as the Greater Jonah, as the Redeemer, where Jesus was carried off in the sea of clouds and taken to the Third Heaven. However, Jesus' divine nature is also the Greater Solomon, Who wants to bring His knowledge, understanding, and wisdom to rule Believers in His eternal Kingdom in the land where the enemy still has a stronghold. Pray that those in the Revival Ekklesia receive the Lord's knowledge, understanding, and wisdom that Believers may participate fully in the Kingdom of God and His dear Son as Ministers, Kings, Lords, Priests, Body, Brothers, Betrothed, Ambassadors, Soldiers, citizens of Heaven and Kingdom, and as members of His *Ekklesia.*

New Wineskins For the Revival Ekklesia is Kingdom community

New Wineskins for the
Revival *Ekklesia* is Kingdom community

BELIEVERS CANNOT POUR NEW WINE INTO
OLD WINESKINS IN THIS END TIME REVIVAL.

Matthew 9:17 says, "Nor do they put new (*neos*- youthful, fresh, regenerate) wine into old (*palaios*- antique, worn out) wineskins, or else the wineskins break, the wine is spilled and the wineskins are ruined (*apollumi*- destroy, die, lose value and effectiveness). But they put new wineskins, and both are preserved (*sutereo*- to keep closely together to conserve, to remember, keep, observe)."

The Greek word for "new" is "*neos*," which means "new in time, recent, newly possessed, youthful, fresh." The "new wine" that Christ poured out through Jesus' divine nature and the new born again spirits of Believers are expressed through a vigorous spiritual Kingdom life with Christ's divine nature, stirring people in the world to join the Revival into a higher life in the Kingdom of God. Furthermore, the rhema word of Christ's divine nature is spirit and life in the Kingdom community that new converts discover during the Revival (John 6:63). Christ's divine nature will energize Believers' new born again spirits with resurrected life of Christ's humanity nature to send this *zoe* life into their souls to enjoy Christ's humanity nature as their Betrothed and future Bridegroom. Christ's divine nature causes the corporate expression of the Body of Christ in the spiritual Kingdom community lifestyle of the new Believers that share the resurrected life of Christ's humanity nature, with the power of the Holy Spirit to do the purpose of God the Father.

In the context of the passage of Scripture in Matthew 9, the word "old" in "old wineskins" is *palaios*, which means "antique, worn out but specifically connotes old religious traditions, practices and rituals, that lack the *zoe* life, such as the fasting maintained by the Pharisees, who were of the old religious order, and by the disciples of John, who are not following Kingdom of God teachings of John the Baptist and established a newer religious order instead of the Kingdom of God. All spiritual traditions and practices, which have become old religious orders are old wineskins, as they lack the ushering in of Christ's divine nature amid the gathering in fellowship of Believers in the Kingdom of God (Matthew 18:20). Jesus is saying that His Kingdom way of life cannot have in it the old rituals way of life of the Pharisees, which among other things required a lot of fasting. If Jesus' "new" Kingdom truths were attached to the Pharisees' old religious traditions and rituals, then it would distort Jesus' truths, and the people would remain in religious bondage.

Jesus is teaching against "syncretism," which is the mixing of beliefs. As Believers, we must reject religion and must completely replace the old religious way of life with the new godly Kingdom way of life and fellowship. Also, Jesus' "new" Kingdom way is righteous and spiritually strong, and it cannot be combined with the "old" sinful and weak religious way of life. They are incompatible. Ephesians 4:22-24 says, "That ye put off concerning the former conversation the old man, which is corrupt according to the deceitful lusts; And be renewed in the spirit of your mind; And that ye put on the new man, which after God is created in righteousness and true holiness."

Sometimes, the old wineskins can have oil of the Spirit massaged in them, and they become more pliable. Then, the old wineskins will not cause the lace strings to break when the new wine is poured in as they discover the real message of Christ, which is the Kingdom of God come and God's Will be done here on earth as it is in heaven and not in man-centered religious rituals (Matthew 6:10). The personal relationship with Christ Jesus, with the presence of His divine nature, is the manifested family and Kingdom community order of God's Kingdom. The new wine put into old wineskins often bursts the wineskins by the fact that the new wine is still fermenting from the activated yeast within. Trying to put new wine into old wineskins is trying to contain Christ's divine nature in religious rituals or practices when Christ's divine nature with the resurrected life of His humanity nature wants to do something new and fresh.

Some denominations will attempt to squeeze the anointing of the Holy Spirit into the structural format of their corporate, unique religious hierarchy to no avail. The Holy Spirit will not be limited by the peculiar established practice of a particular religious denomination. True Kingdom of God lifestyle does not express spiritual life and relationship through religious ritual practices, as many believe. The anointing of the Holy Spirit can be like the oil that makes the old wineskins to expand without breaking. Otherwise, Christ's divine nature will pour the new wine of the Spirit into fresh, new wineskins where Kingdom community relationships in celebration in and of Christ Jesus is expressed in love amongst Believers, where Believers truly love each other and are there to help, encourage, and support each other in righteousness, peace, and joy in the Holy Spirit that define the Kingdom of God (Romans 14:17).

The new wineskins signify the Kingdom community kingdom life in the local fellowships as the container of the new wine, which is the embodiment of the entire Godhead, where the Holy Spirit and Christ's divine nature have jurisdictional authority manifesting Believers' new spiritual life expressed in fellowship with each other with *agape* love. The local Kingdom community in the kingdom of God is built into Christ's *Ekklesia* (Matthew 16:18), and the corporate anointing of the anointed Present One, God the Word, is expressed through the local Kingdom communities in which the Believers live celebrating and witnessing of the transformation of their souls finding their inner satisfaction with the Lord's divine nature as the Present One (Matthew 18:15-20). Believers have born again spirits and constitute the Body of Christ and become the Kingdom community expression of the *Ekklesia* and resurrected life of Christ's humanity nature, as the Ascended One (Romans 12:5; Ephesians 1:22-23). The Lord's resurrected life manifesting in Believers through Christ's divine nature is the new wine and is the inner awakened life that manifests in each Believer and through each Kingdom community of Believers. The Body of Christ celebrating resurrected life in the Kingdom community of the new wineskin, the outer container that holds the new wine.

With the Believers of God's Kingdom community, the new wineskin is not a matter of fasting or any other religious practice, but the matter of experiencing in a living way God's spiritual Kingdom *zoe* life, grace, love, mercy, power, and authority of Christ as their focus of worship of Jesus' humanity nature as the Ascended One and Christ's divine nature as the Present One.

Christ came to earth not to establish earthly religious rituals but a heavenly dynamic Kingdom expressing His life, grace, love, mercy, power, and authority. Thus, the Kingdom life, grace, love, mercy, power, and authority are not found in religious traditions, but in the actual presence of Christ's divine nature in Believers, personally and communally in Believers' midst when they congregate together in worship and to express *agape* love to each other. Christ's divine nature expresses Himself and His humanity nature's resurrected life in the Believers individually and in Kingdom community as the Ascended Christ's humanity nature enthroned as the King of God's Kingdom, and the Savior, the Lord of Lords, the King of kings, the Great Physician, the Bridegroom, the Apostle of our Faith, the High Priest of the order of Melchizedek. Christ's humanity nature's resurrected life is the New Wine for His disciples to partake in celebration and communion, representing the redemption of Believers' sins.

Jesus celebrated His last Passover Meal with His Apostles before His suffering and death. The Jews celebrated the Passover Feast to remember being slaves who God delivered from Egypt, the Law spoken by God at Mount Sinai, God's provision while traversing the desert for forty years, and their entering into the Promise Land. Yet, here Jesus knew that Jews were being ruled by the Romans because they rebelled against God and did not fulfill their covenant with God to be a Kingdom of Priests and a Holy Nation as they had been called to be (Exodus 19:6). Jesus knew that His death and resurrection would allow fallen unsaved people who believe to become born again and receive sinless, perfect, righteous and holy spirits. Then, Believers' souls needed to be spiritually transformed to be better citizens in the Kingdom of God. To do this, Jesus added redemption as part of the Passover Meal. The Promise Land is now the whole earth, where the King of the Kingdom of God becomes the Ruler of all other Kingdoms and peoples in the world (Daniel 7; 13-18; Revelation 11:15). Jesus said in Acts 1:8, "But ye shall receive power, after that the Holy Ghost is come upon you: and ye shall be witnesses unto Me both in Jerusalem, and in all Judaea, and in Samaria, and unto the uttermost part of the earth."

The final partaking of the New Wine is at the Marriage Supper of the Lamb with His multi-membered Wife (Revelation 19:7-9). This will be when the Spouse of Christ will have a sinless born again spirit and a sinless soul, returning to earth with the King to receive a new resurrected body (1 Corinthians 15:23) and to rule and reign with Christ (Revelation 19:7-9). This was a fulfillment of what the Angel Gabriel said to Mary when he pronounced to her of her impending pregnancy of Jesus in Luke 1:30-33, "And the angel said unto her, 'Fear not, Mary: for thou hast found favour with God. And, behold, thou shalt conceive in thy womb, and bring forth a Son, and shalt call His name JESUS. He shall be great and shall be called the Son of the Highest: and the Lord God shall give unto Him the throne of His father David: And He shall reign over the house of Jacob forever; and of His kingdom there shall be no end.'" When Jesus became an adult, His first miracle was the changing of water into wine, representing that He came to receive a bride, Himself. The final paradigm is the bridal paradigm (Revelation 22:17).

The practice of fellowship in the Church is the wineskin into which the new wine of the Revival must be poured, but wine is consumed by living organisms. The Body of Christ, the Believers, which make up the *Ekklesia*, is not some corporation, but a living, breathing organism of Believers joined together in Christ with a common purpose to be followers who are obedient to Jesus Christ's divine nature, and who expresses His power and authority in bringing Jesus' humanity nature's resurrected life to Believers expressing *agape* love as the foundation motive of all ministry.

The new wine is poured out by the Godhead, especially the ministry of the Holy Spirit, but these old wineskins of religious denominations cannot easily oversee the movement of the Holy Spirit very well in the Revival as the Holy Spirit does things in decency and order but is not restricted to structure. The old wineskins are designed usually for the work to be done only by a single Pastor or Teacher and his or her small circle of committed working servants. However, the new wineskin must hold the new wine through an activated Kingdom community of Believers who minister wherever they are, in business, in school, in the marketplace, in home fellowships, or any place where Believers join and are led by the Holy Spirit, God the Word, and Father God to witness to unbelievers and Believers alike. The Lord is calling forth the whole Body of Christ as a Royal Priesthood of Believers living in covenant Kingdom community fellowship to pour out Christ's resurrected life, grace, love, mercy, power, and authority to His Body to make disciples of those lost in this dying and decadent world.

COMMITMENT IN KINGDOM COMMUNITY IS A PLURALISTIC KINGDOM SPIRITUAL REALITY

The gospel of the Kingdom is a pluralistic message, not just an individualistic message, although Believers are individually saved by repentance and remission of sins. The Believer must come into the Kingdom with pluralistic love, pluralistic responsibilities toward other Believers and join others as Kingdom spiritual Ambassadors and Kingdom spiritual Soldiers, but focus less pluralistic on exclusive self-improvement, as iron sharpens iron (Proverb 27:17) that will cause a quicker transformation of the Believer's soul. Individual spiritual transformation of the soul is the work of the entire indwelling Godhead (John 14:16,17,23; John 15:2; Romans 8:13; Ephesians 5:26).

Jesus said in Matthew 28:19, "Go therefore and make disciples of all the nations..." Nations denote a discipleship of pluralism. Discipleship is a deeper relationship with the Lord than is mere conversion. Discipleship motivates maturity of the souls of new born again Believers, and discipleship is a lifelong process of transforming the minds, emotions, and wills in the heart of the souls; so, the Believers become spiritually minded, spiritually emotional, spiritually believing, and spiritually submitted to the will of God.

The gospel of the Kingdom is not a self-actualizing, self-centered "bless me individually" message, even though Believers are blessed mightily when they serve others in God's Kingdom. Believers are saved and forgiven of their sins for a purposeful service as servants dispensing loving compassion to other Believers as they fellowship together in the Kingdom of God. The Body of Christ is a pluralistic membership. Romans12:5 says, "So we, being many, are one Body in Christ, and every one members one of another." The Gospel of the Kingdom is Believers' rebirth as a new creation into God's Kingdom where there is a "chosen generation, a royal priesthood, a holy nation, a peculiar people" (1 Peter 2: 9) who are joined and knitted together in unity in Kingdom community. The pluralistic gospel of the Kingdom with repentance and remission of sins also involves the ongoing spiritual transformation, maturation, and sanctification of each Believer's soul to receive and contribute to a multi-member Kingdom community of Believers for the purpose of recapturing the stewardship of God's creation, which Jesus won on the Roman Cross by defeating the kingdom of darkness (1 John 3:8).

In truth, it is the "goodness of God that leads you to repentance" (Romans 2:4). This "goodness" is that Believers, with created fallen immortal spirits and souls have been reconciled to Father God and become citizens of Heaven and join the family and the Kingdom of God (John 1:2; 1 John 3:12). Believers receive a born again, perfect spirit that is holy and righteous and does not ever sin (Hebrews 12:23; Ephesians 4:24; 1 John 3:9), but their souls are not born again and need to be transformed and renewed (Romans 12:2). Those new Believers coming in through the Joel 2 Third Revival will find the expression of the goodness of God through His *Ekklesia* Kingdom community loving lifestyle. The Lord wants Believers to bring new disciples from the Revival into the vibrant family of God where they are loved and trained to enter the crucifixion of Christ Jesus' humanity nature and to allow Christ's divine nature to live His life in them and through them to touch others. The Lord wants Believers to join the household of faith, learn to love and nurture one another in the Kingdom community of Believers where God the Word, God the Holy Spirit, and God the Father are invited in the spiritual fellowship, learn wise servanthood, and express love and care to those in the world about the goodness of God. This is not some cultist belief of control. This is the truth from Scripture about Believers experiencing the resurrected life of Christ's humanity nature as the Ascended One and Christ's divine nature as the Present One living amid Believers. This is about Believers being led by the Holy Spirit and Christ's divine nature to fulfill the will of Father God as the Kingdom of God is manifested in Believers and through Believers to the world as the gospel of the Kingdom and repentance and remission of sins are both preached.

Ephesians 2:19-22 says, "Now, therefore, you are no longer strangers and foreigners, but fellow citizens (of Heaven) with the saints and members of the household of God, having been built on the foundation of the apostles and prophets, Jesus Christ Himself being the chief cornerstone, in whom the whole building, being fitted together, grows into a holy temple in the Lord, in whom you also are being built together for a dwelling place of God in the Spirit." The Lord's purpose for His *Ekklesia* is to build a dwelling place for the Godhead, with Christ Jesus' divine nature, manifesting the will of God the Father through the presence and power of the Holy Spirit for the manifested Kingdom of God here on earth as it is in Heaven.

As each Believer reaches the full measure of grace in gifting and calling together in Kingdom community sharing, loving, learning, and supporting, then the Kingdom community of Believers become the communal expression of the fullness of Christ's divine nature ruling and reigning in His Kingdom here on earth and directing and ordaining Ephesians 4:11 Ministers "For the perfecting of the saints, for the work of the ministry, for the edifying of the body of Christ: Till we all come in the unity of the faith, and of the knowledge of the Son of God, unto a perfect man, unto the measure of the stature of the fullness of Christ" (Ephesians 4:12-13). However, each Believer must be equipped with the fullness of the Lord's grace according to the measure of Christ's gift (Ephesians 4:7) in order to do his or her part in edifying or building up the Body of Christ, with each Believer supplying what Christ has given as his or her part as a bondservant of Christ (1 Corinthians 12: 12-27), for the benefit of the Kingdom community of Believers and building the Kingdom of God to overcome the influences of the kingdoms of this world.

Therefore, the preaching of the great American individualistic, self-fulfillment gospel of everlasting life or obtaining one's ticket to Heaven is an anemic message, at best, because it leaves out the activating into ministry the gospel of the Kingdom, which is the joining with Christ as family and as participants in the Kingdom spiritual government as Ambassadors and Kingdom spiritual army as good Soldiers (2 Corinthians 5:20; 2 Timothy 2:3-4) for the witnessing to the world system where *agape* love will be the primary motivation and the *zoe* life will be the primary blessing in an economic system in the New Heaven and New Earth (Revelation 21:1) based upon giving and receiving as opposed to buying and selling.

Consequently, the gospel of individual salvation to obtain everlasting life and to go to Heaven instead of hell are blessings but need to be preached with the gospel of the Kingdom. Many new Believers are taught incorrectly there is no work to be done by them personally after initial salvation based upon Ephesians 2:8-9, since Jesus did all necessary work already for their salvation and eternal life. These new Believers are taught that Jesus' death on the Cross and His resurrection are all that Believers need to know following initial salvation. Yet, this is like receiving a gift of a horse by someone who knows nothing about how to care for the horse. The horse was a gift, but you have to actually feed, water, groom, and build a stable for the horse to keep it healthy, store lots of hay, have available a block of salt, and also have to ride the horse to keep the horse tame.

The next verse after Ephesians 2: 8-9 is Ephesians 2:10 says, "For we are His workmanship, created in Christ Jesus unto good works, which God hath before ordained that we should walk in them." Paul was not a schizophrenic because he was speaking of unbelievers obtaining initial salvation that does not require work in Ephesians 2:8-9, but he was speaking to new Believers after initial salvation where God has ordained each Believer to perform good Kingdom works. Similarly, in Philippians 2:12-13, Paul speaks to already saved Believers, "Wherefore, my beloved (Believers), as ye have always obeyed, not as in my presence only, but now much more in my absence, work out your own salvation with fear and trembling. For it is God which worketh in you both to will and to do of His good pleasure."

These new Believers need to perform the obligation to relate with other Believers and submitting to the Godhead to transform their souls by experiencing fellowship on a regular basis with other Believers in loving and caring Kingdom community in God's Kingdom, for the purpose of edifying, engifting, and building up the Body of Christ. This is much more than going to a building, sitting in pews or chairs, worshiping the Lord, listening and taking notes of a sermon spoken by the Pastor or Leader of the congregation, and repeating this tradition week after week for their entire lives. What a pity! There would be little or no rewards before the Judgment Seat of Christ, but at least the Believer has eternal life instead of infernal death.

Trusting fellowship of Believers in the Kingdom community starts on Sunday and continues the entire week. The Kingdom of God is not a religion but is a 24/7 commitment of experiencing the Kingdom of God personally and in fellowship, not just ritualistically in a religious hierarchy. The Kingdom of God sends Believers as Kingdom of Heaven Citizens and as Ambassadors into the marketplace of ideas, employment, businesses, schools, homes, governments, and this is the mandate of Jesus in Acts 1:8.

Learning to love other Believers in the Lord in the same Kingdom community is a revolutionary idea, especially in an individualistic focused society in the natural as in the U.S. and other first world countries. This requires that Believers learn about the history, life, gifts, and needs of other Believers, staying connected with them regularly in the event of health needs or financial needs as part of the responsibility of the citizens in the Kingdom community. In so doing, other Believers in the Kingdom community group will do the same and join and knit together in unity of the Lord in the Kingdom community to supply to others in the Body of Christ with that which Christ has engifted and "graced" everyone. Ephesians 4:7 says, "But unto every one of us is given grace according to the measure of the gift of Christ's (divine nature)." Jesus' humanity nature ate, slept, and did the work of the ministry daily with His disciples, so, His disciples were trained like Jesus had been trained as a Carpenter by His stepfather, Joseph. Jesus called it discipleship training.

Here is my own positive experience regarding loving Kingdom community fellowship. For several years, I belonged to a fellowship of Believers in Rancho Cucamonga, California, at that time called Church of the Foothills, with Pastor David Cunningham, who taught and encouraged spiritual loving fellowship in the Church Kingdom community as a way of life. Believers were there when a fellow Believer was in need and were intimately involved in each other's lives in a loving but not a compulsory or controlling way. This meant when a Believer had to move, the other Believers would come and help him move; mow the Believer's lawn if he had a back injury; come work on an elder or single mom Believer's car if it needed repair; provide food when the Believer was sick; bring to the single mom or family with little income Christmas presents for the children, or come clean the house and help with the older children when a mother just had a baby. These acts of kindness were done while the Believers had a vigorous outreach into the Kingdom community and were encouraged to share their experiences in school, employment, in every place where people gathered. Most people inherently want fellowship with friends, so making friends became the method prior to inviting them to have fellowship. When I had my own *Ekklesia*, I set up home fellowships and encouraged the Believers to take care of each other. I would encourage the married couples to allow a single Believer to go with them to have a fun time at a Pizza Parlor where the children played games, or when they went out to dinner, went to watch a movie, or simply came over to fellowship at the home. All along the Believers were encouraged to invite the presence of Christ's divine nature and speak about the goodness of the Lord and His word and what each Believer thought the Holy Spirit is saying to them that day. Also, it was a time to hear each other's testimonies of the circumstances that led them to accept Jesus as Lord and Savior. I often was surprised to discover what interesting Believers there are in the same fellowship of Kingdom community. There may be Believers in your fellowship that enjoy going to some sports event or like knitting or watching Sherlock Holmes movies. I have had brothers living with me and my family for many years where we daily would center our conversations about the Lord Jesus Christ, studying the living word of God, the discipline of the indwelling Godhead, and the move of the Holy Spirit. Believers helped each other with natural needs, celebrated with other Believers when they had successes, and were in daily prayer for each other when there was a need. The divine presence of the Lord as the Present One was always there when we gathered in fellowship.

Back in the 1960's and 1970's Jesus Movement Revival by the Holy Spirit with the message of love was celebrated even in song in the world and was sung by many artists. I remember the 1971 great song of friendship by James Taylor and Carole King, "You've Got a Friend," with the following lyrics: "When you're down and troubled and you need a helping hand and nothing, ooh, nothing is going right. Close your eyes and think of me and soon I will be there to brighten up even your darkest nights. You just call out my name, and you know wherever I am I'll come running, oh yeah baby to see you again. Winter, spring, summer or fall, all you have to do is call and I'll be there, yeah, yeah, yeah. You've got a friend."

The message to the individual Believers by Paul in 1 Corinthians 12:7 was that "the manifestation of the Spirit is given to each one for the profit of all." The purpose of the engiftment was "for the profit of all" instead of "for the profit of the individual alone."

Similarly, the message of Paul in 1 Corinthians 13:4-8 was that the engiftments to individuals in the Kingdom community of Believers were nothing unless they had love for their brothers and sisters in the Kingdom. He said in 1 Corinthians 13:4-8 that "… (*agape*) love suffers long and is kind; (*agape*) love does not envy; (*agape*) love does not parade itself, is not puffed up; does not behave rudely, does not seek its own, is not provoked, thinks no evil, does not rejoice in iniquity, but rejoices in the truth; bears all things, Believers all things, hopes all things, endures all things. (*Agape*) Love never fails…" By its nature, agape love must be expressed by a Believer to someone else, and as the Believer expresses agape love, the Believer may learn to express *agape* love to his own perhaps separated natural family members and be motivated to repent of being unloving in his life.

In fact, 1 Corinthians 13:3 says, "And though I bestow all my goods to feed the poor, and though I give my body to be burned, but have not love, it profits me nothing." In a comparable message, Paul says to the Body of Believers in 1 Corinthians 14:12, "Even so you, since you are zealous for spiritual gifts, let it be for the edification of the Church (*Ekklesia*) that you seek to excel." Seeking the righteousness, peace, and joy of the Holy Spirit is seeking the Kingdom of God (Romans 14:17).

Are Believers to plead for peace or truce with the fallen world and Satan? No! Is there true Godly "righteousness" in the world under the control of Satan? No! The fallen world outside the Kingdom of God has only the knowledge from the Tree of Knowledge of Good and Evil (humanism) and demonic wisdom from the kingdom of darkness (James 3:15). The true righteousness, peace and joy in the Holy Spirit defines the pluralistic Kingdom of God (Romans 14:17). In whom does the Holy Spirit, along with the whole Godhead, dwell? The Holy Spirit and the whole Godhead indwell the Body of Christ pluralistically and individually. Believers are to have joy and peace and righteousness with each other. "Peace" by its very definition means being at rest or being at a state of no conflict with another person. Thus, true peace is being reconciled with God (2 Corinthians 5:18-20) and with fellow Believers. The joy of the Lord means joy with the Lord and also includes the joy Believers are to share with other Believers. Righteousness is not what the world thinks is right or politically correct, but what God says in His Bible what is His righteousness. Believers are mandated in Matthew 6:33 to seek first the Kingdom of God and His righteousness, not to seek first the kingdoms of this world and its demonic sense of right thinking. Righteousness, peace, and joy are the fruit of the Spirit that need to be the transactional motivations of Kingdom interactions and in every activity in Believers' lives (Ephesians 5:9; Galatians 5:22-23).

Many Believers can have good fellowship with the Lord's divine nature, or the Holy Spirit, but have difficulty in living in close fellowship with other Believers in the household of God. No wonder members of the Body of Christ have divisions and schisms. Believers oftentimes treat people in the world better or the same as they treat other Believers and should not be. All Believers are in their journey to become more Christ like in their souls, but most all Believers have disappointments, losses, traitors, and deaths that cause them to have fractured personalities that need healing and mending. The fish must be caught, but they need to be cleaned after being caught. Yet, before the fish can be caught, the fishermen's nets have to be mended; otherwise, the fish escape. Jesus told Peter, Andrew, James, and John to "Follow me, and I will make you fishers of men" (Matthew 4:19). The repentance and remission of sins message must be preached with the gospel of the Kingdom of God, (although they do not have to be in the same sermon) as Believers will get bored if all they do is go to a building and sit in a pew or chair and do nothing for the work of ministry. Believers' hearts are being tugged by the Holy Spirit to go into the world system and bring the principles of the Kingdom of God into the decadent, fallen world to take possession of all industries, businesses, and professions, along with the earth, plants, birds, animals, fish, and every living thing into the dominion control of the Kingdom of God. When masses of Believers are activated to do ministry in these venues and focuses, then the interests in becoming ministers in the Kingdom of God and the body of Christ will cause revival to come to the *Ekklesia*.

Therefore, when one is saved out of the Kingdom of darkness and conveyed into the Kingdom of the Son of God's love (Colossians 1:13), then the gospel of the Kingdom must be preached to include this new family adoption into the household of God (Romans 8:15). In this new Kingdom community that Believers live, there are family responsibilities of loyalty, love, work, financial offerings, and making sure it is God the Father, God the Word, and God the Holy Spirit that are worshipped and that the Believers must volunteer to become Kingdom government spiritual Ambassadors and Kingdom spiritual Soldiers as part of gospel of the Kingdom of God (2 Corinthians 5:20; 2 Timothy 2:3-4).

It is the whole united Body of Christ which Jesus will return to receive as a Bride, not a group of individuals living as if they do not know each other, do not belong to the Lord's pluralistic Kingdom, or do not love and care for each other. John 17:21-23 says, "That they all may be one; even as You, Father, are in Me and I in You, that they also may be in Us; that the world may believe that You have sent Me. And the glory which You have given Me I have given to them, that they may be one, even as We are one; I in them, and You in Me, that they may be perfected into one, that the world may know that You have sent Me and have loved them even as You have loved Me."

Jesus said in 1 John 4:20-21, "If a man says, 'I love God, and hateth his brother, he is a liar: for he that loveth not his brother whom he hath seen, how can he love God whom he hath not seen? And this commandment have we from Him, That he who loveth God love his brother also."

Jesus further said in John 13:34-35, "A new commandment I give unto you, 'That ye love one another; as I have loved you, that ye also love one another.' By this shall all men know that ye are my disciples, if ye have love one to another." Similarly, Jesus continued in John 15:9-13, "As the Father loved Me, I also have loved you; abide in My love. If you keep My commandments, you will abide in My love, just as I have kept My Father's commandments and abide in His love. These things I have spoken to you, that My joy may remain in you, and that your joy may be full. This is My commandment, that you love one another as I have loved you. Greater love has no one than this, than to lay down one's life for his friends."

The Body of Christ is pluralistic, and the building or edifying of the Body of Christ is a pluralistic mandate (Ephesians 4:12-13). 1 Peter 2:5 says, "You also, as living stones, are being built up a spiritual house, a holy priesthood, to offer up spiritual sacrifices acceptable to God through

Jesus Christ." 1 Peter 2:9-10 says, "But you are a chosen generation, a royal priesthood, a holy nation, His own special people, that you may proclaim the praises of Him who called you out of darkness into His marvelous light; who once were not a people but are now the people of God, who had not obtained mercy but now have obtained mercy."

As Peter stated in the above scriptures, the Lord has called individual Believers joined together in His Kingdom to be the Kingdom children of God, which is an emphasis on both the individual salvation and pluralistic Kingdom community life of Believers who have obtained God's mercy and who become the loving servants of the King in His Kingdom. Believers are Royal Priests individually but expressed communally as a Royal Priesthood. Believers are members of, but communally joined together in, loving fellowship as, a Holy Nation. A nation consists of a group of people who have foundational beliefs in common and are gathered in agreement to support, promote, protect, and defend the rights and care for the needs of each other because of that common bond. Again, the emphasis is upon the unity into One Holy Nation whose individual Believers become matured, but together become Christ's multi-peopled Body and Bride.

The message of the gospel of the Kingdom and repentance and remission of sins is primarily a pluralistic message, and it is what is lacking today in Evangelism; and this practice must change if Believers are going to be in the will of God in His Revival *Ekklesia*. God is calling forth Evangelists who will extend God's grace to people in the world with the invitation to be reconciled with God individually and to be joined to the Body of Christ as members of a new spiritual family with responsible spiritual pluralistic work expanding the Kingdom of God and God's will be done on earth as it is in Heaven. This work has nothing to do with obtaining initial salvation but God directed work after being born-again. Again, the Church is the *Ekklesia* which is a Kingdom pluralistic government assembly (*Ekklesia*) and Kingdom pluralistic military assembly (*Ekklesia*), and each of these two activities are responsibilities of each individual Citizen of the Kingdom of Heaven (Philippians 3:20) while in fellowship with other Believers obeying the Lord's commandment of expressing *agape* love of care to each other (John 13:34-35).

Malachi 4:6 says, "And He will turn the hearts of the fathers to the children, and the hearts of the children to their fathers, lest I come and strike the earth with a curse." Because of an incredible lack of mature fatherhood in many nations, the true gospel of the Kingdom and true message of repentance and remission of sins reconciling mankind to Father God should draw many to become born-again and be born of water and of the Spirit (John 3:3,5) to enter into the Kingdom of God in the great Revival of the end time harvest. In the world where the family unit almost has been disintegrated, the gospel of the Kingdom preached with repentance and remission of sins is the family of God united again under the fatherhood of our loving, covenant making and covenant keeping Father God, who calls many fathers to take care of the fatherless or children of absentee fathers in the Believers' Kingdom community (Malachi 4:6).

BELIEVERS MUST UNITE IN THIS REVIVAL, NOT ACCORDING TO THE FLESH, BUT ACCORDING TO THE NEW MAN IN CHRIST WHO IS THE PERFECT AND SINLESS BORN AGAIN SPIRIT AND JOIN WITH CHRIST AS ONE SPIRIT.

1 Corinthians 6:17 says, "But he that is joined unto the Lord is one spirit." Colossians 3:9-11 says, "Do not lie to one another, since you have put off the old man, with his deeds, and have put

on the New Man, who is renewed in knowledge according to the image of Him who created him, where there is neither Greek nor Jew, circumcised nor uncircumcised, barbarian, Scythian, slave nor free, but Christ is all and in all."

The word "where" starting in verse 11 is a reference to the "new man" in verse 10. It means "in the new man" there is no room for the old natural fallen man still in Adam to be part of the new man creation in Christ Jesus, where seeking Believers find zoe life in Christ's divine nature carrying the resurrected life of Christ Jesus' humanity nature (Ephesians 2:15; 4:24).

THE GREEKS: In the Revival that is coming, Believers should not congregate together only because they like Biblical knowledge and wisdom but include those with other divine mandates. 1 Corinthians 1:22 says in relevant part, "For indeed ... Greeks seek wisdom." The wisdom that the Greeks seek is humanistic wisdom, not the divine wisdom from God. Many Believers are stoic and like me love studying the word of God, acquiring wisdom of the Proverbs, seeking out and applying the principles of the Bible, enjoying learning the Greek and Hebrew meanings behind the words of the Bible, love to be like the Berean Jews who "...received the word with all readiness, and searched the Scriptures daily to find out whether these things were so" (Acts 17:11). There are many Evangelicals and those basically non-Charismatic Christians who love the word of God, and are some of the most knowledgeable Believers. They often live ordered lives and conduct themselves with strict adherence to the laws of the land. Yet, this practice should not be emphasized to the exclusion of others of a different practice to enjoy witnessing signs and wonders because such exclusivity can cause division and elitism. The opposite is also true. In the end time *Ekklesia* Revival, the Holy Spirit in conjunction with God the Word will truly bring unison between the Spirit and the Word, as they have always done, but Believers incorrectly separate the movement of the Spirit and the truth of the Word. It is the partition of beliefs that separate members of the *Ekklesia*, but it is generally because they espouse and teach to others partial truths.

THE JEWS: The Jews were always looking for a miracle, a sign from God, a word of prophecy, or a healing. In some respects, the Jews were like the modern-day Charismatics. 1 Corinthians 1:22 says in relevant part, "For indeed Jews require signs...." A miracle is a substantiation to what is preached that God was in the word preached. Oftentimes, religion needs signs, and the Jews continually looked for them. On the other hand, those movements of the Spirit when the signs manifested later became stale denominations after the signs became less frequent or generally very rare. Many of the old Pentecostal denominations order of today who were once vibrant in allowing the Holy Spirit to move freely in their congregational meetings have legislated out many of the signs and verbal gifts from operating in the open meetings. There can be an overemphasis on signs and wonders as confirming the word preached or decreasing emphasis by limiting the expression of the signs and gifts to the "back room" behind closed doors, to keep the old religious order "user friendly" to attract more people from the world. Both extreme practices grieve the Holy Spirit. It is good that we do not have to see a miracle to believe. Yet, Jesus performed miracles and healings in public, in homes, in rooms, in the Temple courtyard, beside public pools, along the streets, in crowds, or amongst one or two people while he preached or taught the word. These restrictions and circumspection of the Holy Spirit by denominational leaders are nothing more than religious bias and denominational rules to avoid embarrassment from nonperformance and to keep the order of traditional practices in tack. The Holy Spirit is Sovereign God, and He can manifest Himself through the *Ekklesia* Body and does it in an orderly fashion if the *Ekklesia* leaders will allow Him to have free reign. When the word became flesh, God the Word took on personality with Jesus' humanity nature, and everyone may express God's word uniquely through his or her personality. God loves diversity of expression and practice, which happen as Believers are led by the Holy Spirit.

THE BARBARIANS (ROMANS): According to the Greeks, whoever did not speak Greek was considered a Barbarian. The Romans were Barbarians by the Greeks standards because of their warlike characteristics and lack of learned culture. The Romans lacked the culture of the Greeks, so they borrowed much of the Greek culture; for example, by merely changing the names of the Greek gods into Roman gods. The Romans set up their Roman Senate, called the *Ekklesia*, patterned after the Greeks, but they always maintained a King, like Caesar, instead of a purer form of democracy like the Greeks. The Roman Senate was more like a "cabinet" of Caesar, as Caesar would assign tasks for them to do. It is interesting that the Greek democracy only allowed real property owners to vote, as they believed property owners had a vested interest in voting what was in the best interest of the country. The Romans were a clashing, combating, contesting, and confronting group of people. They were cruel, violent, demanded blind obedience, and were much like the strict order of the Nazis of WWII, but did not try to exterminate the Hebrews. They loved the orderly soldiering type lifestyle. Their temperament was to fear the populace and demanded police and military intrusion to keep law and order. Often, I think California is much like the Roman government as it stands for law and order, requiring every business and profession to be licensed and enforce licensure discipline and revocation by the government. On the other hand, Colorado only requires the true professionals, like Lawyers, Medical Doctors, Dentists, Psychologists, Accountants, and Architects to be licensed. Even building Contractors merely put up a bond to build homes in Colorado. California is a police state as it has more police in every city, county, the state, highway patrol, forestry, tax enforcement authorities, than there were in Nazi Germany during WWII. The Romans wanted the conquered people to follow the law. Their law was supreme. They wanted to march, act, conquer their enemies, confront the societies who they conquered with their show of force, allow each culture to continue with its traditions, but stay submitted to the law and order of the Roman Empire government, along with the payment of taxes. Rome was a Code state, as is California and Louisiana. Rome was an unloving culture. Love was secondary to law and order. Today, there are saints in the Body of Christ who want to get things done in the Church. They are the "A Team" type personalities. They do not want to sit around and study the Bible. They want to duplicate the activities in the Book of Acts, today! They see the Body of Christ as an Ephesians 6 Army of Kingdom Soldiers fighting against the forces of darkness. They love casting out demons, going out on the streets to witness, feeding the hungry, clothing the naked, visiting those in prison, sheltering the homeless and fulfilling the social needs along with the spiritual needs of people. These Believers are some of the greatest workers in the Body of Christ. Thus, it is hard to criticize these Believers, but often they blow in, blow up, and blow out without personal fellowship with the local Believers. I especially have seen some Evangelists take offerings using domineering methods that are abusive and somewhat deceitful. Then financial needs come up in the local Church Kingdom community amongst the families, leaving the Pastor to answer complaints and to love and help the people through fellowship.

THE SCYTHIANS (SAVAGES): The Scythians were the unlawful, renegades of society. The Savages looked different. They wore tattoos, dressed like people living on the land, and were unrefined in their cultural and social habits. They would live to fight, get inebriated, and tear down what others built up. In today's Christendom, these Believers would be those who were once drug users, motorcycle gang members, who still have their tattoos, wear their chains, and just change their mottos to "Jesus," like the "Switchblade and the Cross," wear their Christian "colors" that put them in "Jesus' gang." Jesus has united the "Savages" and "Barbarians" with the "Cultural Elite" to create one new man in Christ Jesus. There is room for everybody, and no one is excluded. Yet, instead of pushing their will on others in the Kingdom community, these Scythian Believers must learn gentility and *agape* love and be givers in fellowship instead of being takers in the Body of Christ, while the more conservative have to accept these Scythian Believers in fellowship with love. They may not look like each other, but they both have the image of Christ in their born again spirits.

1 Corinthians 12:6 says, "And there are diversities of activities, but it is the same God who works all in all." God does not want discrimination in the Body of Christ. A Kingdom community cannot be built on a gathering of Believers with only race or historical culture in common. This faulty custom is one of the reasons why there is division in the Body of Christ into White congregations, Black congregations, Korean congregations, Hispanic congregations, and so on. The Kingdom community must drop these racial and cultural differences based on the differences of the flesh and culture and become one diversified Body of Believers. A healthy *Ekklesia* should have red, yellow, brown, black and white Believers. They should have Hispanic cultures mixed with Asian cultures, along with Eastern European cultures intermingled with Western European cultures. Believers must stop gathering in communities based upon color or culture and join in unity by the Holy Spirit into one new man in Christ Jesus and enjoy the Present One in their midst. Old religious order traditionally is built on the flesh based on unique races or cultures not being led by the Holy Spirit in fellowship that is designed by the Lord's divine nature to enhance maturation and *agape* love. Diversity of races and cultures is good and stops turmoil, suspicion, and division. God sometimes puts a Believer with another Believer that rubs the Believer the wrong way to mature the Believer as how to deal with a diversity of personalities. Proverbs 27:17 says, "Iron sharpeneth iron; so, a man sharpeneth the countenance of his friend."

The Godhead does not want to relate to Believers' souls in the flesh, but in the spirit. Romans 8:5-10 says, "For they that are after the flesh do mind (in the soul) the things of the flesh; but they that are after the Spirit (Holy Spirit and born again spirit) the things of the spirit. For to be carnally minded (in the soul) is death; but to be spiritually minded (in the soul) is life and peace. Because the carnal mind (in the soul) is enmity against God: for it is not subject to the law of God, neither indeed can be. So then they that are in the flesh cannot please God. But ye (Believers) are not in the flesh, but in the spirit, if so be that the Spirit of God (Holy Spirit) dwell in you. Now if any man has not the Spirit of Christ (born again spirit from the incorruptible Seed of Christ's resurrected humanity spirit), he is none of His. And if Christ (divine nature) be in you (your soul), the body is dead (mortified by the Holy Spirit per Romans 8:13) because of sin; but the (born again) spirit is life because of righteousness."

Those Believers who have come into the Kingdom of God, who were radicals in the world, should be able to congregate and have fellowship with mainline Baptists or Pentecostals Believers for example. Faith Believers should be able to have Kingdom community with those who are Church of God or Assembly of God Believers in Christ. Why do Believers congregate only with Believers who think, live, and look like them? Are they trying to feel comfortable in their flesh? Perhaps the new wineskin will be a commitment to foster diversity of practice, diversity of color, diversity of culture, and diversity of doctrinal beliefs without suffering foundational doctrinal impurities or divisions.

Believers should only have fellowship based upon the unity of the faith and Spirit, which we share (Ephesians 4:4-6). Believers should have *agape* loving fellowship together in their Kingdom community and as family members in the household of God. Believers should be able to *agape* love each other with the *agape* love of God that is shed abroad in their hearts (Romans 5:5). Believers should stop building the old religious order on the basis of flesh or culture and build on the foundation, which is Christ Jesus, Who died for all races, Who He wants to be the Body and Betrothed of Christ.

Paul emphasizes the need for unity by reminding Believers what they all have in common. Ephesians 4: 4-6 says, "There is one body, and one Spirit, even as ye are called in one hope of your calling; One Lord, one faith, one baptism, One God and Father of all, who is above all, and through all, and in you all."

BELIEVERS SHOULD PRACTICE TRUE KINGDOM COMMUNITY
UNDER THE HEADSHIP OF CHRIST'S DIVINE NATURE

1 Corinthians 1:9-13 says, "God is faithful, by whom ye were called unto the fellowship of His Son Jesus Christ our Lord. Now I beseech you, brethren, by the name of our Lord Jesus Christ, that ye all speak the same thing, and that there be no divisions among you; but that ye be perfectly joined together in the same mind and in the same judgment. For it hath been declared unto me of you, my brethren, by them which are of the house of Chloe, that there are contentions among you. Now this I say, that every one of you saith, 'I am of Paul; and I of Apollos; and I of Cephas; and I of Christ.' Is Christ divided? Was Paul crucified for you? Or were ye baptized in the name of Paul?" Even though Paul continuously preached the gospel of the Kingdom of God along with repentance and remission of sins, he had to deal with divisions, problems, the issue of circumcision, the issue of faith alone, making people understand the true Kingdom government where there are faithful Ambassadors and Soldiers, and dealing with the Jews with their laws and customs instead of salvation by faith alone.

Believers were called into the fellowship with Christ's divine nature as the Body of Christ's humanity nature. Believers are to have fellowship with one another where Christ's divine nature as the Present One is in fellowship with Believers to celebrate Jesus' humanity nature Who sits on His throne in Heaven as the King of kings, the Lord of lords, and High Priest as the Ascended One. Believers enjoy and are satisfied with Christ's divine nature as their portion. Christ's divine nature as the Present One is the unique center of Believers' attention in the spiritual Kingdom community in which they live to celebrate and experience the resurrected life of Christ's humanity nature. Christ-centered loving Kingdom community life resolves all divisions amongst the brethren.

This passage of Scripture unveils, and the rest of 1 Corinthians reveals to Believers, the all-inclusive and all present Christ's divine nature, into Whom Believers have been called to celebrate, praise, and worship His presence as their Kingdom community King as the Present One. 2 Corinthians 3:11 says, "For another foundation no one is able to lay besides that which is laid, which is Jesus Christ." Jesus Christ is expressed as the Head of the Church Kingdom community of Believers (1 Corinthians 11:3; Ephesians 1:22-23) and corporately as the Body of Christ (1 Corinthians 12:12).

Christ Jesus is the gift for all ages, for all seasons, and for every Kingdom community of Believers for their enjoyment. Believers need to focus their attention on Christ's divine nature as the Present One, and all problems regarding division will be resolved. It is into fellowship of God the Father and God the Word through the jurisdictional authority here on earth of the Holy Spirit that brings the grace and love of Christ as the Present One amid Believers' spiritual Kingdom community.

1 John 1:3 says, "That which we have seen and heard we report also to you that you also may have fellowship with us, and indeed our fellowship is with the Father and with His Son Jesus Christ."

The fellowship with Jesus Christ' divine nature and humanity nature while He was here on earth became the fellowship that Apostle John described was the same fellowship Believers were to have with each other. Acts 4:42 says, "And they continued steadfastly in the teaching and the fellowship of the Apostles, in the breaking of bread and the prayers."

2 Corinthians 13:14 says, "The grace of the Lord Jesus Christ and the love of God and the fellowship of the Holy Spirit be with you all." The grace of the Lord is the presence of the Lord's divine nature, Himself, giving resurrected life to Believers for their enjoyment (John 1:17; 1 Corinthians 15:10). The expressed *agape* love of God is the indwelling presence of God, Himself, giving forth the grace of the Lord (1 John 4:8, 16). The fellowship of the Spirit is the presence of the indwelling Holy Spirit, Himself, who transmits the grace of the Lord and the *agape* love of God for Believers' Kingdom community participation. In truth, 2 Corinthians 13:14 reveals that the presentation of the triune nature of the Godhead is not just for a doctrinal understanding of a systematic theology, but for the dispensation of grace and love by the Godhead, Himself, in His triune nature into the Kingdom community of the redeemed. In the Bible, the triune nature of the Godhead is never revealed merely as a doctrine, but as the relationship of God with His new creatures in Christ, and more particularly, in His Jehovahistic, covenantal relationship with His chosen Believers.

Again, 1 Corinthians 1:10 says, "Now I beseech you, brothers, through the name of our Lord Jesus Christ, that you all speak the same thing and that there be no divisions among you, but that you be attuned in the same mind (in the soul) and in the same opinion." Apostle Paul begins to deal with the divisions among the Corinthians. First, he besought them through the exalted name of the Lord Jesus Christ that is above every name (Philippians 2:9) and should be the unique Name among all Believers that would cause every knee to bow down in worship. Paul discerned that the Corinthians were divisive and ranked the names of Paul, Apollos, and Cephas (Peter) as equal with the name of Christ, just as Peter on the Mount of Transfiguration mistakenly elevated Moses and Elijah with the same rank in God's majestic order as Jesus (Matthew 17:1-8).

Believers must not exalt any Believer on a co-equal level with Christ Jesus, as this will cause divisions as to who has the greater stature. There is only One, all-inclusive Christ Jesus, whom is the King of kings, Lord of lords, High Priests of priests, and Jesus as the *Alpha* and the *Omega*. There is none other besides Him Who is the Head of the *Ekklesia* (Ephesians 1:20-23).

In the letter to the Corinthian Believers, Apostle Paul dealt with eleven problems. The first and leading problem was the divisions amongst them, which he refers to as "heresies" translated as "divisions." Divisions are the root of most problems amongst the Believers. The first order of priority amongst Believers in any Kingdom community is keeping in oneness of the Spirit in the Body of Christ (Ephesians 4:1-6).

The Greek word for "attuned" in 1 Corinthians 1:10 is "*katartizo*," which means "to repair, mend, fit, frame, prepare, join perfectly together and restore." The same Greek word was used in Matthew 4:21 when Jesus came to James and John who were mending their nets. Mending is the art of putting things back together which were broken or ripped, so that the restored item can function again in its perfected wholeness. Mending is performed before Believers are perfectly joined together in *agape* love.

The Kingdom community of Believers needs to be mended together, so that as one Body of Believers they are in harmony, having the same mind to speak the same thing, that is, Christ Jesus, His death on the Cross, His resurrection, His ascension, His heavenly Enthronement, His Intercession, and His soon return, along with the fellowship of the entire Godhead, God the Father, God the Word, and God the Holy Spirit, together as One God.

Some people study, study, study, to make them have a razor-sharp mind. On the other hand, caring persons learn how to mend through sewing together relationships. If you try to sew fabric with a razor instead of with a needle, you can cut the garment into pieces. However, trying to mend together people who are not of the same mind causes friction in the Kingdom community of Believers. Believers must agree on the foundational beliefs and not require total acceptance on the elective beliefs. These were the divisions that caused the Corinthians to not be of the same mind.

"I AM OF PAUL." Paul was a thinker. He spent three years in the desert where he was taught by Christ, Himself, of the mysteries that he wrote in the New Testament. He was not a flamboyant speaker, but he knew the word of the Old Testament better than all the other Apostles. Many Believers seek the "Word of God" for knowledge and relate with the writings of Paul. Yet today Paul would chastise Believers who call themselves Lutherans, Pentecostals, Methodists, or other religious denominations with distinct religious practices that they have made additional doctrines. Believers must only be followers of Jesus but remain in Kingdom community fellowship. Paul, being the presumptive writer of the book of Hebrews, stated in Hebrews 6:1-2, "Therefore leaving the principles of the doctrine of Christ, let us go on unto perfection; not laying again the foundation of repentance from dead works, and of faith toward God, of the doctrine of baptisms, and of laying on of hands, and of resurrection of the dead, and of eternal judgment." These doctrines are the foundational beliefs that all Believers should have, and the rest of the experiences and practices are electives. The battle is concerning the special electives that are not foundational beliefs of the Apostles, and these cause divisions and factions that form the foundational differences in various denominations.

For example, Pentecostals should be able to have loving fellowship with Baptists. The Calvinism versus Arminianism issue will never be settled in the finite minds of man. Leaders should not split hairs or Churches over the issue. The Truth is that God is all knowing but not all controlling. Believers need to avoid extreme Calvinism and avoid hyper-Arminianism. God is all knowing but not all controlling. The two extreme positions of Calvinism and Arminianism are not the only positions backing up the saints' beliefs, and only a few Believers take the extreme positions, anyway. Justification by faith does not give a Christian a license to commit ordinary sin; yet ordinary sin already is forgiven so long as it does not become a practice and hardens the heart to the point of apostasy and total rejection of Christ and the entire Godhead. Regardless, these are issues of the untransformed souls, not the perfect, sinless, born again spirits of Believers. Souls never receive absolute perfection in their lifetimes here on earth. Even after initial salvation and receiving a born again spirit, Believers still have the influence of the flesh in their souls and do sin, but their sins are forgiven. 1 John 1:7-10 says, "But if we walk in the light, as He is in the light, we have fellowship one with another, and the blood of Jesus Christ His Son cleanseth us from all sin. If we say that we have no sin, we deceive ourselves, and the truth is not in us. If we confess our sins, He is faithful and just to forgive us our sins, and to cleanse us from all unrighteousness. If we say that we have not sinned, we make Him a liar, and His word is not in us."

"I AM OF APOLLOS." Apollos was a dynamic speaker. He was like well-known ministers today, who can move the crowds with their humor and eloquence. Yet, you must be a disciple of Christ, not a disciple of a man who is still in the process of soul maturation, which is every Minister and Believer.

"I AM OF CEPHAS." Peter was an action-minded Apostle. Peter was the only one who jumped out of the boat to walk on the water at Jesus' bidding. Peter was the one who was revealed who Jesus was and boldly stated, "Thou art the Christ, the Son of the living God." Peter was the one, though, who wanted to build three tabernacles on the Mount of Transfiguration, making Moses and Elijah equal with Christ's humanity nature. Peter was the one who would often be on the streets, whose very shadow falling on people in Acts 5 caused them to be healed. Peter was your man on the street, and a doer of God's word.

"I AM OF CHRIST." To say "I am of Christ" in this way was to exclude the Apostles and their teachings or the rejection of the necessity of belonging to and living in a Kingdom community. I am just a follower of Christ. I do not belong to the *Ekklesia* or a Kingdom community of Believers. I am a lone ranger for Jesus." However, this "I am of" is still divisive, for the Believer would think of himself as an elitist and loner.

The same is a problem today when Believers say: "I am a Lutheran, I am a Baptist, I am a Charismatic, I am a Non-denominational, I am a Catholic, I am an Episcopalian, etc." This is divisive denominationalism. Christ is the unique Head of His *Ekklesia*. Jesus' humanity nature was the only One Who was crucified for all Believers and eradicated their sins on the Cross. Believers are to gather in Kingdom community to enjoy the fullness of Christ's divine nature's expression here on earth as the Present One. Jesus' humanity nature is the Ascended One, sitting on the throne in Heaven, who is the spiritual Father of Believers' born again spirits (Isaiah 9:6; Hebrews 2:13). Jesus was referring to His divine nature, God the Word, when He said in Matthew 18: 20, "For where two or three are gathered together in my name, there am I in the midst of them."

All Believers were baptized to enter the death and resurrection of Christ's humanity nature, as Jesus is the crucified, resurrected, Ascended One and the Sovereign King of His Kingdom community. His unique Name, denoting His office title as Savior, King, Lord, and High Priest has the Name above any other name, and His Name cannot be replaced by a denomination name, or the name of any of their historical leaders.

During the season of the *Ekklesia* in Revival, Believers must not put a name on the revival movement of God. Believers must open their hearts and give all Believers the right hand of fellowship in the love of Jesus. This does not mean Believers have to embrace elective religious rituals or gift operations, but Believers do need to stop forcing on others their "pet" doctrinal ritual practices. It is the divergent practices that often separate Believers, not the fundamental beliefs pertaining the death, resurrection, ascension, intercession, and return of Christ's humanity nature. Some Believers become elitists concerning their elective religious practices, but they must stay humble before God. Peter in 2 Peter 5:5-6 paraphrased Proverbs 3:34 and said "God resists the proud but gives grace to the humble. Therefore, humble yourself under the mighty hand of God, that He may exalt you in due season, casting all your care upon Him, for He cares for you."

Jesus as the Passover Sacrificial Lamb, Had to be Examined

CHAPTER EIGHT

Jesus, As The Passover Sacrificial Lamb, Had To Be Examined

AS THE PASSOVER LAMB, JESUS
HAD TO BE WITHOUT BLEMISH OR SPOT

Referring to Jesus as the true Passover Sacrificial Lamb that had to be examined, Peter said in 1 Peter 1:19, "But with the precious blood of Christ, as of a Lamb without blemish and without spot." Hebrews 9: 25-26 says, "Nor yet that He (Jesus' humanity nature) should offer Himself often, as the High Priest entereth into the holy place every year with blood of others; for then must He (Jesus' humanity nature) often have suffered since the foundation of the world: but now once in the end of the world hath He (Jesus' humanity nature) appeared to put away sin by the sacrifice of Himself (His divine nature as the high priest who offered his humanity nature as the sacrificial lamb of God without spot or blemish)."

Jesus' humanity nature was and is the unblemished Passover Sacrificial Lamb, who was born without sin and committed no sin before and after His death, resurrection, and ascension to Heaven (Luke 1:35; 1 Peter 2:22; 2 Corinthians 5:21; Hebrews 4:15; 1 John 3:5). Jesus is still the sinless and unblemished Passover Lamb, Who sacrificed Himself to bring eternal life to all who call upon His name to avoid infernal death. Jesus chose to be the Passover Sacrificial Lamb out of love. Jesus said in John 15:13, "Greater love hath no man than this, that a Man lay down His life for his friends." Jesus' divine nature, God the Word, performed the duties as the High Priest offering up Jesus' humanity nature as the Passover Sacrificial Lamb. Paul in1 Corinthians 5:7 makes it clear when he says, "For Christ, our Passover lamb, has been sacrificed."

God, Himself, was present and participated in giving life to the First Adam before there was sin, and God was present and participated in bringing a sacrificial death to the Last Adam for the forgiveness of sin. Life and death are outside of religion and can have only its redemptive value in the Kingdom of God, where Jesus' precious blood speaks a better covenant (Hebrews 12:24) and has precious redemptive value to God and for Man (Colossians 1:14,20). Jesus' divine nature "… was clothed with a vesture dipped in blood: and His name is called The Word of God" (Revelation 19:13).

As the Passover Lamb, Jesus had to be "examined" to make sure He was without blemish. Exodus 12:3, 5-7 says, "Speak to all the congregation of Israel, saying: 'On the tenth of this month every man shall take for himself a Lamb, according to the house of his father, a lamb for a household… Your Lamb shall be without blemish, a male of the first year. You may take it from the sheep or from the goats. Now you shall keep it until the fourteenth day of the same month. Then the whole assembly of the congregation of Israel shall kill it at twilight. And they shall take some of the blood and put it on the two doorposts and on the lintel of the houses where they eat it." Exodus 12:3, 5-7 lays the foundation for the Feast of Passover.

When Israelites were enslaved in Egypt, and it was time for their deliverance, the unblemished

Passover lamb was killed, the blood was applied to the two doorposts and the lintel of each Israelite house for the deliverance from death of the firstborn. In Exodus 12:13 the Scripture describes the shedding of blood of the Passover lamb in Egypt for Israel's redemption. The blood of the lamb was placed upon the doorposts and the lintel, out of the sight of the people in the house. The meat of the lamb was taken inside and eaten, but the blood was left outside and out of sight of mankind inside. God said, "When I see the blood I will pass over you." Therefore, the blood was for the seeing by God or the presenting to God, not man.

The firstborn male child was entitled to receive a double portion of the parents' inheritance because the firstborn son had the responsibility commanded by God to fulfill and finish his father's obligations owed to God, along with his own obligations God called him to do.

The passage of Scripture refers to a singular Passover Lamb, not Passover lambs. This is a direct reference to Jesus' humanity nature as the One and Only Passover Lamb. The Passover Lamb reference in Exodus is a type of Christ Jesus, or Messiah, to come and to die a sacrificial death to bring eternal life, instead of infernal death, to God's adopted children in Christ.

In Matthew 21:1-5, Jesus came into Jerusalem in triumph riding a donkey and colt. The donkey represented the fulfillment of the Old Hebrew Covenant under Moses and the prophets. The donkey had been "broken" under the weight of the Hebrew religion; it had been "ridden" many times by others before Jesus. However, the colt was new and "unbroken" and not ridden, which represented the New Covenant which carried only the weight of Jesus and no other.

Since Jesus was the Head of His *Ekklesia* (Ephesians 1:22), and Believers are His body (Ephesians 1:23), Jesus had to be without spot or blemish to cause His Body, His *Ekklesia*, to be without spot or blemish. Ephesians 5:26-27 says, "That he might sanctify and cleanse it with the washing of water by the word, that He might present it to Himself a glorious *Ekklesia*, not having spot, or wrinkle, or any such thing; but that it should be holy and without blemish."

JESUS UNDERGOES EXAMINATION TO QUALIFY AS THE UNBLEMISH PASSOVER LAMB

After His triumphal entry, Jesus spent about six days where He underwent the examination by the religious, political, and social leaders of His day, with the religious leaders not knowing Jesus was the Passover Lamb.

THE FIRST QUESTION WAS BY THE CHIEF PRIESTS AND ELDERS. Matthew 21: 23-27 says, "Now when He came into the temple, the chief priests and the elders of the people confronted Him as He was teaching, and said, 'By what authority are You doing these things? And who gave You this authority?' But Jesus answered and said to them, 'I also will ask you one thing, which if you tell Me, I likewise will tell you by what authority I do these things: The baptism of John-- where was it from? From Heaven or from men?' And they reasoned among themselves, saying, 'If we say, "From Heaven," He will say to us, "Why then did you not believe him?" 'But if we say, "From men," we fear the multitude, for all count John as a prophet.' So, they answered Jesus and said, 'We do not know.' And He said to them, 'Neither will I tell you by what authority I do these things.'"

The Priests were the religious authorities who were chosen by religious tradition to serve their Hebrew religion in the Temple, but ended up being self-righteous and serving themselves. The Elders were those in the Synagogue who were supposed to be the benevolent overseers of God's people in the local Kingdom community, but they put unbearable yokes on the people. Jesus was the Passover Lamb. The religious authorities in the Temple and in the Synagogue were the first to examine the Passover Lamb. In their examination of Him, these religious leaders questioned the authenticity of Jesus' authority by asking, "Who are you? We are the religious leaders who have the authority over religious questions, and we want to know by what authority you say and do these things."

In other words, these leaders were inquiring, "Jesus, what seminary school did you graduate from? Where were you ordained or licensed? What denomination do you belong? Who told you to come and teach and preach here at the Temple? What auxiliary church organization do you belong?"

Jesus' response showed astounding wisdom. When Jesus asked them if John baptized had authority from Heaven or from men, they were trapped. They knew that John the Baptist was the son of a Levite priest, and yet they did not want to recognize him with that authority. Similarly, if they endorsed John as a prophet from God to please the people, then they had to accept Jesus as from God since John's whole ministry was to testify as the forerunner of Christ Jesus. Thus, the religious authorities just lied and said they did not know the answer to Jesus' question. Jesus knew they had lied. He essentially said, "I know you know, but you will not tell Me. Instead, your answer just withheld the truth from me and these people. Unlike you religious leaders, I am not going to tell you I do not know. I will not lie to you; I just am not going to answer your question."

Although the Priests and Elders spoke to Jesus in a foolish way, He decided to give them a teaching anyway. Jesus started teaching them in parables in verses Matthew 21: 28-32. The first was the parable of the two sons, where the disobedient son gave his father mere lip service that he would obey his father. The disobedient son said he would obey but did not obey, just like the Priests and Elders. In Matthew 21:33-46, Jesus then gave the Priests and Elders the Parable of the wicked vinedressers who persecuted all those sent to gather the fruit, and then killed the vineyard owner's son, an obvious reference to Jesus and His Father in Heaven and Jesus' crucifixion. God sent His Only Begotten Son, Who is the Heir of all things, and they were rejecting God's heavenly and divine Heir. Jesus tells them that the Kingdom of God will be given to another. However, in Matthew 21: 42-46 Jesus tells the Priests and Elders the purpose why He was sent. Jesus said He is the Stone the builders rejected. He is the Chief Corner Stone in God's Temple, which are Believers. He came to build God's dwelling place (Believers). "I will build My *Ekklesia*." His *Ekklesia* will be in His Kingdom and family, as His throne is the center of authority of His *Ekklesia* and His family is the most loving family in the universe. His *Ekklesia*, will be His Kingdom spiritual Ambassadors and Kingdom spiritual Soldiers.

Thereafter, Jesus spoke the parable of the wedding feast in Matthew 22:1-14. Here He introduces the Son of Man as the Bridegroom. He is the Chief Corner Stone in the dwelling, and in the house is the wedding feast where the Bridegroom is. The more Believers feast with Jesus as the Bridegroom, the more God's dwelling house is built, where the *Ekklesia* will be as the Bride of Christ.

Joining together in fellowship with Christ and each other gives growth to the living building and betrothed of Christ. 1 Corinthians 3:9-17 says, "For we are labourers together with God: ye are God's husbandry, ye are God's building. According to the grace of God which is given unto me, as a wise master builder, I have laid the foundation, and another buildeth thereon. But let every man take heed how he buildeth thereupon. For other foundation can no man lay than that is laid, which is Jesus Christ. Now if any man build upon this foundation gold, silver, precious stones, wood, hay, stubble; Every man's work shall be made manifest: for the day shall declare it, because it shall be revealed by fire; and the fire shall try every man's work of what sort it is. If any man's work abide which he hath built thereupon, he shall receive a reward. If any man's work shall be burned, he shall suffer loss: but he himself shall be saved; yet so as by fire. Know ye not that ye are the temple of God, and that the Spirit of God dwelleth in you? If any man defiles the temple of God, him shall God destroy; for the temple of God is holy, which temple ye are."

Similarly, 1 Peter 2:2-9 says, "To whom coming, as unto a living stone, disallowed indeed of men, but chosen of God, and precious, Ye also, as lively stones, are built up a spiritual house, a holy priesthood, to offer up spiritual sacrifices, acceptable to God by Jesus Christ. Wherefore also it is contained in the scripture (Isaiah 28:16), 'Behold, I lay in Zion a chief corner stone, elect, precious: and he that believeth on Him shall not be confounded. Unto you therefore which believe He is precious: but unto them which be disobedient, the Stone which the builders disallowed, the same is made the Head of the corner, And a Stone of stumbling, and a Rock of offence, even to them which stumble at the word, being disobedient: whereunto also they were appointed. But ye are a chosen generation, a royal priesthood, a holy nation, a peculiar people; that ye should shew forth the praises of Him who hath called you out of darkness into His marvelous light."

Believers should participate in the communion with Jesus to practice the futuristic participation at the "wedding supper of the Lamb" that should motivate Believers to grow and mature. Through Believers' spiritual maturation they become proper "living stones" for the dwelling house of God. Jesus is the Chief Cornerstone for God's house, and Believers join with Christ and align themselves in position as living stones with the Chief Cornerstone.

THE SECOND QUESTION WAS BY THE PHARISEES AND HERODIANS. The Pharisees were the strongest religious party amongst the Hebrews. The Herodians were a Jewish political party promoting the continuation of the dynasty of King Herod. Religion and politics were joined together. The Herodians were the puppet rulers of the Roman government, which were disliked by the Pharisees, who were the self-proclaimed patriots of the Israel nation. Traditionally, the Pharisees and Herodians were opponents of each other. How could they conspire to work together against Jesus in their questioning Him? The reason they could was they saw Jesus as their common enemy. They feared Jesus came to replace them.

Together, the Pharisees and Herodians formulated a question to trap Jesus, and in Matthew 22:17 their question is memorialized. "Tell us, therefore, what do You think? Is it lawful to pay taxes to Caesar, or not?"

This reference to taxes was to the imperialistic Roman government that had conquered the region. This was different than the Temple tax mentioned in Matthew 17:24-27. The patriotic

Pharisees hated to pay taxes to the Romans. The Pharisees thought that Jesus must be very patriotic since all the ancient Israelites were totally against the paying of tribute to an imperialistic invader. Thus, they felt that Jesus, being true to His countrymen, would give an answer in favor of the historical stand of loyalty to Israel. They thought that Jesus was trapped either way that He answered their question. If Jesus agreed to the payment of taxes to Caesar in favor of the teaching of the Herodians, then the Pharisees could say that Jesus is betraying His country, and people would turn away from Him. On the other hand, if Jesus agreed with the Pharisees to not pay the Roman tribute, then the Herodians would accuse Him of trying to lead people to violate the Roman law requirement of paying taxes to Caesar in their corrupt system. Thus, they had Jesus trapped in a dilemma, or so it seemed.

However, they were talking to the Greatest Master, Himself, full of knowledge, understanding, and wisdom. Jesus did not take the tribute money out of His own pocket. He said to them, "Show Me the tax money." They brought Him a coin. "And He said to them, 'Whose image and inscription is this?' They said to Him, 'Caesar's.' And He said to them, 'Render therefore to Caesar the things that are Caesar's, and to God the things that are God's'" (Matthew 22:19-21).

The image they carried was that of Caesar's, not Jesus. Thus, Jesus said give back to him whose image is on the coin. They came to arrest Jesus, but instead He overpowered them with His wisdom. They came to entrap Jesus but were caught in their own trap. Jesus left no ground for accusation by the Pharisees and the Herodians. He not only answered the question they asked of Him, but He also added to render "...to God the things that are God's." They were surprised. They did not think He could respond with an answer that would totally disarm them. "When they had heard these words, they marveled, and left Him and went their way" (Matthew 22:22).

THE THIRD QUESTION WAS BY THE SADDUCEES. The Sadducees were the ancient modernists. They did not believe in the miracles in the Old Testament. They did not believe in angels or the spiritual world. They did not believe in the resurrection (Matthew 22:23; Acts 23:8). Since the Sadducees did not believe in the resurrection, they presented to Jesus a parable that they felt proved the illogic of the belief in the resurrection of the dead. Their question designed to entrap Jesus, but also to validate their doctrine against resurrection of the dead. The question was whose wife would a woman be in the resurrection who kept marrying the brothers of her deceased husbands while she was alive here on earth. Jesus went further in His answer by teaching the Sadducees the error in their doctrine. "You are mistaken, not knowing the Scriptures nor the power of God. For in the resurrection, they neither marry nor are given in marriage, but are like angels of God in Heaven. But concerning the resurrection of the dead, have you not read what was spoken to you by God, saying, 'I am the God of Abraham, the God of Isaac, and the God of Jacob?' God is not the God of the dead, but of the living." (Matthew 22:29-30). Life after death with God is everlasting life and is foundational in the Kingdom of God.

In other words, since God is the God of the living and not the dead; and since God is the God of Abraham, Isaac and Jacob, then Abraham, Isaac and Jacob will be some day resurrected from the dead and therefore are living and not dead. Jesus basically was saying, "You Sadducees know the letter of the law but not the relevant living spiritual reality from which the law came, as it is about a living God for a living people, not a people that die once and never thereafter live. Thus, the resurrection of the dead is a truthful reality."

These ancient Jewish modernists thought they could trick Jesus, but Jesus quickly answered their question, and then took the opportunity to show them that they needed to know the Scriptures in a way that revealed a living God. The living God the Word, Jesus Christ, was standing in front of them. Since Christ is living, then His Believers, too, must be living, even after they die here on earth.

FOURTH QUESTION WAS BY A LAWYER FROM THE PHARISEES. The Pharisees and scribes conspired together to entrap Jesus. One of them, a lawyer, asked Jesus a question in Matthew 22:36-40 to test Him regarding the accuracy of His knowledge of the law: "'Teacher, which is the great commandment in the law?' Jesus said to him, 'You shall love the Lord your God with all your heart, with all your soul, and with all your mind.' This is the first and great commandment. And the second is like it: 'You shall love your neighbor as yourself.' On these two commandments hang all the Law and the Prophets." The first most important commandment agreed with the Pharisees' interpretation of Scripture, but the second most important commandment was an indictment against the Pharisees as they did not love their neighbor as themselves, as they were dictators, not servants; they were takers, not givers; and they were prideful, not humble.

Again, the Passover Lamb answered their inquisition examination easily. He said that the Law and the Prophets hang on these two commandments. Historically, the rabbinic teachings provided many opinions as to the most important commandments in the Decalogue. They disagreed as to how to interpret Scripture.

These religious leaders examined the Lamb of God with these four questions. The first question related to religion, the second question was about politics, the third question was concerning the faith, and the fourth question was regarding proper Scriptural interpretation.

THEN THE PASSOVER LAMB TURNED THE TABLES ON THE RELIGIOUS LEADERS AND ASKED THEM A QUESTION: The religious leaders all had a chance to ask Jesus the toughest questions they could think, trying to entrap Him. Matthew 22: 41-42 reveals, "While the Pharisees were gathered together, Jesus asked them, saying, 'What do you think about the Christ (Messiah)? Whose Son is He?' They said to Him, 'The Son of David.' He said to them, 'How then does David in the Spirit call Him "Lord," saying: "The Lord said to my Lord, 'Sit at My right hand, till I make Your enemies Your footstool'."' If David then calls Him "Lord," how is He his Son?'" In the Israelite culture, a father or grandfather would never call his son or grandson a Lord, as it was the other way around under the law and Jewish rabbinical teaching.

It is not a question of religion, politics, faith, or scriptural interpretation, but the Person of Christ. Who is Christ? That is the best question worth asking and worth answering. The Pharisees gave Jesus a correct answer by saying that the Christ (or Messiah) will be the Son of David. However, why did the Great, Great, Great Grandfather David call His Greater Son to come as the Messiah his "Lord?" The Pharisees and lawyers had the revelation that the Messiah was the Son of David but had no revelation in the spirit that the Son of Man, Jesus, standing before them, was also the Lord of all as the Son of God, and in the ancestral linage as the Son of David as His humanity nature. They had the knowledge of the scriptural study, but they did not know the real Person of Christ who was standing in their midst.

It is not a matter of biblical teaching, but a matter that the Scriptures of the Old Testament primarily point to the living Christ or Messiah. In fact, the Bible is the living Word concerning the living Christ, who is the living King and Lord of all. The living Christ is the only Mediator between God and fallen mankind (Hebrews 12:24). Religion, politics, faith, and scriptural interpretation must all take a back seat to the all-encompassing living Christ, the Resurrected Christ, the Ascended Christ, and the Enthroned Christ.

In His question, the Lamb of God, the Lord Jesus Christ, asked about Himself. He wanted to know if they really knew Who He was. He is the Son of Man and the only begotten Son of God. He is the Son of David. They did not know Jesus as the Messiah.

Jesus asked the most important question that all Believers need to ask and answer. "Who is Christ Jesus in my life?" Everyone is confronted with this question, especially during the end time *Ekklesia* in Revival. Are you going to worship and serve a religious system or the true Christ, with His divine nature and humanity nature, as the King of His Kingdom, Who is both the Present Christ in His divine nature and the resurrected Ascended Christ in His humanity nature? His divine nature, God the Word, along with the entire Godhead, live inside Believers as God's Temple (1 Corinthians 6:19; 1 Corinthians 3:16; 2 Corinthians 6:16; Ephesians 2:21).

THE LIVING ASCENDED CHRIST

Father God crowned His Son with glory and honor before all in Heaven and the angelic hosts (Hebrews 2:7 9; 2 Peter 1:7). The everlasting Kingdom of God will be the manifestation of the glory of the resurrected, Ascended Christ who is called the Lord Jesus Christ (Numbers 14:21; Daniel 7:14; Matthew 13:34; Mark 9:1; 2 Thessalonians 1:9-10). Christ is now the King of Glory (Psalm 24:7- 10). Jesus' resurrected, glorified humanity nature is the sample of what the saints will share and be in Christ for all eternity when He returns for His Bride and then sets up His everlasting Kingdom here on earth with His Spouse (1 Corinthians 15:40-44; Philippians 3:21; Revelation 21:9).

Christ Jesus' exaltation involved His enthronement as the Seated Prophet who speaks Truth and Word of God to mankind and Who sent the Holy Spirit to perform the word of God (Deuteronomy 18:15; Matthew 13:57; Luke 13:33; 24:19; John 6:14,26-51; 8:38,40; 12:49-51). He was and is enthroned as the seated great High Priest in the Order of Melchizedek (Psalm 80:1; 99:1; John 17: 1-4; 19:30; Romans 3:25-26; Hebrews 1:3; 4:14; 5:10; 6:20; 7:15-17,21; 8:1; 9:11; 10:11-13; 12:2), Who ministers to God on behalf of mankind as the Mediator between God and man (1 Timothy 2:5-6; Hebrews 8:6), Who is the Reconciler and Head of the *Ekklesia* directing the ministry of reconciliation (2 Corinthians 5:19-21; Ephesians 1:20-23; Colossians 1:20-21), Who is the Advocate of the New Covenant (Luke 22:20; Hebrews 7:22; 1 John 2:1), Who is the Intercessor on behalf of the brethren (Hebrews 4:15; 7:25; 9:11-28; 10:19-22), and Who is the Minister in the Holy of Holies in the heavenly Tabernacle (Hebrews 4:16; 7:25; 8:2; 9:13-14; 10:12-14).

He is enthroned as the seated King of kings at the right hand of God as a place of greatest honor with authority as Ruler, King of the Kingdom, Lord over all creation, Governor over the *Ekklesia* and all created things and creatures in the three Heavens, on the earth and under the earth, in the natural realm and spiritual realm (Psalm 24:7-10; 72:11; 74:12; 93:1; 96:10; 97:1; Isaiah 16:5; 32:1; 33:22; Matthew 22:41 46; 27:37; 28:18-20; Romans 14:17; 1 Corinthians 15:24-28; 54-57;

Ephesians 1:20-23; 1 Timothy 1:17; 6:15; 1 Peter 2:5-9; 3:22; Revelation 3:21; 11:15-19; 15:3; 19:16; 22:1).

He was and is enthroned as the seated Judge (John 5:19-30; Acts 17:31), Who is the Discerner and Rewarder of all thoughts, words, motives, and deeds of all mankind. Christ will judge all unbelievers at the Great White Throne Judgment and determine the rewards for each Believer at the Judgment Seat of Christ (Romans 14:10; 1 Corinthians 3:10-15; 2 Corinthians 5:10; Hebrews 4:13; 11:6; Revelation 20:11-15).

Christ's exaltation also included His receipt of the Name above all other names, which makes Him the seated Lord of Lords Who is the Great Steward of all creation (Mark 2:28; Luke 24:34; Acts 2:32-36; 10:36; Romans 10:9,12; 1 Corinthians 15:47; Philippians 2:11 Jude 4; Revelations 17:1; 19: 6,16). He is the enthroned and exalted God Man who is worthy of all glory, honor, adoration, praise and worship (Ephesians 1:20-23; 1 Timothy 1:17; 6:15; 1 Peter 2:5-9; 3:22; Revelation 3:21; 11:15-19; 15:3; 19:16; 22:1). As to His divine nature, He was always the Lord God, God the Word (Luke 2:11; John 1:1; 1 Corinthians 15:47), but His humanity nature was exalted for Jesus Christ to be The Lord (Philippians 2:9-11). Jesus is now the Lord Jesus Christ which is the greatest name and title in all creation (Genesis 19:24; Psalm 110:1-5; Mark 16:15-20; Acts 2:34; 10:36; Revelation 3:12). Confession of Jesus as Lord over yourself and everything else in your life is necessary to become born again, to see and enter the Kingdom of God and for salvation unto eternal life (John 3:3,5,16; Acts 9:1-6; Romans 10:9,13; 1 Corinthians 12:3). Jesus' exaltation of His humanity nature to the right hand of God makes Christ also the Lord over the living and the dead (Romans 14:9).

The exaltation of Christ's humanity nature seated Him on the Throne in Heaven at the right hand of God to presently reign in session, and His glorified humanity nature, which includes His glorified body and precious blood, are the holiest things in the Third Heaven and in all finite creation. Jesus' glorified humanity nature, especially His glorified physical body and precious blood, give the Ascended Christ all authority to be seated on His Throne in His offices as Most High Prophet, Most High Priest, Most High King, Most High Judge, and Most High Lord to rule and reign over all created things and all creatures in all the natural and spiritual worlds (Matthew 19:28, 28:18; Ephesians 1:20).

The Revival *Ekklesia* consists of Believers who legally are seated in Christ Jesus in heavenly places in daily relationship with Him by virtue of Christ's omnipresent divine nature, God the Word (Ephesians 2:6). The Revival *Ekklesia* consists of Embassies that send forth Christ's Ambassadors throughout the earth (2 Corinthians 5:20). As new creatures in Christ, Believers gather in loving fellowship with other Believers, not in religion. Believers are citizens of heaven that live here on earth and live and find their destiny in the King as Believers are translated into the Kingdom of God's dear Son (Philippians 3:20; 2 Corinthians 5:17; Colossians 1:13).

PLEASE UNITE WITH ME IN THE FOLLOWING PRAYER: Father, in the name of Jesus, help us Believers to be one in love, purpose, and Kingdom community in the Kingdom of God. Draw us together in loving Kingdom community where Christ Jesus was our Passover Sacrificial Lamb and is the center of our worship, affection, and attention, as He is the benevolent King of His Kingdom, Who is the divine Present One when Believers gather in fellowship. Father God, make us one in Christ, even as Christ and the Father are One. Thank You, Lord, for sending the

Holy Spirit, that we may be committed through Him to You, the Kingdom of God, and to each other in loving fellowship. Be the center of our fellowship. Jesus, we lift up Your Name, as the only Name that is worthy of being exalted and as defining your position as King of the Kingdom of God and the Head or Your *Ekklesia*. Father deal with the divisions in the *Ekklesia*. Cause us to drop our differences. Deal with us as Your children. Help us not be religious, but in true fellowship in the Kingdom of God, cause us to be loving, caring, and perfectly joined as You mend us together in love. God the Word, disciple us to become Your spiritual Ambassadors and spiritual Soldiers of your heavenly Kingdom that has come here on earth and manifests inside of us. Christ Jesus, please help us to know You and Your true nature and authority as the Ascended Christ, Who is seated on Your heavenly Throne in Your offices of Most High Prophet, Most High Priest, Most High King, Most High Judge, and Most High Lord to rule and reign over all created things and all creatures, both in the natural realm and spiritual realm. Holy Spirit we pray for Revival to come to the Christ Jesus' *Ekklesia*. Lord, Jesus, the Spirit and the Bride says, "Come!" In Jesus' name. Amen.

Consecration of the Believer's Body for the Revival Ekklesia

CHAPTER NINE

Consecration of the Believer's
Body for the Revival *Ekklesia*

BELIEVERS' SPIRITS, SOULS, AND BODIES
WERE PURCHASED BY JESUS WITH HIS
PRECIOUS SPILT BLOOD

1 Peter 1:18-19 says, "Knowing that you were not redeemed with corruptible things, like silver or gold, from your aimless conduct received by tradition from your fathers, but with the precious blood of Christ, as of a lamb without blemish and without spot." Similarly, Revelation 5:9 says, "...And have redeemed us to God by Your Blood...." Our redemption was paid for by the blood of Jesus' humanity nature. Our everlasting life was purchased for us by Another, the Son of God, Jesus Christ the Anointed.

It was Sinless Blood, shed by Jesus' humanity nature, as the sacrificial unblemished Lamb of God that paid the redemption price to redeem Believers from the kingdom of darkness and to reconcile them to God (Ephesians 1:7; 1 Peter 1:18; 2 Corinthians 5:18). Death on the Cross of Jesus' humanity nature represents the crucifixion of the old man in Adam and the forgiveness of sins in Christ (Romans 6:6). Additionally, by Jesus' suffering and death on the Cross, Believers are released from the curse of the requirements of the law (Galatians 3:13). Although Believers have been purchased by the Lord's precious blood, He allows Believers free choice whether to serve Him after initial salvation or to follow their own choices (Deuteronomy 30:19-20; Proverbs 16:9; Mark 8:30; John 7:17; Galatians 5:13; Revelation 22:17). Believers' good or bad sowing affects their eternal reaping of rewards (Galatians 6:7-8), but not their initial salvation (1 Corinthians 3:14-15). 1 Corinthians 3:23 says, "And ye are Christ's; and Christ is God's." Believers are spiritual children of Christ Jesus' resurrected humanity nature (Isaiah 9:6; Hebrews 2:13), but Believers are also the adopted children of Father God through Christ Jesus (Romans 8:15). Believers must voluntarily submit themselves in their souls to obey and do the assigned good works of God after initial salvation (Ephesians 2:10; Philippians 2:12-13). In Father God's own timing He will pour out His Holy Spirit to bring Revival to Christ's *Ekklesia* to wind up the *Ekklesia* Age (Joel 2:28).

Romans 14:8-9 says, "For whether we live, we live unto the Lord; and whether we die, we die unto the Lord: whether we live therefore, or die, we are the Lord's. For to this end Christ both died, and rose, and revived, that he might be Lord both of the dead and living." As Believers, we are the Lord's and should no longer make decisions by ourselves. As Believers, we are commanded to obey the commandments of our Master and must not follow the things of this world, the lust of the eyes, the lust of the flesh, and the pride of life, that lead to wrong relationships and the wrong attachments to things and actions in this world.

Believers sometimes wonder why Christ Jesus and God the Father seem to be at a distance to them, but they ignore and fail to obey scripture. If you do not obey the Lord's commandments, it effects your intimacy with the Lord and God the Father. Jesus said in John 14:15, "If you love

Me, keep My commandments." Jesus emphasizes the point in John 14:21, "He that hath My commandments, and keepeth them, he is that loveth Me; and he that loveth Me, shall be loved of My Father, and I will manifest Myself to Him." Similarly, Jesus said in John 14:21, "If ye keep My commandments, ye shall abide in My love; even so I kept My Father's commandments and abide in His love." The First Commandment of the Lord is in Mark 12:30, "And thou shalt love the Lord thy God with all thy heart, and with all thy soul, and with all thy mind, and with all thy strength: this is the First Commandment." Then Jesus stated the Second Commandment in Mark 12:31, "And the second is like, namely this, Thou shalt love thy neighbour as thyself. There is none other commandment greater than these."

Additionally, in John 13: 34-35, Jesus gave His disciples a New Commandment, "A new commandment I give unto you, That ye love one another; as I have loved you, that ye also love one another. By this shall all men know that ye are My disciples, if ye have love one to another." This New Commandment to *agape* love one another, it is not just giving money to other Believers who do not know biblical economics or have divine wisdom as to how to handle investments, money, riches, and wealth, as this would be like giving drugs to a junky to some new Believers who are trying to overcome their sinful habits and disobedience to God and His scriptures. It means caring enough to disciple Believers into the ways of the Kingdom of God, into intimate fellowship with humanity nature of Jesus, God, and the other Believers, and into searching scriptures to fill their hearts in their souls with the word and mysteries of Christ. Fellowship means much more than greeting each other on Sunday morning as you enter the same building week after week. It means from Monday through Sunday being in fellowship and being led by the Holy Spirit to be Christ's servant to whomever the Holy Spirit leads you to minister.

As Believers, we were redeemed by the Lord and thus belong to the Lord. We owe our gift of everlasting life to the Lord. He owns us as His love servants. This means He has the authority and right to tell us what to do, where to go, and how to live. Although this is the biblical truth, the fact does not set well with most Believers who are bent toward self-exaltation, rights orientation, self-actualization, and independent thinking. People in America and Europe most always have natural Plan B just in case God's Plan A does not work in the timing they want. Plan A would be to seek first Christ as King in the Kingdom of God for your needs. Plan B is an independent natural plan just in case God does not answer your prayer, or you get tired of waiting or you did not perform the conditions the Holy Spirit directed you to perform prior to the blessing coming. This is one of the reasons Believers in America and Europe rarely see miracles today because they have their independent Plan B. They do not put their whole faith in God for healing, finances, or relationship repair, because their Plan B is to choose the best medical doctor, work more overtime to increase income, seek a divorce instead of fixing the marriage by changing and becoming a more loving spouse. Some Believers do not want to submit to anyone, including God, and are rebellious in their souls by nature. These Believers in their rebellious independence believe they should have the freedom to think, emote, and believe what they want. However, rebellion leads to bondage, not freedom. Galatians 5:1 says, "Stand fast therefore in the liberty wherewith Christ hath made us free and be not entangled again with the yoke of bondage." Freedom comes from the activation of Christ's spiritual law. Romans 8: 2 says, "For the law of the Spirit of life in Christ Jesus hath made me free from the law of sin and death." Similarly, Jesus said in John 8:32, "And ye shall know the truth, and the truth shall make you free." Yet, there is no bondage in the Kingdom of God. Where the Spirit of the Lord is, there is liberty (2 Corinthians 3:17). God wants you to exercise your freedom to submit to Him, wholeheartedly.

Paul taught that freedom, which comes from two words, "liberty and dominion," is a result of intimate companionship with the Lord, as the Lord shares His *agape* love. When the Lord's divine nature, God the Word, is present, His love permeates Believers' souls; and Believers abide in His love. 2 Corinthians 3: 6, 17-18 says, "Who also hath made us able ministers of the New Testament; not of the letter, but of the spirit: for the letter killeth, but the spirit giveth life… Now the Lord is that spirit: and where the spirit of the Lord (reference to Jesus' omnipresent divine nature) is, there is liberty. But we all, with open face beholding as in a glass the glory of the Lord, are changed (in our souls) into the same image from glory to glory, even as by the spirit of the Lord."

Ephesians 1:18 says, "The eyes of your understanding being enlightened; that you may know what is the hope of His calling, what are the riches of the glory of His inheritance in the saints." We are the Lord's inheritance. Our bodies are made of clay from the earth. Our bodies are His temple which has become His abode (John 14:23). The Lord wants to set His Revival *Ekklesia* on fire to burn with the desire to serve Him and He wants His Body, totally consecrated to Him, to bring His grace, love, hope, faith, and power to a lost and evil world by preaching the gospel of the Kingdom of God and preaching repentance and the remission of sins.

1 Corinthians 6:17-20 says, "But he who is joined to the Lord is one spirit with Him. Flee sexual immorality. Every sin that a man does is outside the body, but he who commits sexual immorality sins against his own body. Or do you not know that your body is the temple of the Holy Spirit who is in you, whom you have from God, and you are not your own? For you were bought at a price; therefore, glorify God in your body and in your spirit, which are God's."

We, as Believers, are not our own, but the Lord's. Therefore, the Lord has all rights over our spirits, souls, and bodies, not us. Since we no longer own our souls and bodies, then we have no right to commit sin with them. Fortunately, our born again spirits do not commit sin (1 John 3:9), but the entire Godhead works to remove the influence of the flesh in our souls to transform our souls to become spiritual and no longer carnal (John 15:2; Ephesians 5:26; Romans 8:13).

Romans Chapters 1 through 8 declare the compassion and mercies of God. Believers were formerly sinners in Adam, and Jesus Christ came and died on a cross, spilling His precious, sinless blood for our redemption; so, we who believe would be in Christ. Romans Chapters 3 & 4 are focused on the redeeming blood of Christ, while Chapter 5 is focused on God's forgiveness of our sins. Romans Chapter 6 through 8 are concerning the effects of sin, the law of sin and death, how the Cross dealt with sin, and how the law of life in Christ overcome the law of sin and death and that Believers through grace are saved. Born again Believers became citizens of Heaven, along with Kingdom spiritual Ambassadors and Kingdom spiritual Soldiers. The blood is for the forgiveness of sins; whereas the cross is for the crucifixion of the old man and self-focused that was in Adam. Then, in a chronological progression of thought, the Holy Spirit through the Apostle Paul speaks of consecration of the body and the transformation of the soul in (Romans 12:1-2).

Because of the compassion and mercies derived from Jesus' spilt blood and death on the Cross and resurrection, as Believers we are encouraged to consecrate ourselves to the Lord. Yet, we cannot do it alone; we need the entire Godhead to do a spiritual transformation in our souls. We were naturally born and spiritually born again for God's purpose, which He destined before the foundation of the world for the manifestation in this time (Ephesians 1:4-5; Revelation 13:8). God's purpose is that those in His *Ekklesia* in Revival express the life of God's only begotten Son and partake of His glory and *zoe* life during these end times. Jesus wants to wrap up the Church Age and energize His Revival *Ekklesia* to bring in the world harvest of souls as the Holy Spirit is poured out on all flesh (Joel 2:28).

Before the foundation of the world, Believers' names were written in the Lamb's Book of Life for God's special purpose (Ephesians 1:4,11; Revelation 13:8). In eternity past God had the purpose that from His only begotten Son would come many born again Believers as part of the Second Man. In fact, Romans 8:29 says, "Because those whom He foreknew, he also predestinated to be conformed to the image of His Son, that He might be the Firstborn among many brothers." As God the Father's children by adoption, believers must be conformed to the image of God's Son, Christ Jesus. Thus, Believers' redemption was for the purpose of sonship to enter in the daily spiritual transformation of Believers' souls to make ready the Bride of Christ. Consecration and transformation of Believers' souls is to make spiritual servants of all who work in God's Kingdom and *Ekklesia*, so they will have the new man nature of true righteousness and holiness.

Therefore, as far as Believers' redemption is concerned, Christ Jesus owns all Believers. God has delivered Believers from the power of darkness and translated Believers into the Kingdom of His dear Son (Colossians 1:13) as His *Ekklesia* that are Kingdom spiritual Ambassadors and Kingdom spiritual Soldiers. Jesus bought Believers with His own precious blood and death (1 Corinthians 6:19-20; 1 Peter 1:18). Believers have become citizens of Heaven (Philippians 3:20) and now belong to the household of God (Ephesians 3:15). Believers have a Master and King, Christ Jesus, who Believers must exercise their wills and volunteer to serve and must volunteer to follow the leading of the Holy Spirit who leads Believers into the harvest field as the Lord's *Ekklesia* enters Revival.

IT IS THE AGAPE LOVE OF THE LORD IN OUR HEARTS THAT MOTIVATE US TO RECEIVE CONSECRATION OF OUR BODIES

2 Corinthians 5:14-16 says, "For the love of Christ compels us, because we judge thus: that if One died for all, then all died; and He died for all, that those who live should live no longer for themselves, but for Him who died for them and rose again. Therefore, from now on, we regard no one according to the flesh. Even though we have known Christ according to the flesh, yet now we know Him thus no longer."

Jesus Christ loved Believers that were chosen by God before the foundation of the world (Ephesians 1:4-5). Christ Jesus' humanity nature died for as the Passover Sacrificial Lamb of God, while His divine nature served as the High Priest offering up the Passover Lamb of God as the sacrificial offering on the Cross to relieve Believers from the curse of the law, and for redemption and forgiveness of their sins, and to make a way to remove believers from being in the first Adam (Romans 6:6; 1 Corinthians 15:22; Galatians 3:13). Then Christ Jesus' humanity nature was risen from the death as the Second Man, so Believers would become new creatures in Christ (2 Corinthians 5:17; 1 Corinthians 15:47). Believers became new creatures in Christ Jesus' humanity nature by the power of God by becoming and receiving born again spirits as children of Christ Jesus' humanity nature (Isaiah 9:6; Hebrews 2:13).

As Believers, we have the resurrected *zoe* life of Christ Jesus' humanity nature living inside us. The consecration of our bodies is our repayment to Him for the love He has shown to us by laying down His natural humanity life (*psuche*) for us (Luke 23:39; Luke 24:7; John 10:15; John 15:13; John 20:27). His love of Believers is their motive for submitting to the work of the Godhead to consecrate them by removing the influence of the flesh out of their souls. The love of Christ, through His divine nature will always be with Believers, along with the *agape* love of the entire Godhead. The Godhead together always will love Believers and will transform Believers' souls, so that Believers may be holy and righteous in Christ and worthy of being chosen by Father God to be His children by adoption, citizens of the Kingdom of Heaven, and Kingdom spiritual Ambassadors and Kingdom spiritual Soldiers, kings of the King lords of the Lord, and priest of the High Priest, Christ Jesus, of the order of Melchizedek (Hebrews 6:20).

Romans 5: 5-6,8-9 says, "And hope maketh not ashamed; because the (*agape*) love of God is shed abroad in our hearts by the Holy Ghost which is given unto us. For when we were yet without strength, in due time Christ died for the ungodly.... But God commendeth His (*agape*) love toward us, in that, while we were yet sinners, Christ died for us. Much more then, being now justified by His blood, we shall be saved from wrath through Him." It was Jesus' humanity nature that was the Sacrificial Passover Lamb that died for us on the Roman Cross, but because Jesus' sinless life caused His death to be unjustified, God's sense of justice caused God to raised Jesus' humanity nature from the dead with new resurrected *zoe* life. Jesus' incorruptible seed was implanted by the work of Jesus divine nature, God the Word, into Believers' born again spirits when Believers accepted Jesus as Lord and Savior (1 Peter 1:23).

Since Christ died on our behalf, Believers do not have to die an infernal death. However, Christ purchased Believers' bodies for God's temple, a dwelling place here on earth. When unbelievers accept Jesus as Savior and Lord, then they accept His divine nature, along with the entire Godhead to come and live in and own their bodies as the Temple of God (1 Corinthians 3:16). Therefore, Believers' bodies need to be consecrated to God, so Believers do not defile the Temple of God (1 Corinthians 3:17). 1 Corinthians 6:19 says, "What? Know ye not that your body is the temple of the Holy Ghost, which is in you, which ye have of God, and ye *are* not your own?" In exchange for Believers' everlasting life in Christ, they gave up the ownership of their bodies unto God.

So religious scholars can't argue that I teach a gospel with required works for initial salvation. The Holy Spirit led works are afterward as faithful servants of the Lord in His Kingdom. Only that which is from the Lord can be consecrated back to Him. Believers' salvation is from the Lord. Therefore, Believers out of love should give back to the Lord what He gave to them, which was their resurrected *zoe* life. Believers need to accept the Lord's resurrected life of His humanity nature in their souls, and then exercise their wills in their souls to give their transformed souls to the Lord for all of eternity.

Believers become the Betrothed of the Lord. Romans 7:4 says, "Therefore, my brethren, you also have become dead to the law through the Body of Christ, that you may be married to another-- to Him who was raised from the dead, that we should bear fruit to God. For when we were in the flesh, the sinful passions which were aroused by the law were at work in our members to bear fruit to death." The Lord desires His *Ekklesia* as His Betrothed now while she is being prepared as His Bride in the future. Ephesians 5:27 says, "That he might present it to himself a glorious *Ekklesia*, not having spot, or wrinkle, or any such thing; but that it (she) should be holy and without blemish."

Because the Lord purchased Believers, He owns them. Yet, His love for Believers allows them to go free. Believers must make voluntary choices to serve the Lord and the Godhead after initial salvation. When Believers have a revelation of sonship, then they will understand the love of a Father to those who were or are prodigal sons. Sonship uses Jesus, as God's only begotten Son, as the Pattern for obedience to God the Father. God the Father, God the Word, and God the Holy Spirit are in perfect agreement as to the pattern to use for discipline, the goal for the discipline, and the Three-in-one God doing the discipline. The purpose of the Lord's discipline in making disciples of all nations is the process of making spiritual sons and daughters in Christ who will be transformed into His Revival Church and the Bride of Christ.

As a Believer, if you want to serve mammon, He will allow it. If you want to serve the lusts of your flesh, He will allow it. If you want to serve the world, He will allow it. If you want to serve idols, He will allow it. The Lord is after spiritual sons and daughters who voluntarily submit themselves wholeheartedly to Him. He wants you to say, "Lord, I am your love slave because I love you and You love me. I am not Your slave just because You purchased me. I am your love slave because I love You." As Believers, we are not the Lord's bondservants just because He purchased us, but experientially through intimate fellowship with the Lord, we become His love servants only on the day we voluntarily say, "Lord, I submit to your consecration of my body to be the temple of the Godhead, and I offer myself as Your obedient child and love slave because I love you with my whole heart."

In Exodus 21: 2-6 the "love slave" under Jewish law is established. "If you buy a Hebrew servant, he shall serve six years; and in the seventh he shall go out free and pay nothing. If he comes in by himself, he shall go out by himself; if he comes in married, then his wife shall go out with him. If his master has given him a wife, and she has borne him sons or daughters, the wife and her children shall be her Master's, and he shall go out by himself. But if the servant plainly says, 'I love my master, my wife, and my children; I will not go out free,' then his master shall bring him to the judges. He shall also bring him to the door, or to the doorpost, and his master shall pierce his ear with an Aul (Awl); and he shall serve him forever."

The doorposts and lintel were the place where the blood of the Passover Lamb was applied, so that the plague of death of the firstborn would not strike (Exodus 12:7, 12-13). Christ's humanity nature was the Passover Lamb, and we, as Believers are led to the Cross where the Lord's blood was spilt to choose to become a love slave to the Lord forever as the infernal death will pass over us and be replaced with everlasting life with the family of God. Christ, Himself, consecrates us to God the Father. Christ's humanity nature says He is the Way, Truth, and Life (John 14:6). God's only begotten Son purchased us to set us free, so that we would voluntarily come to Him and give our hearts and love back to Him. John 8:36 says, "Who the Son sets free is free indeed."

There is a story about a young slave girl in the Middle East during Biblical times who was being auctioned off as a slave to the highest bidder. Evil men were bidding for her, and the price was going up. The slave girl knew that she would suffer no matter which of the three men bought her, so she began to weep and grieve in her heart. Suddenly, a fourth man started bidding against the other three and outbid them all. He bought the slave girl. He immediately called in a blacksmith and broke her chains, and he then set her free. The fourth man said to the slave, "I did not purchase you to be my slave as I bought you to free you. My purpose was to liberate you out of bondage, so you could enjoy freedom." Then the fourth man turned and walked away. The girl was astonished, bewildered, and dumbstruck. She was shocked at the gesture of kindness afforded her by this compassionate man, whose heart saw a captive that he was compelled through compassion and mercy to grant freedom. In about two minutes she turned around and came running up to the man and said, "From this day forward until the day I die, I will be your servant of my own free will." This servant girl grew to love her master, and he grew to love her. They eventually married, and she became the bride of the man who gave her liberty and set her free from the bondage of slavery by paying the price to purchase her freedom.

This is the *agape* love of the Lord towards you as His Believer, child, disciple, brother, Betrothed, and all other relationships with Him as written in the word of God. He purchased you to set you free to keep the devil from owning you as his slave. He only wants you to be His bondservant to love Him in return for the gesture of kindness and great love in being crucified and dying on the cruel Roman Cross that you may live with liberty. He wants you to desire to become His love servant with your own free choice. The Lord is waiting to hear these words from you, "From this day forward through all eternity I will serve You Lord with my whole being as your love servant." Then, the Lord will want you to become His Bride, where you will live eternally with the One who liberated you from the bondage of sin and the hold of the devil. The end time Revival will be not only to bring liberty to the captives, but also to prepare the Bride without spot or wrinkle, that she may be glorious, ready for the wedding ceremony with the Lord (Ephesians 5:26-27; Revelation 19:9).

THE SIGNIFICANCE AND PURPOSE OF CONSECRATION

Romans 12:1 says, "I beseech you therefore, brethren, by the mercies of God, that ye present your bodies a living sacrifice, holy, acceptable unto God, which is your reasonable service." This Scripture speaks of a total consecration of Believers bodies to do the will of God. As Believers, we are to present our bodies as living sacrifices unto God as qualified, transformed workers in His Revival *Ekklesia*. When God has our entire consecrated bodies, then He can do with us what He wills.

Consecration of the influence of the flesh in our souls is a most important step in sanctification, which transforms our souls into the image of Christ. Consecration is the act of the wills in our souls to submit to the Godhead in the work in removing the influence of the flesh and reigning in the continuous temptations of the flesh to make our bodies the temple of the living God.

Becoming the image of Christ allows Believers to partake of His glory and fellowship with His divine nature. This does not make Believers God, but it allows Believers to have an intimate relationship with God. It does allow Believers to be joined with Christ as His glorified Body, so Believers are then useful for the Master's service when the Spirit of the Lord moves in this end time *Ekklesia* in glorious Revival. Believers will never be able to remove completely the sin principle out of their bodies (Romans 7:20-23); but Believers ought to continuously buffet the flesh and keep it under subjection to make their bodies deemed to be crucified with Christ; so, the flesh's influence in Believers' souls has been lessened (1 Corinthians 9:27; Galatians 2:20). After death, eventually, when Jesus returns (1 Corinthians 15:23), Believers receive new glorified resurrected bodies suitable to live in the new Heaven and earth.

Unlike the saints in the Old Testament who offered dead sacrifices to the Lord, when we as Believers submit to God's consecration to make us God's holy temple, we present ourselves to Him as *living sacrifices*. Believers should voluntarily submit themselves to be the love servants of the Lord, but the problem is that as living sacrifices we want to crawl off the altar of sacrifice because being baptized in fire to burn up the flesh's influenced in our souls is painful and change is often uncomfortable. Yet, the Lord promises not to leave us during our fiery ordeals in our lives that make us more submissive, humble, and Christ like. As Believers, we need to submit to the Lord and accept that we are the love servants of the Lord, and that we are not our own. Romans 6:16 says, "Do you not know that to whom you present yourselves as slaves for obedience, his slaves you are whom you obey?"

As Believers, we separate ourselves unto the Lord as living sacrifices for His use. Our sacrifice unto the Lord satisfies His heart's desire for our love returned out of free choice. To present our living bodies as sacrifices unto the Lord is a most "reasonable service" in the eyes and heart of the Lord. Such "reasonable service" does not depend as much on our working for the Lord but on our satisfying the heart of God. He knows if He has our hearts, He has our wills. God and Christ's humanity nature judge men by their hearts, not their work. God wants to do a work in us and through us. He wants to direct and lead His moving tabernacle of our consecrated bodies, housing our souls and spirits, along with the Godhead, to make His Revival *Ekklesia* have His presence throughout the land. The Lord wants to take what He has put inside Believers to go outside and touch others and take dominion of the things of the earth to bring possession back to God's Kingdom.

BELIEVERS ARE GOD'S BURNT OFFERING

Numbers 28: 2-3 says, "Command the children of Israel, and say to them, 'My offering, My food for My offerings made by fire as a sweet aroma to Me, you shall be careful to offer to Me at their appointed time.' And you shall say to them, 'This is the offering made by fire which you shall offer to the Lord: two male lambs in their first year without blemish, day by day, as a regular burnt offering.'" Similarly, Leviticus 1:9 says, "...The priests shall burn all on the altar as a burnt sacrifice, an offering made by fire, a sweet aroma to the Lord." The burnt offering is an offering unto sanctification.

In the Old Testament, God required burnt offerings to Him. In the New Testament, we, as Believers, belong to the Lord and should offer ourselves as burnt offerings daily to God for His pleasure and our affection for His returned *agape* love. In the Old Testament the sacrificial animal was dead, but in the New Testament we who belong to the Lord must present ourselves as *living sacrifices* daily to God for His satisfaction as burnt offerings. What we must do is satisfy the Lord, not just do a work for Him. We are the Lord's, and our wills are obliged to become totally submitted to God's will. Our thoughts should become what He is thinking. Our feelings need to match what the Lord is emoting. Our hearts need to love other Believers as Christ loved us. Our very souls have to become submitted similar to how our new born again spirits are perfectly submitted to Him. Our born again spirits are already consecrated to God. Our souls and bodies need the same consecration to do the will of God.

God will make Believers a burnt offering unto Him. He, Himself, will set us on fire to burn out the thorns and thistles and the briars and brambles. He will purify us by exposing us to the light of His fire. "God is a consuming fire" (Hebrews 12:29). Jesus came to baptize us in fire (Matthew 3:11) and therefore we become burnt offerings unto God. There is no time to retire from God's work. We need to refire, not retire.

2 Corinthians 5:15 says, "And He died for all, that those who live should live no longer for themselves, but to Him who died for them and rose again." The purpose of our consecration to the Lord is to live "to Him" not just "for Him." Living "to Him" is a higher call than living "for Him." Living "to Him" means we are joined with Him as one spirit in His resurrected, perfect, sinless humanity nature and His soul where His mind, emotions, heart, and will reside in His humanity nature has become our minds, emotions, hearts, and wills. 1 Corinthians 6:17 says, "But he who is joined to the Lord is one spirit with Him." Believers souls must become spiritual and no longer carnal (Romans 8:6).

Since as Believers our born again spirits are joined to the Lord as one spirit, Believers become part of the Body of Christ. Believers take not only the resurrected life of Jesus' humanity nature, but also, are joined with His humanity nature as His body. As His body, we as Believers are no longer our own body. We as Believers have become part of the makeup of the very Person of His humanity nature. Jesus, being the Head, has a right to command His body to do whatever He thinks in furtherance of His purpose. Jesus saved us, so, like Him, the entire Godhead lives in us. Christ through His divine nature can live His life in us and through us to touch others with His resurrected *zoe* life. In our natural bodies, from the brain comes every nerve down our spinal column. Every cell has a nerve from the spinal column for proper communication from the head. Likewise, every member of the Body of Christ is directly connected to the Head, Christ Jesus, through His divine nature; and we must take God's orders through and from Him.

Why must Believers consecrate and sanctify their bodies unto the Lord. The reason is that Believers very bodies are the Temple of our holy God (1 Corinthians 6:19; 1 Corinthians 3:16; 2 Corinthians 6:16; Ephesians 2:21). Believers are mandated to keep holy their bodies as the Temple of God. Leviticus 20:26 says, "And ye shall be holy unto Me: for I the LORD am holy, and have severed you from other people, that ye should be Mine." Peter stated in 1 Peter 1: 15-16, "But as He which hath called you is holy, so be ye holy in all manner of conversation; Because it is written, Be ye holy; for I am holy." Paul stated in 1 Corinthians 3:16-17 "Know ye not that ye are the Temple of God, and that the Spirit of God dwelleth in you? If any man defiles the Temple of God, him shall God destroy; for the Temple of God is holy, which Temple ye are."

In all of our living as a pluralist Kingdom community of Kingdom Believers, as Christ's Revival *Ekklesia*, and as citizens of the Kingdom of Heaven, we must submit, consecrate, and sanctify our daily living to the purpose of seeking and manifesting God's holy Kingdom, which means Believers must present "your bodies a living sacrifice, holy, acceptable unto God, which is your reasonable service" that we "may prove what is that good, and acceptable, and perfect, will of God" (Romans 12:1-2). As Believers present their bodies as living sacrifices unto God they subdue the influence of the flesh as the Godhead, together, transforms Believers souls by weaning the souls from receiving stimuli from the body and the five senses.

As God's holy Temple and Tabernacle, wherever we travel and engage in the service of the Lord, the Lord's divine nature will express Jesus' resurrected life through us to bring Revival to the land. Ephesians 2:10 says, "For we are His workmanship, created in Christ Jesus for good works, which God prepared beforehand that we should walk in them." The wording of this Scripture gives us a choice to work for the Lord. Thus, we must offer ourselves to Him as living sacrifices. This is another one of the purposes of our consecration, so that God can do His good, holy works through us.

Again, 1 Corinthians 6:20 says, "For you were bought with a price; therefore, glorify God in your body." The purpose of consecration is to bring glory to God in our bodies. Since God lives inside of us, everything we do has to be God's Kingdom purpose with the Lord's delegated *exousia* authority and the Holy Spirit's anointing and *dunamis* power. Otherwise, Believers are living their lives in the futility of their carnal efforts, which will have no eternal fruits or rewards.

Romans 6:5-6 says, "For if we have been planted together in the likeness of His death, we shall be also in the likeness of His resurrection: Knowing this, that our old man (in first Adam) was crucified with Him, that the body of sin might be done away with, that we should no longer be slaves of sin. For he who has died has been freed of sin." The reasons why Believers' souls are into sin after initial salvation is because they have not accepted fully the death of Jesus on the Cross to eradicate the influence of the sins of the flesh from the body that are habitual actions in their souls. If you have been "united in the likeness of His death" then you have accepted that you have also entered into the "likeness of His resurrection." If you are united with Christ, then you have a body which is now owned by Christ as His body and where the Godhead lives as His Temple.

Believers' "self" awareness in their souls can experience Christ's death to mortify the influence of their sinful flesh in their souls. Some Believers still allow their pleasure-seeking bodies to dictate to their minds, emotions, and hearts where their wills reside in their souls as the body's fleshly desires energize their actions to sin instead of submitting their bodies to the Lord and the Godhead for consecration and sanctification. Your soul must exercise her will to allow Father God to prune away the sinful flesh out of the soul (John 15:2), submit to God the Word who cleanses the flesh and sanctifies the soul by washing of the word of God (Ephesians 5:26), and submit to God the Holy Spirit who mortifies the deeds of the flesh in the soul for more *zoe* life (Romans 8:13).

Romans 6:13-14, 18-19 says, "Neither yield ye (soul) your members as instruments of unrighteousness unto sin: but yield yourselves (soul) unto God, as those that are alive from the dead, and your members as instruments of righteousness unto God. For sin shall not have dominion over you (soul): for ye (soul) are not under the law, but under grace.… Being then made free from sin, ye (soul) became the servants of righteousness. I speak after the manner of men because of the infirmity of your flesh: for as ye (soul) have yielded your members servants to uncleanness and to iniquity unto iniquity; even so now yield your members servants to righteousness unto holiness." Is habitual sin reigning in your life? If so, you must enter into the crucifixion of Christ and no longer present your members as instruments of unrighteousness to sin but submit your body unto righteousness of God. Your soul must exercise her will to the will of God to allow your soul to undergo spiritual transformation. It will not happen overnight; it may take most of your life to mature spiritually, but it is well worth it; for there are crowns to be earned and even in this life.

3 John 2 says, "Beloved, I wish above all things that thou mayest prosper and be in health, even (no more than and no less than) as thy soul prospereth."

How do Believers yield their members in their bodies to righteousness unto holiness? The position as Indenture Bondservants is we have agreed to submit to a Master because the Master paid off the infernal debt we owed to God. This relationship is by agreement. In the Kingdom of God, it is a heart issue because you voluntarily become a Kingdom Indentured Servant because you fall in love with the Lord Jesus Christ. The Indenture is a covenant binding one party to the service of another for a specified term. In the case of Believers, the term is for eternity. Believers are the Lord's *doulos* and are His Bondservants for all of eternity, and there is no greater submission, no greater love, and no greater contentment than in being the Lord's *doulos*.

Colossians 2:14 says, "Having wiped out the handwriting of requirements that was against us, which was contrary to us. And He has taken it out of the way, having nailed it to the cross." The word "handwriting" is commonly used to refer to a monetary obligation that is acknowledged by a debtor. It means a signed confession of indebtedness, bond, or self-confessed civil liability or criminal indictment. Thus, when Jesus wiped out or obliterated the handwriting of our indebtedness by hanging it on the cross, He became the owner of the indebtedness. We now owe Christ Jesus everything because He paid off our indebtedness. We became His indentured bondservants because He paid off our infernal indebtedness to God.

The ultimate purpose of consecration is stated in Philippians 1:20 which states: "...So now also Christ will be magnified in my body, whether by life or by death." When Christ is magnified, we are diminished in our self-wills. Philippians 3:21 says, "Who shall change our vile body, that it may be fashioned like unto His glorious body, according to the working whereby He is able even to subdue all things unto Himself."

Romans 6:12-23 instructs Believers to consecrate their members of their bodies to God. Likewise, Romans 12:1 instructs Believers to consecrate their entire bodies to God as living sacrifices unto Him, which means to God the Father, God the Word, and God the Holy Spirit. By such consecration, Believers yield their bodies to stop influencing the soul with carnal thoughts, emotions, and beliefs brought in from the natural world stimuli through the body's five senses.

The consecration of Believers' members in Romans Chapter 6 is for Believers' own benefit to bear the fruit of righteousness. Romans 6:13 says, "Neither yield ye your members as instruments of unrighteousness unto sin: but yield yourselves unto God, as those that are alive from the dead, and your members as instruments of righteousness unto God." In this consecration, Believers are to be delivered from sin to be a love servant to God to bear fruit unto sanctification. Romans 6:13 is for Believers' personal soul sanctification, with the help of the Godhead to subduing the influence of the flesh in the soul; so, sin does not have a stronghold over your mind, emotions, heart, and will in your soul. The Kingdom of God is a place where your soul has dominion over sin instead of sin having dominion over your soul.

The consecration of Believers' entire bodies in Romans 12:1 is for the Believers' benefit to do the will of God and bear the fruit of righteousness. In this consecration, Believers are to please God and prove God's good, well-pleasing and perfect will.

Consecration is putting ourselves in the hand of God as His Revival *Ekklesia*. Believers cannot be His Revival *Ekklesia* unless they are an *Ekklesia* actually experiencing the Revival. Yet, this is a voluntary act on Believers' part. It must come out of Believers' *agape* love for the Lord under the Godhead. The Lord and the Godhead do not act in a criminal way. Likewise, the Holy Spirit's ways are the opposite of Satan's ways. The Holy Spirit will not trespass your will. If the Holy Spirit cannot get you to come to Him voluntarily and be revived, He is not going to force you, but He will allow you to activate the law of sowing and reaping if you choose (Galatians 6:7-8). The problem you can choose the sin you commit but you cannot choose the consequences as a result of that sin.

WHAT ARE THE PRACTICAL STEPS LEADING TO CONSECRATION TO BE A PURE WORKER IN THE REVIVAL *EKKLESIA*?

Colossians 3:5 says, "Therefore put to death your members which are on the earth: fornication, uncleanness, passion, evil desire, and covetousness, which is idolatry."

Romans 8:13 says, "For if you live according to the flesh you will die; but if by the Spirit you put to death the deeds of the body, you will live." Life or death is a choice of how you want to live. It is an exercise of your will-- you must choose life over death, but you need to die to your self-centered soul to obtain Jesus' intimate relationship. You should starve your soul from partaking of continuous carnal stimuli from the fallen world through your body's five senses. Because your soul becomes hungry and thirsty for things of God, you will choose spiritual stimuli brought first to the heart in the soul by the born again spirit and Holy Spirit, which your soul will find most satisfying. Your soul will turn less to the body for stimulus nourishment.

Your body is like these telemarketers; they keep calling over and over. You can try to stop these telemarketers, but once you are on their list, they are relentless and will hound you with telephone call after telephone call every day. Once your body goes through consecration, the body decides to cooperate with your soul to enter into worship during the times of fellowship, will pick up the Bible and focus its eyes for the soul to read and study scriptures, will allow the soul to pray daily, will allow the soul to take notes when the Pastor is teaching, will allow the soul to listen to Christian music, will allow the soul to think with Bible Correctness instead of the fallen world's Political Correctness, will allow the soul to witness to others about the Kingdom of God, will allow the soul to lay hands on the sick and pray for healing to see them recover, will allow the soul to preach the gospel of the Kingdom of God, and will allow the soul to teach the word of God prepared by the soul through the leading of the born again spirit and the entire Godhead.

1 Peter 5:10 says, "But may the God of all grace, who called us to His eternal glory by Christ Jesus, after you have suffered a while, perfect, establish, strengthen, and settle you." As Believers, while we are being discipled as *doulos* unto the Lord during the time the *Ekklesia* is in Revival, we need to learn to submit to the leading of the Holy Spirit. It will require our submission to some suffering and maybe persecution during the time of Believers' consecration, maturation, and sanctification. The more independent Believers have been in the past from authority, the more time of suffering, disciplining, and consecration it will take for them to be matured, established, strengthened, sanctified and settled in their souls where sin no longer has dominion over my soul.

The secret to consecration and sanctification is submitting, learning, and taking in our souls the fruit of the Spirit of longsuffering. If you have an urge to sin in the flesh, you must suffer for a while (Hebrews 11:25). The way to stop drinking alcohol is to suffer for a while. The way to stop smoking is to suffer for a while. The way to stop overeating is to suffer for a while. The way to stop watching too much television is to suffer for a while. The way to stop lust of the flesh, lust of the eyes, and pride of life is to suffer for a while. You must be willing to suffer the displeasure of the illumination and the revelation of your own flesh's self-centered, selfish motivation in your thoughts and actions. The problem is Believers are often taught they need not suffer once they are saved.

The good news is that after you have suffered for a while, then the Godhead will perfect your ways to conform your soul to His ways, will establish you on God's Kingdom journey, will strengthen your resistance when temptation comes again, and will settle you on the better foundation of God's word. However, do not allow temptation around you while you are on the altar of the Lord's consecration and sanctification. Romans 13:14 says, "But put on the Lord Jesus Christ, and make no provision for the flesh, to fulfill its lusts." How does a believer stop sinning? You enter into the crucifixion of Christ and stop living to sin. You put on the new man, which is your sinless born again spirit who is joined to Christ and enter into a life of continuous prayer and reading the Word of God. You invite and submit to the leading of the Holy Spirit. Resist the devil and he will flee (James 4:7).

Paul said in 1 Corinthians 9:27 that: "I discipline my body and bring it into subjection, lest, when I have preached to others, I myself should be disqualified." Discipline refers to training. Training means ongoing study and accepting God's word as the foundation of your beliefs, and then preaching the gospel of the kingdom of God, repentance and the remission of sins, and teaching God's word to others. Our souls will become washed by the water of the word of God (Ephesians 5:26). Our souls must become spiritually minded and no longer carnally minded (Romans 8:6). Consecration includes taking on the Godly habits of the Holy Spirit as He leads us. Our touch, seeing, hearing, smelling, and tasting of our five senses in our bodies must be consecrated to God and for the Master's good pleasure. Our soul's cleansing and sanctification must become spiritually minded, spiritually emotional, and spiritually heartfelt, so our wills are exercised to follow the leading of the born again spirit, led by the Holy Spirit. The good pleasure of Lord's divine nature, God the Word, is to do the will of God the Father. His good pleasure is for righteousness and holiness. His good pleasure is to build His Revival *Ekklesia* as an irresistible force of love here on earth. His perfect will is to manifest the Kingdom of God and God's will here on earth as it is in Heaven (Matthew 6:10).

Galatians 5:16-17 says, "I say then: 'Walk in the spirit, and you will not fulfill the lust of the flesh. For the flesh lusts against the spirit, and the spirit against the flesh; and these are contrary to one another, so that you do not do the things that you wish.'" Walking in the spirit means that you are walking in step with the Holy Spirit as He leads you. Sonship through Christ Jesus invites discipline by God the Father (Hebrews 12:7-11). The Kingdom of God and the Lord's *Ekklesia* in Revival will be filled with Spirit led Believers who have gone through the process of consecration and sanctification. What pleases God eventually will become your good pleasure.

The training and disciplining through crucifixion of the flesh must start first with the tongue.

James 3:6 says, "...The tongue is so set among our members that it defiles the whole body and sets on fire the course of nature; and it is set on fire by hell." To discipline the tongue, one has to change one's heart. Matthew 15:18-19 says, "But those things which proceed out of the mouth come from the heart, and they defile a man. For out of the heart proceed evil thoughts, murders, adulteries, fornications, thefts, false witness, blasphemies." Thus, the heart must put on the New Man and become holy and righteous for your will to act with righteousness and holiness (Ephesians 4:24).

The heart in your soul is where your library of beliefs is stored and where the will is, and volutary longsuffering in the soul is the forbearance of sinful actions. This means that your soul willingly has to be deprived of the body's sinful pleasures and the stimuli from the world. You must consider the body as you would a horse or anything else that is rebellious and undisciplined. You must strive to get control of your body and reign it in. You need to buffet your body. Make it obey you. Teach it to die to its own desires and to be led by the spiritually minded, spiritually feeling, spiritually heartfelt love of your transformed soul, which in turn is submitted to the new born again spirit, who in turn is totally submitted to the Holy Spirit, who in turn is strictly submitted to the Lord Jesus Christ, who in turn is perfectly submitted to God the Father. This is the redemptive order that will rule and reign in the Revival Church.

As Believers, in order to have Jesus' humanity nature's exchanged resurrection life; we must suffer the implantation of an exchanged crucified death from Christ Jesus (Galatians 2:20). 2 Corinthians 4:10-11 says, "Always carrying about in the body the dying of the Lord Jesus, that the life of Jesus also may be manifested in our body. For we who live are always delivered to death for Jesus' sake, that the life of Jesus also may be manifested in our mortal flesh." We must enter into the crucifixion of Christ, which is the process of dying by the Lord Jesus Christ in order for us to experience death to self. It is not the actual stroke of death of our flesh that we apply to our souls; it is the vicarious death of the Lord's crucifixion that must be applied. As Believers, our souls must receive the resurrected life of Christ Jesus' humanity nature that is carried and implanted by His indwelling divine nature, God the Word (1 Peter 1:23). As we prosper spiritually in our souls, it brings healing and financial prosperity to meet our need (3 John 2). Jesus said He felt His virtue leave Him when the woman with the issue of blood merely touched the hem of His garment (Luke 8:46). The Lord's spiritual virtue in your soul will permeate through your body to minister to others, as this process becomes the manifested anointing from the Holy Spirit.

Submission unto concentration and unto sanctification is a process that God wants all Believers have to endure. Galatians 5:24 says, "And those who are Christ's have crucified the flesh with its passions and desires." You should stop the body from sowing carnal thoughts, emotions, and natural fallen stimuli in your mind, emotions, and heart of your soul. Galatians 6:8 says, "As For he who sows to his flesh will of the flesh reap corruption...." Crucifixion is a death process, not death itself. Jesus was crucified at 9:00 a.m., but the stroke of death came at 3:00 p.m. How does one enter Jesus' crucifixion? It will do no good to try to crucify the influence of the flesh in your soul with your own will. Be led of the Spirit and seek the Lord to exchange His sacrificial crucifixion and death for your temporary flesh or carnal life. The only crucifixion that works is the appropriation of Christ's crucifixion in our lives. Romans 6:5-8 says, "Knowing this, that our old man (in Christ) is crucified with Him, that the body of sin might be destroyed, that henceforth we should not serve sin. For he that is dead is freed from sin. Now if we be dead with Christ, we believe that we shall also live with Him (with His resurrected life)."

As Believers, we cannot consecrate our bodies and souls by ourselves. The Messianic Believers of the Old Testament through the sacrifice of animals could not accomplish salvation or consecration; instead, they had to believe in the coming Messiah as their Lord and Savior. Yet, we have received the personal sacrifice of Christ's humanity nature and received His compassion and mercy that led to salvation, so His divine nature consecrates Believers to the entire Godhead through His humanity nature's identification with us, our submission to Him, and His resurrection life by the word of the Kingdom imparted and implanted as seed in the heart of our souls.

SPECIFIC THINGS TO CONSECRATE
TO THE LORD OURSELVES:

As a Believer, the first thing you need to do after initial salvation is start the process of dying to self in your soul and submitting your soul to consecrate your soul and body to God. Submit to the consecration of your flesh's influence in your soul as a living sacrifice unto God. Commit your will to do God's will and not your own will. Commit yourself to be a worker in His Revival *Ekklesia*. Submit your soul and body to the Head, which is Christ Jesus, with His humanity nature and divine nature. Obey the Lord's divine nature who is always with you, especially as you enter fellowship with other Believers in Kingdom community (Matthew 18:20) and when you are making disciples of unbelievers that become Believers, baptizing them, and teaching all that the Lord commanded (Matthew 28:20).

As Believers, when we consecrate our souls and bodies to God, God wants Believers to accept His will as their will to be done here on earth as it is in Heaven. Sometimes, life is good and other times it is not so good. Sometimes its blessing and other times its suffering. You must be willing to take life as it comes. You must always seek first the kingdom of God and His righteousness, and all things of God through Jesus Christ will be added to your life (Matthew 6:33). When our souls feel down and troubled, God assures us in Romans 8:28, "And we know that all things work together for good to them that love God, to them who are the called according to His purpose."

As Believers, when we submit our souls and bodies to God, we present our bodies as living sacrifices unto the Lord to be used in His Kingdom as Ambassadors and Soldiers, as Ephesians 4:11 office gifts, as Believers who are using the biblitarian Kingdom economics and God's imparted knowledge, understanding, and wisdom to run all businesses or professions, as stay home mothers. Believers have the indwelling Godhead, so believers will be exercising their spiritual gifts with the "Bread Basket" anointing during the season of the Joel 2 Revival *Ekklesia*. God and Christ Jesus' humanity nature own our bodies, souls, and spirits. We are not free anymore to sin with our souls and bodies. We have become the Temple of God, Who is holy, righteous, just, full of mercy and grace, and is love personified. 1 Thessalonians 5:23 says, "And the very God of peace sanctify you wholly; and I pray to God that your whole spirit and soul and body be preserved blameless unto the coming of our Lord Jesus Christ." Similarly, Mark 12:30-31 says, "'And thou shalt love the Lord thy God with all thy heart, and with all thy soul, and with all thy mind, and with all thy strength:' this is the first commandment. And the second is like, namely this, 'Thou shalt love thy neighbour as thyself.' There is none other commandment greater than these."

The Bible never talks about the consecration and sanctification of just the heart in the soul where your library of beliefs is stored, but rather your whole body and whole soul. As Believers, we must "present our bodies a living sacrifice, holy, acceptable unto God, which is your reasonable service" (Romans 12:1). As Believers, we willfully must allow the Godhead to consecrate our whole body and soul to the Lord, just as our born again spirits are already consecrated, perfect, sinless, righteous, and holy (Hebrews 12:23; 1 John 3:9; Ephesians 4:24).

Galatians 5:16-18 says, "This I say then, 'Walk in the Spirit, and ye shall not fulfill the lust of the flesh. For the flesh lusteth against the Spirit, and the Spirit against the flesh: and these are contrary the one to the other: so that ye cannot do the things that ye would. But if ye be led of the Spirit, ye are not under the law.'"

Thus, our mouths are not our own. We must speak the words of God; we must become Biblitarians. Our ears are not our own. We should only listen to music and the words of the Lord. We need to consecrate our eyes. We should look at things that are pure. We need to consecrate our hands. We should use our hands to heal and touch people with Christ's love. We should consecrate our feet. We should carry the gospel of the Kingdom and repentance and remission of sins wherever the Lord sends us. Our bodies are not our own. Therefore, we cannot use any part of our bodies to satisfy our own fleshly lusts. We are the Body of Christ, so our bodies are the Temple of God and must maintain holiness and not be defiled. God has a right as Creator and Jesus as Lord to decide what we must see, speak, taste, listen, touch and where we must go.

Once an offering was taken in church and the plates were passed. When it came to a twelve-year-old girl, she kept asking the usher to lower the plate. When the plate was all the way down on the carpet, the girl stepped into the offering plate. She had no money, so she gave what she had which was her entire spirit, soul, and body as an offering unto the Lord.

It is important to remember that God is the Almighty, All Knowing, Immutable, Always Present Sovereign King by His right as the Creator, over the entire spiritual and natural universes or worlds; and He speaks with absolute authority in His Kingdom as Sovereign King.

God's words come to Believers' soul through God's redemptive order of communication, which is as follows. God's redemptive order of communication follows the redemptive flow of His authority, power, knowledge, understanding, and wisdom, which all are motivated by God's redemptive love (*agape*). In other words, Jesus, consisting of His divine nature as God the Word and His humanity nature as the only begotten Son of God, receives and only speaks what He hears Father God saying (John 7:16-18; 14:10). Then God the Word transmits Father God's words to God the Holy Spirit. In furtherance of God's redemptive order of communication and transmission of His authority, power, wisdom, knowledge, understanding and love, the Holy Spirit only says to your born again spirit what He hears God the Word saying. John 16: 13-14 says, "....when He, the Spirit of truth, has come, He will guide you into all truth; for He will not speak on His own authority, but whatever he hears He will speak; and He will tell you things to come. He will glorify Me, for He will take what is Mine and declare it to you."

The Holy Spirit declares the words spoken by God the Word as *rhema* to the born again spirit, who then communicates the *rhema* of God to the soul, first in the heart of the soul. Galatians 4:6 says, "And because ye are sons, God hath sent forth the spirit (joined with) His Son into your hearts, crying, Abba, Father." The resurrected spirit of God's Son gave birth to your born again spirit, which is joined with Jesus' resurrected spirit by Jesus' divine nature, God the Word (1 Corinthians 6:17). Jesus' resurrected humanity spirit is in heaven but is joined with your born again spirit inside of you; and he comes into your heart, into your whole being joined to Jesus' resurrected humanity spirit. Thus, Paul says his Son's spirit comes into your heart. The soul gets nourishment and transformation as she submits to the word of God. The word coming from God's redemptive order of communication is full of spirit and life (John 6:63). Thus, when you hear that God wants you to consecrate your body to Him, this redemptive communication is profoundly serious and comes down from Father God through His redemptive order of communication, and you have to take it with the solemnity that it deserves.

Jesus said in Matthew 4:4, "Man shall not live by bread alone, but by every (*rhema*) word that proceedeth out of the mouth of God." As Believers, we must serve the Lord with our whole bodies and whole souls, being led by our born again spirits, who is led by the Holy Spirit, Who is communicated the *rhema* of Father God by God the Word, Who repeats what He hears from God the Father. When God revives us with a new born again spirit, He commissions us to be laborers in His harvest for the expansion of His Kingdom here on earth. Yet, the entire Godhead wants us to decide voluntarily to serve Him in love. Jesus said in Matthew 22:37, "You shall love the Lord your God with all your heart and with all your soul and with all your mind." The Lord's divine nature asks each of us, "Do you love Me?"

If you dedicate yourself to the service of the Lord in the Kingdom of God, then all other things will start lining up in proper priority. It is easier to let go of relationships and things once you give yourself to the Lord and King of His Kingdom. You are not your own. You were bought for a very costly price, and you must give yourself to God wholeheartedly. When you do, your reward will be greater than you can acquire from this three-dimensional fallen world. As the spirit of God's Kingdom becomes your spiritual reality, then serving God with your whole spirit, soul, and body becomes routine as God continuously sends the rewards of righteousness, peace, and joy in the Holy Spirit. Romans 14:16-19 says, "Let not then your good be evil spoken of: For the kingdom of God is not meat and drink; but righteousness, and peace, and joy in the Holy Ghost. For he that in these things serveth Christ is acceptable to God and approved of men. Let us therefore follow after the things which make for peace, and things wherewith one may edify another."

OTHER PEOPLE:

As Believers, we should pray that our family members who are saved submit to the consecration of their bodies and souls to God. We are required to put God before our families, spouses, children, parents, brothers, and sisters and distant relatives as we work in the Revival Ekklesia to bring in the harvest. We must seek God and His Kingdom first in our daily routines. In the natural, a Soldier may not be able to come home to his family for Christmas. An Ambassador may not be able to return home because she is working on behalf of her government in very important negotiations with other governments. Therefore, Believers are the "called out ones." This is why Jesus said in Luke 18:29-30, "Verily I say unto you, 'There is no man that hath left house, or parents, or brethren, or wife, or children, for the kingdom of God's sake, Who shall not receive manifold more in this present time, and in the world to come life everlasting."

Many human sentiments bid you to return to family reunions, childhood commitments, and the like. At times you may be able to attend, but if there is God's Kingdom issue or problem, you need to obey the leading of the Holy Spirit, not your calendar or the bidding of family members. You must let the dead bury their dead when the harvest comes (Matthew 8: 22). These natural sentiments are okay until they interfere with God's ministry assignments. If any activities are so important to you that it leads you away from following the King and His Kingdom, then you need to set better priorities and make these other things of less importance. If God gave you a particular Kingdom ministry assignment that He thinks is important, then, you should consider it of significant importance to you.

In your consecration, you must put all your relationships on the altar, and your commitments to those relationships must forever be in second place after your commitment to God. God wants a consecration of everything you touch, think, and seek after. He wants purity in Believers' hearts, emotions, and minds; so His children in the Revival *Ekklesia* are not corrupted by the influence of the flesh, the natural world, and the kingdom of darkness.

Sometimes, the Lord insists you drop certain current friends and directs you to go to a new place and acquire new relationships who are strong Believers who will help each other to mature spiritually in their souls. Sometimes, it hurts to leave friends, to lessen time with family, and to leave your neighborhood. Yet, if they are not consecrated to the Lord where they become secondary in your life, then you will have to lessen your time with them to participate fully in the Revival *Ekklesia*. God is your Father by adoption and running His Kingdom is a big job; and He will not take second place to anyone or anything. God is a jealous God. He wants your whole heart, attention, and service.

If the people you love and are intimately involved are not consecrated, you cannot fully satisfy or serve God. You should leave them for a season to do God's work. You are a missionary, Kingdom Ambassador, and Kingdom Soldier; you are called-out to serve the King in His Kingdom. As God brings Revival to the Lord's *Ekklesia*, He is calling His people to repentance, bodily consecration, and soul sanctification. God forbids anything of the flesh to interfere with the work of the *Ekklesia* in Revival. He wants you to be spiritually minded, spiritually emotional, and spiritually believing.

David was a man after God's own heart (Acts 13: 22). As the singing King, David prepared a song in Psalm 73:25, "Whom have I in Heaven but Thee? And there is none upon earth that I desire beside Thee." King David had the right heart. Jesus said in Matthew 5:48, "Be ye therefore perfect, even as your Father which is in Heaven is perfect." The Greek word for perfect is *teleios* which means complete and mature in your spiritual labors, spiritual growth, moral character and are continuously seeking the King and the Kingdom of God with faith that with God all things are possible.

In obedience to God, Abraham offered up Isaac to the Lord to show God that he would not hold anything back from God. There can be no human being who captures your heart with the same intensity as God captures your heart if you are going to be used in the Revival Church in an intense way. Often, God chooses elderly Believers because they are available and not burdened with demanding jobs and raising children that lessen their work in His Revival Church.

WORLDLY ACTIVITIES:

Many lukewarm Believers do things to feed their soulish desires, pride, and lusts. Believers enroll into school, planning to get the top grades, the best jobs, and higher salaries. Believers run after things such as sports, music, art, and other types of activities without first seeking the Lord that takes away time spent in Kingdom community fellowship, studying the word of God, visiting those who are sick, and being servants of the Lord's Kingdom. If any activity is so important to you that it leads you away from the King and His Kingdom, then you need to set better priorities, boundaries, and make these natural things less important. Seek first, not second or third, the Kingdom of God and His righteousness (Matthew 6:33).

As Believers, allow the Holy Spirit to lead you; otherwise, you will run after the things in the fallen world and will miss the things of God and the work in His Kingdom. This is all involved during movement of the Holy Spirit in the Revival *Ekklesia*. Nothing you do, even though it seems good in the eyes of the fallen natural world, will have eternal value if it is not directed by God to be done by you.

As a Believer, you may put a lot of time in your career, but without an intimate relationship with the Lord, you will rarely profit from the career. Without Christ being Lord in your life, there will be little or no satisfaction in the career after years of work. You will not find rest in the career, even if you make a lot of money. Your business, job, profession, or career in the world is designed to burn you out. It will zap you of your energy. It will harm your health. It will cause you to stumble. You will run and get weary. You will faint from your weariness. You will have no joy and no sense of accomplishment. Jesus said in Matthew 11: 28-30, "Come unto me, all ye that labour and are heavy laden, and I will give you rest. Take my yoke upon you and learn of me; for I am meek and lowly in heart: and ye shall find rest unto your souls. For my yoke is easy, and my burden is light." Only the Lord's divine nature, God the Word, can bring you true spiritual rest. The Revival *Ekklesia* cannot use your fleshly talents and skills. It can only use your compliant heart, your spiritual gifts, and your time to the work of the Lord. Whatever you do for the Lord lasts if the Godhead is directing your steps in your journey.

For example, in my own life, I always believed in Jesus and God. Yet, I "back slid" for years while going through college and law school, and I became a lawyer at age of 25. I thought there was going to be a "pot of gold at the end of the rainbow" once I became a lawyer. I dreamed of becoming a lawyer even from the fifth grade, but I did not know the reality of long hours, competitiveness, injustice, overhead expenditures, and the continuous acquisitions of new clients, and all these unforeseen difficulties, that together were the biggest let down in my life. I thought that once I became a lawyer, I would have lots of money, assets, and prestige, but then I found people jealous, resentful they had to pay me money to get them out of legal problems; and I had to deal with other unsaved lawyers and judges with ego problems. I was missing the Lord in my life and failed to consecrate my business to the Lord. I did not know why my life's career dream was not making me happy, or at least satisfied. I lost my joy for life.

Although I came back to the Lord in 1979, it was not until 1987 that I earnestly started serving the Lord again with my whole heart as I had done as a young boy and teenager. I dedicated my life to serve the Lord. I practiced law, and at the same time I had a ministry. I found fulfilment in my law practice. Since then, my life has been full of the Present One and the Holy Spirit, and I have lived the most important years of my life with an intimate relationship with the Lord. The

Lord's divine nature, God the Word and the Holy Spirit put everything in order when I turned my heart over to the Lord and consecrated myself to His service. I found out who I really was in Christ Jesus. God revealed to me my engiftments to write teachings and books that minister God's word. I attuned my entire belief system to the word of God. I became a Biblitarian. I have studied the word of God daily since 1987. I have ministered hundreds if not a thousand sermons to people. I had radio programs. Yet, my greatest thrill is that every day I find something interesting in the word of God to ponder and write about. I pray for the sick all the time. I give my business clients the wisdom I have learned from the word of God, especially if they are non-believers without necessarily informing them of the source of my wisdom. If they inquire of the source, I often lead them to the Lord right then and there.

I have had many personal tribulations that most Believers would have given up years before me, but through it all the Lord's divine nature has been with me. If fact, the entire Godhead has been there. I feel the pleasure I give to the Holy Spirit when I write; and He gives me new illuminations from the word of God, along with His anointing. I have learned to hear the *rhema* word of the Lord from His *logos* word, "For the (*logos*) word of God is quick, and powerful, and sharper than any two-edged sword, piercing even to the dividing asunder of soul and spirit, and of the joints and marrow, and is a discerner of the thoughts and intents of the heart." My desire is to serve God with all my might and soul. I was born in 1949, and I do not know what the Lord has planned for me, but I am ready; I am His love servant. He has never left me nor forsaken me, and I will never leave Him. I live to serve Him. To some this may sound religious, but it is not. I am not religious. I am Jesus' bondservant, and I write and teach the word of God.

OBJECTS:

Any object, car, boat, jewelry, stamp collection, coin collection, clothes, hair and/or anything which has preoccupied Believers' time, thoughts, money, or energy should be consecrated to the Lord. Anything that is put ahead of God can become an idol, and our God will not have other idols before Him. The Revival *Ekklesia* will not exalt idols, but rather the Lord Jesus Christ.

Some Believers have only a small thing of influence of the flesh that needs to be consecrated. Others have something that has consumed their lives like drug or alcohol addiction. Believers must be careful of any clubs that they belong in the world, such as antique cars or any of the social clubs. Believers have to research before joining any social media or clubs. Believers alt to be careful not to pick up and start using slang or vulgar language just because it is popular in the world. Such can cause you to sin by you becoming too involved at the expense of your ministry calling. Believers need to submit to consecration of their bodies and souls and say, "These hands, feet, eyes, mouth, ears, and my soul are not my own; they belong to the Lord." I know it is hard to let go of some of these relationships and things, but Believers must be serious with God in His Revival *Ekklesia*. Believers must dedicate and submit themselves to the consecration and sanctification to the entire Godhead and always seek first the Kingdom of God. Believers must make their bodies obey their souls and spirits, not the other way around. Believers' souls must put on the born again spirit, the new man of righteousness and holiness (Ephesians 4:24). Believers must make no provision for the flesh's influence in their souls. Romans 13:14 says, "But put ye (soul) on the Lord Jesus Christ, and make no provision for the flesh, to fulfill the lusts thereof."

Turn away from the things in this world that consume your life and turn to God, the Life Giver.

Submit yourself to follow the Holy Spirit, then you will be consecrated to God the Father's use in Jesus' Revival *Ekklesia* as His child by adoption. Be about the Father's business (Luke 2:49) in God's Kingdom here on earth and be one who is led by the Holy Spirit, as sons of God (Romans 8:14), and not by the most popular ideas of this world. You belong to the Lord Jesus Christ not the fallen world.

Personally, I remember that the national pastime of baseball used to take a lot of my life's energies before I came back to the Lord. When I was single living in Orange County, California, I use to go to almost every Angel game in Anaheim, California. When I was growing up, I played baseball during recess and after school, in a High School league, during picnics and at every family reunion. I used to collect baseball cards as a hobby. I would memorize statistics of ball players of my favorite teams. As a young teenager, baseball players that I liked were guys like Mickey Mantle, Yogi Bear, Don Drysdale and all the other great baseball players of the sport at that time. I loved the St Louis Cardinals, the New York Yankees, and eventually the Anaheim Angels. I even went to the Dodgers games when they were doing well.

Then, one day I met "Jesus in the outfield" and realized that I had to consecrate my love for baseball to the Lord. I had moved to the Inland Empire, California, so it was not that convenient anymore. When I came back to the Lord, baseball stopped having its pull upon me. It did not seem important anymore. The desire for consecration comes as a byproduct of spiritual maturation and transformation of the soul that continues with a closer walk with the Lord.

However, when I came back to the Lord, I still had some things hanging in my mind, emotions, and will that have interfered with my complete consecration unto the Lord. Even though I was saved, I still had a preoccupation in my soul for making money in the secular world. Getting involved in international "deals" became imbedded in my mind, emotions, and heart and kept me away from God. The financial activity became more important than God. However, in January of 1987, I gave up their control of me. I let go and gave them to the Lord. The Lord suddenly became my all-consuming love and compassion. I can tell you it felt so good to get rid of the things that were holding me back from Jesus and the Kingdom of God. While I was refusing to consecrate my business activity to God, I could not hear from God because I had no intimate relationship with God, although I was saved. Later, God showed me how to consecrate my business to Him, and He made my law practice a ministry outreach and my professional part of my ministry calling. Hundreds of lives have been touched through my law practice and my prayers, teachings, sermons, and books over the many, many years, as my law practice became the place where I met and ministered to hurting people.

When the Israelites left Egypt, they took all their animals and things with them, and they consecrated them to the Lord. The people gave the gold, silver, scarlet cloth, and other precious things liberally to build the Tabernacle in the Wilderness. When you come to the Lord, you need to consecrate your house, your car, your hobbies, your job, your business, even your golf clubs. Use them for the Lord. Give the Lord charge over them. God's purpose is to make Believers' bodies as the Temple for Himself to live within the revived Believer that is becoming the Revival *Ekklesia*, which is the primary living organism in His Kingdom.

You may have a career or profession that you need to consecrate to the Lord. You may have a hobby that you need to consecrate and give to the Lord. God can use anything you give Him for

His purpose of building His Revival *Ekklesia* and His Kingdom. With Moses, God used what he had in his hand for forty years, his shepherd's staff, to perform miracles and signs of the Lord's presence and the Lord's authority given to Moses.

I always consecrate every house I have ever lived. I go around the house with oil and anoint the doorposts, lintels, windows and every room to dedicate them to the Lord. I have given away cars, sound equipment, a beautiful glass pulpit, much personal property, and lots of money to other ministers doing the Lord's work as I was led by the Holy Spirit. I have given my law practice to the Lord, so I am His servant. Only those things you give to the Lord can be blessed and be a place of blessing. I have allowed traveling Evangelists to live with me for years to help support them while doing the Lord's work when they needed a home.

More than anything else, when I gave all these things to the Lord, the things did not hold me. I am freed up to serve the Lord as a leader in His Revival *Ekklesia.*

PLEASE SAY THIS PRAYER WITH ME:

Lord Jesus, magnify Yourself in my soul, so the influence of my flesh does not dominate by mind, emotions, heart, and will. Purify my mind, emotions, and heart, so I will have the right thinking, emoting, and believing. God, consecrate my body to You that I may be an effective leader in the Body of Christ, a zealous king and priest under Your authority in Your Revival *Ekklesia*, and a mature citizen in Your Kingdom. I accept your promise with faith that when I am weak in the influence of my flesh in my soul, You become strong in me because of my submission and dependence. God help me resist the temptations of the flesh from dominating my soul. Help me be spiritually minded rather than carnally minded. Help me from sinning with my body. Lord, help me not to entertain any provision of the flesh. God, I dedicate my body to you. God, consecrate my eyes, ears, mouth, hands, and feet to do your will in building Your Revival *Ekklesia* and Your Kingdom. You own my body. God, you have chosen my body as your Temple in which to live. Consecrate Your temple. I thank you for saving me and redeeming me. Lord Jesus, exchange your crucified life for the life I have in my soul that I may partake of your resurrected life in my soul and live to serve You as a citizen of Your Kingdom and as a Minister in Your Revival *Ekklesia*. Father God, I submit the influence of my own body in my soul to Your pruning. God the Word, I submit the influence of my flesh in my soul for your cleansing word. God the Holy Spirit, I submit the deeds of my flesh in my soul to your mortification. Help me suffer for a while, so that I can enter the crucifixion of Christ Jesus and be rid of the habitual sin of my flesh in my soul. Holy Spirit, I ask You to touch my body, heal it, and consecrate it. Lord Jesus, consecrate my body to Yourself that I may receive Your holiness in my soul without the influence of the flesh. God, cleanse your Temple. God, receive my consecrated body and soul as your love servant from this day forward through all eternity. God, use me to do Your work when you pour out Your Spirit on all flesh to establish, manifest, and dedicate Your Revival *Ekklesia* and Your Kingdom. In Jesus' name, I pray. Amen.

Believers in Christ are the true Spiritual Jews and Spiritual Israel

Believers in Christ are the true Spiritual Jews and Spiritual Israel

The terms, Hebrews, Israelites, and Jews, all refer to the same people, which constitute the nation that came from the loins of Abraham through Isaac and then Jacob, that are a nation promised and chosen by God in the Old Testament (Genesis 12:1-3).

The term Hebrew is first used in the scriptures to refer to Abraham (Genesis 14:13). Then it is used to refer to Joseph (Genesis 39:14,17) and then the other descendants of Abraham through Isaac and Jacob (Genesis 40:15; 43:32). The word Hebrew has the meaning "to cross over the water" which refers to Abraham leaving Ur and crossing over the Euphrates River to come into the Promise Land. Afterwards, the nation of people that came from Abraham through Isaac and Jacob were called Hebrews. Paul said that he was a Hebrew and Israelite (2 Corinthians 11:22). Hebrew became the language and writings that were developed by the descendants of Abraham through Isaac and Jacob.

Genesis 32:22-30 describes an event where Jacob wrestled with the Angel of the Lord or Pre-incarnate Christ, and Jacob said in verse 30, "I have seen God face to face, and my life is preserved." Hosea 12:3-4 confirms that Jacob struggled with a Person who was God and a Messenger, or Preincarnate Christ. Jacob asked to be blessed, so the Angel of the Lord changed Jacob's name to Israel. The twelve sons of Israel were called Israelites (Exodus 9:7; Judges 20:21; 1 Samuel 2:14; 2 Corinthians 11:22).

When the nation of the Israelites divided as two nations, the ten northern tribes called their nation Israel. The two southern tribes of Judah and Benjamin called their nation Judah. The ten tribes of Israel of the Northern Kingdom were taken captive by the Assyrians and were scattered throughout the known world at that time. The two tribes of the Southern Kingdom, Benjamin and Judah, were taken captive by the Babylonians, but were not scattered; and many returned to their homeland. When the United Nations declared and recognized the new nation of the Hebrews, Israelites, or Jews in 1948, more of the Israelite tribes who were scattered they felt would come to the nation of Israel instead of Judah, so they named this new country, Israel, to attract those Israelites who were scattered in other nations.

The tribal name of Jews was first used to describe the inhabitants of Judah, the name taken by the two tribes of the Southern Kingdom after the division (2 Kings 16:6; 2 Kings 25:25). Returning from Babylon to their homeland, the name Jew or Jews was used to call all the inhabitants of the homeland.

Jew or Jews is used by the writers of the New Testament to distinguish them from the Gentiles, Samaritans, and other people living or traveling in Israel at the time of Christ Jesus and after His death, resurrection, and ascension (John 4:9; Romans 2:9; Acts 2:10). Thus, the Hebrews, Israelites, and Jews were written in the New Testament to designate the natural flesh descendants of

Abraham, Isaac, and Jacob (John 4:9; 2 Corinthians 11:22), but Christ Jesus decided to create in the tribe of Judah and the family of David new spiritual Jews of both Jews and Gentiles. This was a great mystery revealed to Paul that the Body of Christ consists of both Jews and Gentiles, not just Jewish people alone (Ephesians 3:13-18).

John the Baptist said in Matthew 3:9, "And think not to say within yourselves, 'We have Abraham to our father:' for I say unto you that God is able of these stones to raise up children unto Abraham." Jesus said in John 8:37-40,44, "I know that ye are Abraham's seed (by the flesh); but ye seek to kill Me, because My word hath no place in you. (38), I speak that which I have seen with My Father: and ye do that which ye have seen with your father (devil). (39), They answered and said unto him, 'Abraham is our father.' Jesus saith unto them, 'If ye were Abraham's children, ye would do the works of Abraham. (40), But now ye seek to kill me, a man that hath told you the truth, which I have heard of God: this did not Abraham.' (44), Ye are of your father the devil, and the lusts of your father ye will do. He was a murderer from the beginning, and abode not in the truth, because there is no truth in him. When he speaketh a lie, he speaketh of his own: for he is a liar, and the father of it." Both John the Baptist and Jesus said that being Abraham's natural children does not by itself cause a Jew in the flesh to be saved. A Jew in the flesh can be saved only by being in Christ.

Likewise, Paul said in Romans 3:9, 29 "What then? Are we better than they? No, in no wise: for we have before proved both Jews and Gentiles, that they are all under sin.… Is He the God of the Jews only? Is He not also of the Gentiles? Yes, of the Gentiles also." Similarly, Paul said in 1 Corinthians 12:13, "For by one Spirit are we all baptized into one body, whether we be Jews or Gentiles, whether we be bond or free; and have been all made to drink into one Spirit."

Paul wrote in Galatians 3:28-29, "There is neither Jew nor Greek (of the flesh), there is neither bond nor free (of the flesh), there is neither male nor female (of the flesh): for ye are all one (spiritually) in Christ Jesus. And if ye be Christ's, then are ye Abraham's Seed, and heirs according to the promise." Through the Seed of Jesus Christ, the Jewish Messiah's humanity nature, Believers become spiritual Jews by receiving born again spirits. God's promise was given to Abraham and reasserted to Isaac and Jacob that through their Seed (Christ Jesus, the Hebrew, Israelite, and Jewish Messiah) all nations on earth would be blessed. This was a reference to the birth of the Jewish Messiah supernaturally born as a descendant of Abraham, Isaac, Jacob, tribe of Judah and family of David by Mary, the mother of Jesus' humanity nature. Yet, Jesus was also the Son of God, so His seed came from God, Himself. Jesus also had two natures. Jesus has a humanity nature as the great-great-great grandson of Abraham, Isaac, Jacob, and David but He also has a divine nature, God the Word. Jesus' humanity nature was the only begotten Son of God.

The mystery of Christ Jesus as the Jewish Messiah was to reconcile fallen mankind, whether Hebrews, Israelites, Jews, or Gentiles, to God, as we all are natural children of Adam and Eve. Through Christ Jesus' humanity nature Believers receive Christ's spiritual Seed of His resurrected humanity nature and become born again new creatures in Christ (Isaiah 9:6; 1 Peter 1:23; 2 Corinthians 5:17) and therefore are spiritual Jews and spiritual Hebrews.

Thus, upon Jesus' death, resurrection, and ascension, there was born a new spiritual creature in Christ as the Second Man in Christ (2 Corinthians 5:17; 1 Corinthinas 15:47), which are Believers' born again spirits, who are spiritual Jews, spiritual Israelites, and spiritual Hebrews.

Paul said the promises to Abraham were that by his Seed through Isaac and Jacob, which was the Messiah, Christ Jesus' humanity nature, all nations would be blessed (Genesis 12:1-2; Galatians 3:8). Paul said in Galatians 3:16-19, "Now to Abraham and his Seed were the promises made. He saith not, 'And to seeds,' as of many; but as of One, 'And to thy Seed,' which is Christ. And this I say, that the covenant, that was confirmed before of God in Christ, the law, which was four hundred and thirty years after, cannot disannul, that it should make the promise of none effect. For if the inheritance be of the law, it is no more of promise: but God gave it to Abraham by promise. Wherefore then serveth the law? It was added because of transgressions, till the Seed (Christ Jesus, the spiritual Jewish Messiah) should come to whom the promise was made; and it was ordained by angels in the hand of a mediator."

All nations of both Jews and Gentiles would be blessed by the majority accepting Christ Jesus as Savior and Lord. Paul made God's purpose clear in Ephesians 2: 14-18, about one New Man, which says, "For He is our peace, Who hath made both (Jews and Gentiles) one, and hath broken down the middle wall of partition between us; having abolished in His (Jesus' humanity nature) flesh the enmity, even the law of commandments contained in ordinances; for to make in Himself of twain one New Man (1 Corinthians 15:47; 2 Corinthians 5:17; Ephesians 3: 13-18; 4:24; Colossians 3:10) of both (Jews and Gentiles), so making peace; and that He might reconcile both (Jews and Gentiles) unto God in one body by the Cross, having slain the enmity thereby: And came and preached peace to you which were afar off, and to them that were nigh. For through Him we both (Jews and Gentiles) have access by one Spirit unto the Father."

Now, let us conclude this Jewish and Israel spiritual heritage based on what has been written in the chapters of this book. First, Jesus was of the Tribe of Judah (Hebrews 8:8) and family of David (Romans 1:3) through Jesus' humanity nature's mother, Mary (Matthew 1:18-23; Luke 2:7). The Jewish Messiah, Christ Jesus' resurrected humanity nature, is the spiritual Father of Believers' born again spirits (Isaiah 9:6; Hebrews 2:13). It was Jesus' humanity nature Who supplied the incorruptible Seed to cause new Believers to have born again spirits (1 Peter 1:23). The descendants of the Jewish Messiah, Christ Jesus, are Believers' born again spirits as spiritual Jews and spiritual Israel. Born again Believers are New Creatures in Christ (2 Corinthians 5:17) as the Second Man in Christ (1 Corinthians 15:47).

Paul wrote of a new spiritual Jew in Romans 2:28-29, "For he is not a Jew, which is one outwardly (in the flesh); neither is that circumcision, which is outward in the flesh. But he is a Jew, which is one inwardly; and circumcision is that of the heart, in the spirit, and not in the letter; whose praise is not of men, but of God."

Additionally, Paul wrote of a new spiritual Israel in Romans 9:6-8, "Not as though the word of God hath taken none effect. For they are not all Israel, which are of Israel (in the flesh). Neither, because they are the seed of Abraham (in the flesh), are they all children (of the promise): but, in Isaac shall thy Seed be called. That is, they which are the children of the flesh, these are not the children of God: but the children of the promise are counted for the Seed." Galatians 3:28-29 says, "There is neither Jew nor Greek, there is neither bond nor free, there is neither male nor female: for ye are all one in Christ Jesus. And if ye be Christ's, then are ye Abraham's seed, and heirs according to the promise."

The natural Jews were from the seed of Abraham, the Tribe of Judah, and family of David. However, the spiritual Jews are born again spirits of Believers from the incorruptible Seed of Jesus' resurrected humanity nature (1 Peter 1:23).

Believers were chosen before the foundation of the world to be spiritual Jews and spiritual Israel in Christ Jesus, as the incorruptible Seed of the Jewish Messiah's humanity nature was used to give birth to Believers' born again spirits. Ephesians 1:4-5 says, "According as He hath chosen us in Him before the foundation of the world, that we should be holy and without blame before Him in love: Having predestinated us unto the adoption of children by Jesus Christ to Himself, according to the good pleasure of his will."

BIO
Dr. Nova Dean Pack

Dr. Nova Dean Pack's father left the family when he was 3 years old, and at age 10 his mother died at age 32, leaving six children behind. Dr. Pack and his brothers and sisters were raised on his grandparents' farm where there was continuous hard work as chores - taking care of 120 acres, along with feeding many cows, pigs, chickens, ducks, geese, and other animals and milking two to three cows morning and night, along with yearly soil preparation, seed planting, cultivating, the harvesting of hay and crops. For solace, on the farm, was a beautiful wooded area where Dr. Pack spent many hours alone praying and seeking God and reading his bible. The farm life was very tough, but the work ethic was engrained in Dr. Pack's foundation of beliefs. Southern Illinois was part of the Bible Belt; so, most everyone went to an old religious order as a lifestyle, although it was mostly a religious experience.

After his mother died, Dr. Pack, at age 11 was born again and had a very intimate relationship with Jesus and the Holy Spirit. He taught Sunday School from the Bible to other students near his age and baptized several people his age and younger in the creeks of Illinois at age 13 and onward.

Dr. Pack moved to California at age 15. He worked his way through college and graduated from Cal State University Long Beach in 1971. He graduated from Pepperdine University School of Law, a fundamental Christian based top rated law school, in 1974. He passed the State Bar exam on the first sitting also in 1974. He immediately started practicing law with other partners, but he left the partnership and started his sole practice of law in 1981.

Dr. Pack personally was ordained by two known prophets in California in 1992; namely Dr. Chuck Flynn and Dr. Richard Maiden. Dr. Pack received ordination papers with the Independent Assemblies of God International (IAOGI), Santa Ana, CA in 1993 and has been the corporate attorney for IAOGI since that year. Dr. Pack was the Senior Pastor of a Church fellowship from 1994 through 1999 in Redlands, CA. Dr. Pack was overseer of two ministries from 1993 through 2020 and ministered monthly at those ministries, along with other *Ekklesia*. In 2004, the Holy Spirit inspired Dr. Pack to use the name "Biblitarian," so Dr. Pack formed the ministry called "Biblitarian Ministries."

Dr. Pack broadcasted a radio talk show entitled "Business in Ministry" in San Bernardino, CA., for two years from 1992 through 1994 where he taught business men and women how to make their businesses a place of ministry. In 1994 through 1996, Dr. Pack taught a daily radio teaching that aired in Riverside and San Bernardino Counties, California, where his ongoing sermons in Church became the subjects of radio broadcasts.

During this period, Dr. Pack conducted monthly teachings for 50 straight weeks at several *Ekklesia*, teaching men and women that their businesses were their venue of ministry. Dr. Pack sees his law practice as a place and opportunity for ministry to those in need, where he witnesses to the unsaved, prays for the sick, takes care of those in need, and educates his clients and employees on the Biblical principles of business and economics and estate planning. Dr. Pack is one of the very few attorneys at law that actually brings the wisdom and principles in the Bible into his law practice for the benefit of his Christian clients and all those seeking his advice.

Dr. Pack is a prolific writer, having written over 30 Christian books on various spiritual topics (most of which have not, as yet, been published), some directly for the Believer in business. Also, he is an accomplished public minister who teaches under a strong anointing. Dr. Pack has learned how to bring the dynamic of intellectual endeavor under the authority and anointing of the Holy Spirit. He has preached and taught more than a thousand messages over the years.

Dr. Pack's ministry focus is preaching the gospel of the Kingdom (Matthew 24:14) and the message of repentance and remission of sins (Luke 24:27), which Jesus commanded to be the dual priority of preaching and teaching. He also is an inciteful teacher in the transformation of the soul and how to bring biblical wisdom, knowledge, and understanding for practical use in daily living.

Dr. Pack sends his regular teachings to Believers in over 65 different countries. Dr. Pack currently broadcasts his podcasts under the name "Biblitarian Ministries" on the priority of seeking first the Kingdom of God and His righteousness, God's grace extended for repentance and remission of sins, and the receiving of benefits of living in the Kingdom of God. Biblitarian Ministries can be viewed on The Marketplace Network, a Christian media network broadcasting on Amazon Fire TV, Facebook, YouTube and Twitter platforms. Dr. Pack may be contacted at ***packnovapack@aol.com.***